# How to COOK a DRAGON

## LIVING, LOVING, AND EATING IN CHINA

*Linda Furiya*

SEAL PRESS

HOW TO COOK A DRAGON
Living, Loving, and Eating in China

Published by
Seal Press
A Member of Perseus Books Group
1700 Fourth Street
Berkeley, California

Library of Congress Cataloging-in-Publication Data

Furiya, Linda.
 How to cook a dragon: living, loving, and eating in China / by Linda Furiya.
 p. cm.
 ISBN-13: 978-1-58005-255-9
 ISBN-10: 1-58005-255-X
 1. Furiya, Linda. 2. Women food writers—China—Biography. I. Title.

 TX649.F86A3 2008
 641.5092—dc22
 [B]
    2008020820

Cover and interior design by Domini Dragoone
Printed in the United States of America by Maple-Vail
Distributed by Publishers Group West

In order to respect the privacy of individuals mentioned in the book, the author has changed their names.

*To Manfred Ichiro*

# CONTENTS

# Chapter 1

# The
# CRICKET'S
# Song

IF IT WEREN'T FOR the Beijing duck dinner that July evening in 1997, I never would have met the cricket peddler.

It was my first night out since I'd arrived at the Beijing International Airport less than a week before. I had taken a three-month leave of absence from my job to be with my then boyfriend Eric, who lived and worked in China's capital city. The first few days, I slept like a dog. When I couldn't sleep, I walked around Eric's apartment in a drowsy blur. Around midnight, I'd awake, wide-eyed, and eat salami sandwiches and instant noodles in front of the TV. I watched *The Simpsons* and CNN Asia until the sky went from black to gray. All the while, Eric snored away in the bedroom.

*The Beijing duck restaurant* Eric took me to for my first dinner out was a typical sprawling, banquet hall–style Chinese restaurant with massive round tables, each with a lazy Susan at its center. In the entranceway were photos of foreign ambassadors and dignitaries who had eaten there over the years.

Using my chopsticks, I picked from a small dish of peanuts, boiled with star anise and heavily salted. These delicious nuts were served with drinks at almost every restaurant; Eric had corrected me when I'd first picked them up with my fingers.

Although we had dined together at home during the week, I was surprised by how shy we were on this first official date. We were familiar with each other, and yet wholly unfamiliar. Eric was already living in China when we first started dating; he'd visit San Francisco, where I was living, for business meetings every couple of months. I couldn't help but feel overwhelmed by the fact that we were virtual strangers.

And yet here I was, embarking upon something pretty huge, given the circumstances. After I'd secured my leave of absence, I subleased my apartment in San Francisco's Mission district. What outcome would result from our time together, I didn't know; all I was certain of was that Eric wasn't committed enough to our relationship that I was willing to sacrifice all my ties to San Francisco.

I had known Eric for almost three years, mostly as a work friend. We met while working at an investment bank in San Francisco's financial district—I as a receptionist and he as an analyst in the bank's bullpen. During our relationship, whenever anyone would ask us how we'd met, Eric would say that I'd had a boyfriend at the time—a man I later married and quickly divorced. "And then she was available again," he was fond of saying.

Our workplace was a breeding ground for difficult attitudes, inflated egos, and insecurity. But the Eric I knew then was above Ivy League name dropping and didn't fit the stereotypical image I secretly had of a status-conscious upper-class person. He was down to earth and gravitated toward the mailroom guys and the front-desk ladies; he rode a motorcycle to work. In a world of one-upmanship, capitalism, and shaky value systems, Eric was a sincere, regular guy.

The summer of my first divorce, I began working on a novel to get my life back on track. Eric was working at the bank's Shanghai office. That fall and winter I spent time healing by hanging out with my friend Gill, swimming in the San Francisco Bay, and riding my motorcycle in the hills of Marin County. Over many margaritas sipped under the year-round Christmas decorations at the Mexican restaurants La Rondalla and Cantina, I tried to figure out what had gone wrong, and how my dreams of having a husband and a family had slipped away from me.

The first hint of spring was in the air the afternoon I ran into Eric, who was traveling a lot at that point, in the executive kitchen. He was back in the States for a week of meetings. I think it was then that I really saw him for the first time—his intensely dark chocolate-drop eyes and light freckles that I hadn't noticed until I got up close. He somehow appeared taller, too. "The skinny white guy with the runny nose" was how he charmingly described himself; his wit, self-deprecating sense of humor, and unpredictable goofiness captured my heart. And for most of our relationship, I lovingly saw him as the funniest, sexiest man I knew.

We met for drinks that very night at a smoky, semidark dive bar in the Mission; the Counting Crows played loudly through the speakers. Over my wheat beer and his scotch and soda, we discussed our life goals. Mine was to pursue writing; Eric's was to make money. Love, marriage, and children, we agreed, would follow naturally. From there, we started a rocky yearlong relationship and saw each other whenever he was in town. Each visit was an exciting social whirlwind, crammed with ski weekends in Tahoe; after-work dinners at hip, expensive restaurants; and drinks at the cool bars and cocktail lounges that were sprouting up on every corner of San Francisco on the eve of the prosperous dot-com era. But then we'd be separated for three weeks to a month at a time—sometimes longer. The distance and stretches of time we spent apart made me paranoid that Eric was seeing other women, and although I was already head over heels in love, I called it quits after a year and a half.

Eric arrived in San Francisco that New Year's Eve and appeared on the doorstep of my new apartment in the Mission. Before the clock struck midnight, I agreed to give it another try. Six months later, I applied for my three-month unpaid sabbatical, found someone to sublease my apartment, and was on a plane to Beijing, where Eric had relocated permanently and taken a job as the chief financial officer of a Chinese software company.

*While we waited for our food,* a young man wearing a traditional Mandarin tunic and tasseled hat came to our table to pour tea. With a flourish, he presented a metal teapot; a long, knitting needle–like spout sent a lively stream of eight-treasure tea into my cup. Afterward, he strode around the banquet room, carrying the teapot like a watering can, on the prowl for more cups to fill.

I took a drink of my beer and barely touched the sliced-cucumber appetizer because I was anticipating the duck. The richness of this traditional duck dish was more appropriate for hearty autumn and winter appetites, but I'd heard so much about it that I'd insisted Eric take me someplace where I could try it. It's a once-in-a-lifetime culinary experience to dine on this imperial dish, which has been refined and improved over the centuries to achieve a near mythical reputation. The Chinese use a technique that separates the skin from the body to achieve the perfect crispness. Each duck restaurant has its own secret spice rub, which is massaged liberally into the ducks' carcasses. Fragrant fruit-tree wood, such as date, peach, and pear, is used in the roasting process for an additional layer of flavor.

When I lived in San Francisco, I never felt inclined to seek out Beijing duck, though I regularly saw the shiny roasted birds hanging from restaurant windows on Kearny Street in Chinatown. So now I waited, rather impatiently, as I smelled the mouthwatering sweet aroma of roast duck from the tables around us. I couldn't resist craning my neck to take a look at the feast that would soon be laid out at our very own table—the dark, tender meat and the shiny, crisp amber skin I'd been told tasted like bacon.

I was delighted to finally see a chef pushing a trolley cart toward our table. As if bearing a vintage wine, he lifted the platter and presented the plump duck for our approval. I nodded at the skin's glistening veneer; I looked at Eric and smiled.

The chef placed the duck on a cutting board and chopped it into 120 pieces. The skin cracked like peanut brittle at the touch of his knife.

As I watched the chef show off his knife skills, a waitress wearing a *qipao* (Mandarin dress) brought out a plate of thinly sliced scallions, plum sauce, and a steamer basket filled with *heyebing* (thin Chinese pancakes).

I watched as Eric smeared the steamy pancake with the dark plum sauce. He added a couple of slices of scallion and a sliver of duck meat, topped with the skin. He rolled the pancake up tight, and I waited for him to sink his teeth into the juicy roll; instead, he handed it to me, and I didn't hesitate to grab it.

All those centuries of work came together in that first perfect bite. There was nothing I could think of that compared with the smoky duck meat mingling with the sweet plum sauce and clean, piquant scallion. I ate it in two bites.

After my fourth roll, I felt satisfied enough to hold a conversation with Eric. I asked him if we were going out after dinner.

"Andrew asked us to meet up with him and some friends," he responded. "He wants me to meet another guy who went to Exeter. We'll take a cab over to Uighurville, where they're having dinner, and then we'll probably go to Sanlitun." Andrew had been an underclassman when Eric attended Exeter, a prestigious East Coast prep school; they had reconnected not long after Eric arrived in Beijing.

I had taken a big porcelain spoonful of the corn-and-pine nut side dish. I had never had this combination before, and I was enjoying the contrast between the pine nuts' rich, bold flavor and the corn's sweetness. Despite the taste sensations, I felt a sudden stab of homesickness. Friday nights in San Francisco, I would meet friends for dinner, drinks, or a movie. Here, I had yet to create a life.

Eric had stopped talking while I was lost in my reverie, and I began to feel acutely self-conscious about the expanding silence. Finally, he asked me casually about my week, and my response was like that of horses being set loose on a race track. To allay my deep nervousness, I began talking nonstop, describing every minute detail of my unpacking and the tea store I had discovered one afternoon.

When I couldn't wring out another bit of information about my week, Eric said, "I hope that you take this time to really write."

*What a thing to say,* I thought.

"Yes, I know," I responded, immediately aware of my defensive tone. "We talked about this before I came."

"And I—"

"I also know I shouldn't expect anything to come out of my stay," I interrupted, "because you don't know how long you'll be in China, or if it will even work out with the company." I parroted back statements he'd been making ever since we started dating. I was well aware that this discussion couldn't lead anywhere positive, and I felt sluggishness wash over me. The combination of the dinner and the conversation left me feeling as if I were still suffering from jet lag.

*Eric's inability to commit* to our relationship was a sore spot for me. I had expressed the "L word" to him that winter, when we'd decided to be exclusive to each other, but he hadn't said it back. Perhaps it was the excitement of his periodic visits, his international lifestyle, or his being so different from the type of man I generally found myself attracted to that made me know in my heart that I wanted to take our relationship as far as it would go. Rather than take the safe route in a relationship as I always did before, I made a conscious choice to cast security aside.

"I wasn't going to say that," he said gently.

"What were you going to say?" I asked.

Putting his hand over mine, Eric looked deep into my eyes. "I just meant that I hope you're going to take advantage of this time and write. I think you could be a good writer. I don't want you to be afraid of going for it."

I felt myself loosen as all the reasons I loved Eric came rolling back to me like gentle morning surf. I loved the way he smelled of soap, garlic, scotch, and cigarettes. I found it charming how he ate his sandwiches in a circular direction, starting at the crust and making his way around and around until he finished. I liked how when I stood next to him and he put his arm around me, the entirety of me seemed to tuck perfectly into his armpit. It was my favorite way to walk next to him or sit beside him on the couch at the end of the day. I felt protected and safe, like a child sheltered in the crook of a towering tree.

I refused to let him off the hook about commitment, though. "I'll do what I can about my writing, but don't forget, I'm here to spend time with you. We're now a part of each other's daily life. My plan is to finish the first draft of my novel, but I have to admit," I added hesitantly, "I am glad I have my job waiting for me back home."

Eric withdrew his hand from mine and leaned back. I felt the tenderness of the moment evaporate like summer fog. "That's another thing," he said. "I think you're wasting your time, stalling your life. Answering phones? What kind of job is that? This is the time in your life to make changes. You're divorced, thirty years old, and in a dead-end job. You have nowhere to go but up."

The defiant independent woman in me, the one who rode a motorcycle to work and swam four days a week in the San Francisco Bay, puffed up with anger. I felt the emotion lift me out of my chair. I felt as if it would carry me right out of the restaurant had Eric not announced, "I love you."

Which was exactly what I loved and hated about Eric. He often said infuriating, insulting things and then followed them with words that would stop the romantic in me dead in my tracks. My anger deflated as quickly as a popped balloon. "Go on," I said cautiously.

"You know I love you, but I can't be with you if you settle for whatever life hands you. I can't be with you if you don't quit your job. I'll take care of us while you break into writing."

Every cell in my body was rejoicing at hearing him finally say he loved me, but part of me was rebelling at the same time. His claim that he wanted to take care of me swept me up in some kind of girlish fantasy. It felt like the joy and relief of hearing the blessed sound of raindrops tapping steadily on a roof during a summer drought. And yet he wasn't just telling me to quit my job back home; he was saying that he couldn't—wouldn't—be with me if I didn't. And yes, it was a dead-end job, but I didn't have a trust fund or rich parents to bail me out of my mistakes. My heart felt full and elated, but my stomach cramped as if it were stuffed with thorns. Not only would I be in a foreign country where I couldn't speak a word of the language and had no friends, but I also wouldn't have a job to support myself.

"This is too much," I said shaking my head. "You can't do this to me. You know I love you, but whether you approve or disapprove of my job, it pays my bills. I still have a life in San Francisco. You're asking me to give that up in hopes that things will work out between us. And if they don't, you'll still have your stock options and your job. I'll go home with a broken heart and an empty bank account."

He didn't say a word; he just looked at me.

Our waitress, who had stalled on bringing us our last course, a large tureen of duck soup, apparently determined that the coast was finally clear. I could drink only a few sips of the rich, cloudy duck stock and seasonings that night, but during the next year in Beijing, that soup would become my cold remedy.

*Getting lost in Beijing's Inner City*, among the honeycombs of old *hutong* (alleyways) filled with *siheyuan* (courtyard homes), is a cinch. Entering a *hutong* is like stepping into a labyrinth: Where you step out is often not where you began. Eric and I strolled through this neighborhood to walk off some of the duck, not bothering to pay attention to where we were going. Each doorway was like a captivating face. Many were papered with red and gold decorations announcing some special family event; others were stark and weathered, with a single ornate door handle. We peeked into garden courtyards where birdcages hung alongside laundry, and where the air was filled with the smells of dinner, the sounds of a child practicing violin, and the cheerful chatter of conversation.

We emerged from the *hutong* by simply turning a corner in a quaint residential neighborhood, and found ourselves confronted by the noise and grime of urban Beijing. In addition, we'd been deposited onto a narrow concrete island that separated the bicycle lane from the cars.

Eric looked up and around, scanning as if watching a bird fly, only he was looking for a street sign to tell us where we had led ourselves.

The longer we stood there, the denser and more oppressive the vehicles, bicycles, and people became. I felt as if I were stranded on a rock as high tide rolled in. All I knew was not to lean too far forward, or I'd get punched in the ribs by a passing bicyclist, and not to lean too far back, or I'd get scraped by a car's side mirror and whisked into the road.

"Let's make a run for it," Eric said, meaning we had to just jump into the street and dash toward the opposite sidewalk. I recalled the disturbing advice he had dispensed the very morning I'd arrived: "If the walk sign says GO, stop. If it says STOP, go." With that in mind, I debated our current situation. Being evacuated by air to a hospital in Hong Kong wasn't how I wanted to spend my time in China. I rationalized that if we stayed on the traffic island long enough, rush hour would run its course. There was plenty to see—like the old man riding the grown-up tricycle with the hand pedals, or the little toddlers wearing split pants instead of diapers, who flashed their bottoms every time they bent over.

Eric was determined to go across, though. I looked down the boulevard to see if it was safe. What I saw there filled me with awe, so much so that my mouth went dry. Literally thousands of bicyclists swayed and moved away and toward us in one wave, like a gigantic school of fish.

Beijing's network of bicycle lanes and roadways was impressive. In addition to its sizable bike lanes, the city had bicycle-only roads where cars were denied access. Life on these roads was like another world: Riders smoked cigarettes, ate, and even read while pedaling. Mothers wearing dresses and four-inch heels pedaled while their babies sat behind them wearing no safety belt, holding on to just a bar. Boyfriends pedaled while their girlfriends sat sidesaddle on the back rack, reading magazines and sipping soda.

Curbside, pedicabs rigged with wagons sold bike accessories: seats, baskets, rain ponchos, and infant seats. Bike vendors peddled produce, beer, snacks, books, and magazines. You never had to worry about getting a flat; every few hundred yards, a tire-repair person was set up to do business with a basin of water, a patch kit, inner tubes, and hand tools for less than a penny.

*As the hordes of bike commuters* rode in close formation like professional racers, the street chaos was interwoven with zigzagging taxicabs, the grinding gears of construction trucks, and brave pedestrians scurrying across the street to the shoulder-to-shoulder-packed sidewalk. And then I heard something strange. Barely audible, it was a living, chirping, rhythmic sound that rose above the racket and was getting closer. The crowd parted like a flock of grazing sheep, and from it emerged a cheerful-looking old man with orb-shaped baskets of crickets, pedaling slowly, as if he were taking a back road in Provence, rather than being stuck in a throng of people that was nearly paralyzing me.

The air was still and stifling; the only breeze came from the whizzing bikes and cars. Even as the sun descended, sweat and soot trickled down my temples. But the old man looked cool and fresh in his wide-brimmed straw hat, loose gray short-sleeved shirt, and matching pants rolled up at the ankle, above his flip-flops. The basket hanging across his handlebars held a book, a fan, and a glass jar containing water and floating tea leaves. His back fender was rigged with a bamboo pole; from a distance, the object dangling from it resembled part beehive, part misshapen piñata.

I gravitated toward the old man and his crickets, perhaps because the insects' music sounded familiar. It was the only comforting thing I could turn my attention to. Crickets' chirping always commences at the best time of a summer day, in those fleeting moments before darkness falls, when the color of the sky deepens from turquoise to lapis to navy. Often accompanied in Indiana, where I grew up, by the high-pitched squeals of bats striking at mosquitoes in the cool, dark calm, the lull of the cricket song rose like a Buddhist chant.

"Watch out!" Eric yelled.

"What?" I answered, shaken from my daydream. Eric winced as a teenage bicyclist wearing headphones, blue jeans, and a T-shirt flew past me.

The old man pulled over to the curb on the other side of the street to secure his bamboo pole. I stepped off the curb without looking, keeping my eyes focused on the old man and his bike. I knew that if I looked at the oncoming bicyclists, I would freeze like a startled rabbit. *They can go around me,* I told myself.

I walked purposefully and steadily, saying a prayer under my breath as a young woman in a skirt and blouse gracefully swerved to avoid careening into me, and a middle-aged man slowed down to curse at me in Mandarin. Finally, I stepped onto the opposite curb. "*Ni hao,*" said the old man, nodding at me. He had two teeth missing in the back, and a gold crown on his right bicuspid.

"*Ni hao,*" I greeted him. His eyebrows arched noticeably.

I turned my attention to the objects hanging from his bike. There were dozens of small, covered, billiard ball–shaped straw cages, each one holding a single singing cricket. The cages were woven out of bamboo in a seamless rickrack style, with no apparent doors or way to get the crickets out.

As if in greeting, the insects began their wave of singing; it rose and fell, vibrating the entire length of the old man's bike.

Just as the old man bent over slightly to tighten a rope, anchoring the pole to his bike, I watched Eric dash across the street to meet me. My hand shot up to my mouth while I watched for the inevitable disaster.

"It's about time," I joked when he made his way to me unscathed. He wasn't amused.

"Check out this guy with the crickets. Each basket is holding just one!" I peered into one of the bamboo containers and saw tiny antennas and sharp legs clinging to the sides.

The old man's eyes widened when he heard me speak English. He said something, clucked his tongue behind his gold-capped tooth, and laughed. When Eric responded in Chinese, his eyes widened again and he let out a belly laugh. I could imagine what he was thinking: *This Chinese girl is speaking English, and this* laowai *(foreigner) can speak Mandarin.*

As if to confirm that we were playing a joke on him, the cricket peddler said something in Mandarin to me again.

Looking at him, I said, "I'm so sorry. I wish I could talk to you, but I can't speak Chinese, and I don't understand one word you're saying."

I could make out that Eric was explaining to him that I am not Chinese, but Japanese American.

His curiosity satisfied, the old man was eager to move on and try to sell us some of his wares. Eric and the old man haggled back and forth. Eric told him one was enough, but the old man insisted we needed five because they are small and needed each other in order to sing.

The old man skipped nimbly to the back of the bike and dug under the baskets in search of something. He brought out a cage noticeably larger than the others.

Eric told me the old man had said that he had two crickets that didn't fight when they were together, and so Eric had agreed to buy both—a compromise. As Eric counted out his money, the old man began talking to me as if I understood what he was saying. I stood there, holding the cage. The basket vibrated in my hand as the pair of insects picked up on the cacophony of the chirping chorus.

When he was finished, the old man stared at me, unblinking. "Eric, he keeps looking at me. What's he saying?" I asked.

"He's telling me some of the history of the crickets. He wants you to remember that they sing in the summer and autumn, and die in the winter."

"I kinda figured that." I mumbled. "I did grow up in Indiana."

Eric paused as the old man added something. "I think he's going into all this because you're a visitor, but he wants me to tell you about concubines in the Forbidden City." I watched the old man rattle on as Eric translated: "Apparently, the emperor had three thousand concubines. Their material needs were taken care of, but not their emotional needs. He's saying something about the concubines' keeping a cricket in a small cage made of real gold. That their singing symbolized sadness and loneliness."

I felt that hair-rising-on-the-back-of-my-neck sensation, like when a fortune teller brings up a shred of personal information you've never shared. But I disguised my surprise well. "Huh," I said. "That's a depressing story. Ask him what this has to do with me."

Eric asked and the old man played deaf, slowly counting his money before pocketing it. He then bowed to me, a Japanese gesture for my benefit. He climbed onto his bike saddle, waved, and pedaled off down the street. The two caged crickets kept chirping in my hand long after the louder, more raucous sounds of the city drowned out their brothers' and sisters' orchestra.

*It was seven o'clock* by the time our rickety taxicab bumped and rattled down the narrow one-lane road, squeezing past cars as we went deeper into the alleyway. I had no idea where we were—I knew only that we were going to a restaurant on the west side of the city, where a community of Uighurs, the Muslim minority group of China's Xinjiang Province, lived.

I stared out the window at the daily life on display in the neighborhood streets. Groups of men wearing boxer shorts, undershirts, and flip-flops stooped on low stools. They sipped from tall bottles of beer and fanned themselves as they played cards. I could almost smell the shampoo and taste the toothpaste as a young woman washed her hair and another brushed her teeth at an outdoor spout. A few feet away, a middle-aged woman scrubbed away at a whole chicken in a basin of water.

The cab stopped at the entrance to yet another back alley. There were fewer cars in this area, and Eric pointed out the people we were meeting, sitting at three tables set close together, away from the dust of the road. Children ran back and forth, and women carrying baskets of vegetables stared as they passed. An old man wearing a navy blue Mao suit, his face lined like a map, stood by the table with his hands behind his back, taking in the table of expatriates and a few young Chinese before walking away.

After Eric and I greeted everyone, I looked around at the empty beer bottles, ashtrays filled with cigarette butts, and stacks of dirty plates and bowls littering the table. There were seven of us: a sandy-haired American who was the China correspondent for an American weekly news magazine, with his Chinese girlfriend; a Swiss guy named Tulley and his Chinese girlfriend; Eric's friend Andrew; Eric; and me.

A striking young Uighur woman with a high forehead, almond-shaped eyes, and pale, freckled skin took our drink orders. The odor of petrol and rotting garbage mingled with the scents of cooked garlic and onion, sweet roasting mutton, and burning coal from the restaurant.

The waitress brought out classic Xinjiang fare—hearty spiced roast mutton, platters of fresh naan (round, flat leavened bread), and tomato-based noodles fragrant with onions and peppers. I was disappointed that I felt too full to try some of the delicious-looking dishes.

Conversations stopped when a car horn tooted—the sound of a fast-approaching vehicle, followed by a cloud of dust as it skidded to a stop.

"The China hand has arrived!" Andrew yelled as the doors of a black Volkswagen Santana opened, blaring the crooning of a Chinese pop singer. A Caucasian man and his entourage of Chinese friends poured out, like grains of rice spilling from a bag. Andrew explained to me later that a China hand was an expat who spent several years studying or working in China. But I would learn during my time here that it meant much more than that.

The group quickly dispersed; some went into the restaurant, others went to get more chairs. Andrew introduced Eric to the China hand, Craig. I anticipated that the three would swap stories, but they clustered around the American journalist and Tulley, leaving me to my own devices.

I found myself grouped with the guests at the other end of the table, who happened to be the Chinese who'd just arrived with Craig. A woman who had given herself the English name Allison struck up a conversation with me, peppering me with questions about America. I'd learn later on that speaking English attracted locals who wanted to practice.

Within that group of Chinese, I didn't hear one Chinese name, but I did meet a Yolanda, an Apple, a Sunny, and a Dixon—their chosen English names. As an English speaker who had my own associations with these words, I couldn't help but raise my eyebrows at some of these monikers. During my time in China, I found—especially among the younger set—that universities and learning institutions were a popular source of names, too: I met several Harvards and Yales and one Parsons, after Parsons School of Design. I came to understand that speaking a new language meant you could become anyone or anything that you aspired to be.

Later, when I began studying Mandarin, my teacher insisted that I give myself a Chinese name based on the sound of my real name or some aesthetic character. After a while, we came up with Fuling Li: Fu for my last name, Furiya; and Ling, which is like Linda but means "dawn" or "new beginning." And if a Chinese girl could name herself after Madonna or Nicole Kidman, I could add a Li, after the gorgeous, talented Chinese actress Gong Li.


*Aside from the interesting names I learned,* I was amazed by how beautiful Allison's hair was. I could almost see each individual strand, glossy and thick as fishing line. She worked at a state-run publishing house that printed schoolbooks and academic works. To be polite, I asked her questions about her life: whether she had any hobbies, where she had traveled, what she and her friends did for fun. She was the first local Chinese girl I had ever spoken to.

She said her hobby was playing the piano. When she told me she had competed nationally as a pianist, I commented that it was more of a vocation than a hobby. She shrugged and said the piano playing had ended when she fractured a bone in her hand after she fell off her bicycle. She had never traveled abroad, because it's difficult for Chinese to leave their country. And she and her friends spent their free time window shopping or gathering at a local teahouse.

Allison spoke very calmly, and I could tell by the way she looked downward, as if she were reading off a page, or upward, as if in search of a word, that she was putting much thought into her responses. Suddenly she looked up past my head, and her mouth spread into a wide smile.

I turned to see Craig behind me. He pulled up a chair and sat down between us. I looked to see where Eric was and found him laughing uproariously in response to Andrew, who was sitting forward and telling a story. The Chinese girlfriends were seated some distance away from their men, talking amongst themselves. I took a sip of my warm beer just to do something.

As I was planning to make a move to the mixed couples' end of the table, Craig turned around as if he were startled, which, I was starting to figure out, was just the way he moved.

"*Ni hao,*" he greeted me, as if I had just appeared out of nowhere. He pointed at my cricket basket and asked a question in Mandarin that I didn't understand.

I held up my hand and shook my head. "I don't speak Chinese."

Astonished, he made a jerky movement again, like a cartoon character. I couldn't help but laugh. Craig, like Eric and Andrew, was a regular-looking white man with clean-cut brownish hair and fair, slightly freckled skin.

He pointed his finger at me. "You're American."

"That would be right!" I said. I rolled my eyes, like any American gal would.

Laughing, he said, "I was like, for a second, *Man, there's no way you could get that accent listening to English tapes.*"

"I'm Japanese American, born and raised in Indiana," I responded, with a bit of an edge. I didn't like my niggling compulsion to explain my ethnicity to total strangers, many of whom I'd never see again, but I'd discovered that it actually served me well. Because I spoke directly to my American origins and Midwest farm-town roots, and because I'd grown up in a Japanese family, I found that I answered people's questions all at once. To Westerners, I thought I conveyed a sturdy foundation to start from, and to the Chinese, my explanation represented a *yes, we may look alike, but it stops there*. Looking back, I realize that I certainly would have responded differently if I'd been an American-born Chinese or if I'd been in Kyoto instead of Beijing. But I hadn't even been there a whole week, and I was already feeling the pressure of being constantly mistaken for Chinese.

I asked Craig what city he was from. His eyes looked faraway for a moment, as if he hadn't thought about that in a long time.

"Maine. Portland, Maine," he answered.

"When was the last time you were home?" I asked.

"About a year and a half ago. I consider China my home," he said, extending his arms broadly, as if children were going to run into his embrace.

"I heard you were here during the Tiananmen Square situation." I remembered hearing this from Eric, who'd heard it from Andrew.

"Yeah," Craig said in a modest voice, looking away as if I'd uncovered that he was actually a celebrity.

"Wow, that's a long time."

"I've seen lots of changes. How long have you been here?"

"Less than a week."

He raised his eyebrows in a *no kidding?* way.

"I'm with Eric, over there."

"Are you here to study Mandarin?"

"No . . . well . . . I mean, yes, when I get the time. I need to finish a book I'm writing first."

"You can't live here if you don't speak the language."

"I'm sure I'll pick it up along the way."

This comment sent Craig off on a monologue about how we, as foreigners, as visitors, must embrace the centuries-old Chinese culture.

"I've been here for almost thirteen years, and I still feel I have so much to learn from this country. The true way of tapping into the soul of the Chinese," he said, pausing, "is to master the language. It's hard work, and frustrating, but it's the most satisfying thing in the world."

Trying to interject a thought of my own was as difficult as putting toothpaste back into its tube. Craig's voice became more pronounced and measured, as if he were giving a lecture. It was when he began speaking in Mandarin and then translating his own words into English that I looked up and saw that he wasn't doing it for my benefit. He had caught the attention of the Chinese sitting at our end of the table. Actually, a small group from the neighborhood had gathered. I could tell by their smiles and nodding heads that they were impressed by Craig's vernacular and ideas. I recognized the look, having seen the same expression of admiration on my parents' faces anytime a white person spoke Japanese fluently.

Craig had his pulpit and was on fire. He completely dropped the English. At the end of his oration, I thought he was going to take a bow while the audience applauded.

I was amazed by how the Chinese listened to Craig. If he'd behaved like this in the States, his grandiosity and bravado would have sent listeners into flurries of excuse-making to get away from him, but here, he had eight Chinese hanging on to his every word—and I don't believe they were being polite.

This was the first time I really began to understand a different kind of attraction the Chinese might have to certain types of expatriates who were here to find themselves, or to ditch the mediocre suit they'd worn in their home country for a shiny new one. Seeing Craig bask in the attention, I could see the draw of mastering the language and learning about the culture and customs.

I sighed internally with relief when the waitress returned with a tray and began cleaning up the table. The crowd at the other end stood up and stretched, indicating that the evening had come to an end. Andrew announced that we would break up into groups and head to Sanlitun's Jiuba Jie, or Bar Street.

I hopped into a taxi with Eric and Andrew. It had cooled off, and the street was teeming with people eating outside, strolling, or just people-watching on the curb. A loudspeaker played symphony music in a small park; couples ballroom-danced to its murmurs, and I saw one man leading an invisible partner. In another part of the park, groups of elderly fan dancers practiced to the beat of banging cymbals and drums.

"It looked like you were having a lively conversation with Craig over at your end of the table," Eric commented. I focused my attention on the rearview mirror, where a red tassel with a portrait of Chairman Mao was hanging. Despite the atrocities the deceased leader committed, many workers still believed he had done right by the common Chinese.

"Yeah, he thought I was a local Chinese girl," I said, laughing to refrain from showing my indignation. "I didn't appreciate the lecture he gave me about how I needed to embrace the Chinese culture, the language, and the people."

"Well, there are three factions of expats living here," Eric said. But before he could continue, Andrew finished the thought for him: "There's the Colonialist White Man, the China Soul, and the Living in Denial. Do you have anything to add to that, Eric?" Andrew asked, leaning forward and looking at him.

"Nope, sounds pretty accurate to me," Eric said.

"The Colonialist White Man is self-explanatory," Andrew continued. "Exploiting the economy and the women, living here until the opportunities run dry. Doesn't give a damn about the history or the culture. The China Soul is someone who comes innocently enough to China to study the language, but then gets engulfed in the culture, which is so much more rich and textured than that person's boring old Anglo-Saxon heritage. More often than not, they're the ones who end up marrying a Chinese woman and never going home. And last, there are those I call Living in Denial. You'll see this a lot in the older, multinational guys who have the bucks to support this kind of lifestyle. They live on compounds on the outskirts of town that literally look like a neighborhood in the States. A driver takes them to and from work, they wouldn't dare eat at a local restaurant, and they socialize only with Westerners. I know some guys who have been here for five years and can't speak a word of Chinese." Andrew started reexamining the crickets chirping happily in the basket, peering into the little rickrack holes as he spoke.

I was captivated by his descriptions and prompted him to tell me more. "What's Craig?" I asked, though I already knew the answer.

"Craig fancies himself the China Soul type. He believes he's Chinese, especially because he was here before Tiananmen Square. He thinks he can speak for them, like Kevin Costner's character in *Dances with Wolves*. There's an element of exploitation, too, though. Don't you think, Eric?" Andrew asked, raising his voice at the end so Eric would hear him.

"Whatever you say, Andrew," Eric said with a chuckle. I looked back and forth between them. I sensed that Eric felt uncomfortable, but Andrew forged on.

"Craig is one of those guys who devour Chinese women. He literally walks into a room and scans it to see which ones he wants, then makes his move. He feasts on them the way hungry person eats a bag of chips or a bowl of popcorn."

"That's creepy!" I nearly shouted. "Is it because he comes across as something special here, and back home he's average?" But I didn't get an answer. The cab pulled up to the bar, and I lost Andrew to this new distraction.

*During the day,* the cafés and restaurants along Sanlitun's Jiuba Jie set out tables and chairs so that customers could dine alfresco, though the experience was hardly relaxing, as passing taxis and trucks kicked up dust constantly. A German butcher and a couple of tiny grocery stores catered to Westerners looking for white bread, European cheeses, and meat shipped from overseas.

At night, the beer joints opened up and the street became one long party strip. We walked down a narrow alleyway to an establishment called the Hidden Tree Bar. I didn't know that behind the *hutong* walls were families crammed into one-bedroom apartments, putting up with rowdy bar noise night after night.

Before we entered the bar, Eric pulled me aside.

"Listen, I have to ask you a big favor," he said, looking away from me as he spoke.

"What is it?"

"Craig asked me to help him out. He's supposed to meet a woman here for a drink, but then this other woman who doesn't know about the first woman is also coming."

"So? What does that have to do with you?" I was starting to figure out why Eric had seemed uncomfortable when Andrew was talking about Craig's appetite for Chinese women. *Andrew had probably been trying to warm me up for this,* I thought.

"Because I speak Chinese, he wants me to occupy the woman inside the bar while he talks to the other one outside."

"Is this what you and Andrew were giggling about in the taxi?" I asked.

He nodded sheepishly.

As Eric waited for my answer, Craig stuck his head out the door.

"Hey, Eric, you're on!" he said, wearing a big grin.

Eric gave me a weak smile and followed Craig inside.

The bar was cramped and dimly lit. An air-conditioning unit wheezed in the window, barely making a dent in the place's moist warmth. The stuffiness strengthened the stink of cologne, cigarettes, and roast meat from the kebab vendor outside, along with the ubiquitous undertones of sour beer. I couldn't help but notice that the crowd was predominantly white Western men with Chinese women.

I sipped my beer and bobbed my head to the rock 'n' roll music, trying to appear comfortable standing alone. Eric was over at the bar, talking to Craig's girlfriend, who smiled, laughed, and bobbed her chin coyly up and down all the while. I looked out at the back courtyard and saw Craig sitting at a table with the other woman. He didn't look like he was going anywhere. I knew Eric was mine, but the woman he was entertaining was far from unattractive.

It seemed that most of the women in the bar were quite beautiful and dressed in sexy outfits. Naively, I'd imagined the women in Beijing to be pigtailed, cap-wearing country bumpkins. Almost all of them had the same silky hair Allison had. It cascaded against their bare arms, which appeared pale and cool. When the Swiss guy's girlfriend flipped her hair, it smelled like sweet berries.

These women stood with their hips jutting out and strolled with long, confident strides, as if working a catwalk. I felt as if every woman in the room except me had been trained at a Barbizon Modeling Center.

One of the young women in the group leaned toward me and yelled something to me in Chinese.

"I'm sorry, I don't speak Mandarin," I yelled.

"What?" she said, surprised. "You're not Chinese?" She had only a slight accent.

She shared this information with her friend, whom I didn't remember having seen in Uighurville. Her friend looked me up and down, but not in the lascivious way a man would, or even in the critical, head-to-toe way a woman sometimes does when she's checking out another woman's outfit. No, it was more a bewildered, *Why didn't we notice this alien in our midst?* look.

The women exchanged more words. And then the one who had been speaking to me initially—whose name, I later found out, was Miranda—yelled in my ear, "Why don't you speak Mandarin?!"

"I'm Japanese American," I answered.

"Japanese. Ah," she said, as if I suddenly made sense. "*Konichiwa.*"

"I'm not . . . " I started to explain. "Aw, forget it."

Miranda was wearing denim shorts, a pink scoop-neck top with puffy cap sleeves, and high-heeled cowboy boots. All she needed was a piece of hay between her teeth, and her country-girl look would be complete. Her friend had on a short, black, dancer's-style wraparound skirt and a low-cut, clingy raspberry tank top with SHORTCAKE printed across it in rhinestones. I seemed to be the only Asian woman there that night who could have confirmed the rumor that all Asian women are flat chested. With a big, welcoming smile, Miranda leaned in again. "You look like us," she said, pointing to herself, then to her friend. Her friend smiled, too.

I wasn't sure if I should feel flattered. I caught a reflection of myself in the long mirror over the bar. My long hair cascaded down my back just like theirs did. The short, lime-green floral-print sundress I was wearing had looked light and festive in the small Mission-district shop where I'd bought it, but now it seemed skimpy and tawdry.

It was the time of night when men begin to wear beer goggles. Alone again, I looked around and noticed some white guys leering at me. I looked around for Eric and saw him deep in conversation across the room with Craig and his two girlfriends. They looked like they were on a double date.

I didn't know what to do, but I had to get out of the loud bar. Cradling my cricket basket, I was practically run over by two Chinese women screeching with delight as a young blond man followed them in hot pursuit.

His tight, shiny, sapphire-blue shirt was unbuttoned down his chest. He was even wearing a gold necklace. At first I thought the fact that he was dressed like John Travolta in *Saturday Night Fever* was a joke, but I remembered the thematic getups of Miranda as a country gal, and her friend as a dancer in training. As he passed me, the blond stopped. "Whoa, *Xiaojie!*" he said in a European accent I couldn't decipher.

I rolled my eyes at him and went outside.

The air was magnificently cool. No one was on the street except for a local man in his cotton pajama bottoms, tank top, and slippers, walking a Pekinese. I sat on a gritty step beneath a *hutong* doorway.

As I debated whether to go back inside the bar, the blond man came out the door. He lit a cigarette and walked my way.

"*Ni hao,*" he said, exuding a finesse I imagined he'd gained from his many conquests.

"Y'know what? I don't mean to be impolite, but I'm really tired and I don't speak Mandarin, so I'd appreciate it if you left me alone," I said, not caring whether he understood me.

The strong cologne he wore stung my nose. His demeanor changed after I spoke. "What? You're not Chinese?" he asked. I still couldn't place his accent—Polish, maybe Russian.

"No, I'm not Chinese. I'm American." I could feel my voice shaking and getting louder. "And if one more person asks me why I don't speak Chinese, I swear I will scream bloody murder." I was exhausted and way past feeling tolerant.

"Okay, okay, relax," he said, stepping away. "You look Chinese, okay? We're in China, right?" He paused for a moment, taking me in. "Okay, so if you're not Chinese, then what are you?" he asked.

*What am I?* I hadn't heard that question in so long, living as I did in a politically correct city with lots and lots of Asians.

"I'm Japanese American," I answered.

"Oh, you're Japanese," he said.

He knew he'd said something wrong when I flared my nostrils.

"No, I was born and raised in the United States. I grew up there."

"That explains your American accent. You speak good English," he said with a big smile.

I stopped myself from launching into another explanation by asking, "So, where are you from?"

"Russia," he said, rolling the "R" lusciously. He said it with so much pride and bravado that I couldn't stifle a grin.

"What are doing here, besides chasing skirt?" I asked, only half joking. He looked at me, puzzled. "Never mind," I said. "Are you working here? Studying? Traveling?"

"I'm studying Mandarin," he said, and then uttered a word that I imagined was the name of a school, as he followed it with a look of overt pride. He paused, waiting for me to react, but I'd never heard of the school, so he informed me that it was the premier language school in Beijing.

"Great," I replied. He looked dejected, a feeling I don't believe he was accustomed to.

"And why are you here?" he asked.

Amid the constant mix-ups about my nationality, this was one question not one person had asked me yet.

"You really don't want to know," I said.

"Sure I do," he said, and I believed him. Who knows why I chose to divulge so much in that dusty doorway across from the loud bar—maybe it was because of the day I'd had, or because Eric was in there flirting with girls, or because I doubted my reasons for being here. I told the

Russian about my divorce, about my long-distance, soap-opera relationship with Eric, and about my coming to Beijing. I didn't tell him that I'd never thought about China when I was growing up in a white farm town, or how I had my own issues about it because I'd been mistaken constantly for a Chinese person when I was growing up, and I didn't want to be associated with the country.

"You didn't answer my question," he said, rubbing his chin.

I looked at him blankly.

"You just told me how you got here, but not why you're here."

I thought about this for a second.

"Well, why are you here, then?" he repeated.

I looked at him again, more closely this time, at the way the humidity had curled his blond Prince Valiant hairstyle into angelic golden ringlets.

Without hesitating, I said, "I'm here to be with the man I love and to write."

With those words I made a commitment to follow my heart, to sever my ties with the job and the apartment that bound me to my old life in San Francisco. I understood what Eric had been trying to convey to me at dinner—that for us to have a future together, I needed to risk living with him in Beijing indefinitely.

"That wasn't so hard, was it? I would have screamed if you had told me you were here to study Mandarin."

I actually laughed sincerely.

We left it at that. I didn't ask for his name, and he didn't ask for mine.

Eric finally came looking for me. All my earlier insecurities and annoyances were gone. He looked at me suspiciously when he found me laughing with my new friend in the alleyway.

After I said goodbye to the Russian guy, Eric asked me who he was.

"He's just someone I struck up a conversation with," I said innocently.

*On the cab ride home,* Eric told me that the two women Craig was trying to juggle knew each other. In the end, they'd left Craig to continue partying.

I was certain the poor crickets were deaf by the time we made it home that night. Before bed I found a shoebox and punched some holes in it. I threw in a couple of leaves of iceberg lettuce and some slices of red pepper. Then I released the crickets from the close quarters of their bamboo baskets by lifting the basket from its base.

As I lay in bed, I could hear the cycle of chirping crickets. Drifting in and out of sleep, I had a recurring dream of running through the *hutong* and getting nowhere.

The next morning, I opened the shoebox and found one cricket mounting the other. I knew from having dogs that this was a form of domination, but I also decided that I couldn't go another night with our new pets. After a hangover breakfast of eggs, bacon, toast, and potatoes, Eric and I decided to take a cab to Ritan Park, where we would free the unhappy crickets in a sparsely wooded area.

We rode in silence in the cab, each of us lost in our own thoughts. There was no air-conditioning in the Xiali cabs back then, and the warm air whipped through the windows, making me drowsy. The more I thought about it, the more I dwelled on the idea that if two animals are put in a box, one will dominate and the other will submit. I applied this notion to my own situation, considering what happens when two people end up in a country where one speaks the language and the other doesn't.

After paying a couple of RMB at the park entrance, we strolled past the plastic-toy and beverage vendors. The grass was worn in many places from heavy foot traffic. We headed toward a quiet area with a pagoda-style gazebo surrounded by a rock garden. Near a clearing of trees with a patch of bushes, I knelt down and opened the shoebox.

The stronger cricket was tearing the weaker one apart now; part of the victim's leg was missing. Eric and I each lifted one cricket out and placed it carefully on a tree trunk. We stood back and watched as the insect with the missing leg appeared to linger and hop after the other one. The stronger cricket disappeared, with one big jump, onto a leafy branch.

*The next Monday,* late in the afternoon (morning in San Francisco), I called the human resources office at the investment bank and left a message saying I wasn't coming back. I also left a message for the person subletting my apartment, telling her that she could have the place if she wanted it. Making these phone calls wasn't easy, but afterward I felt light, and free to do whatever, and go wherever, I wanted. Except for the clothes I'd brought with me, I had no other possessions. I had begun downsizing after my first divorce, and then I'd sold off nearly all my household items and furnishings before leaving for Beijing, so I wouldn't have to store them. My most treasured personal items—photos, journals, books, and small personal effects—I mailed to my parents' home.

I moved the boxes cluttering the desk in Eric's office. I hung photos of my friends and family on the wall and set up my laptop.

Long after the crickets were gone, I swore I could hear their song in the squeaking of the air conditioner or in the hallway when the janitor was about. And the cricket peddler's ominous story of the lonely concubines turned out to be a place to which my distracted mind often wandered in the months that followed.

## CORN, PINE NUTS, and ROASTED RED and YELLOW BELL PEPPERS

*To enjoy the full flavor of this dish, don't skimp on the pine nuts.*
*Serve as a side dish with grilled meats, like steak and lamb.*

INGREDIENTS:

2 cups fresh corn kernels

1 cup pine nuts

1/2 yellow bell pepper, seeded and cut lengthwise into thirds

1/2 red bell pepper, seeded and cut lengthwise into thirds

3 tablespoons chicken stock

1 tablespoon sake

2 teaspoons red wine vinegar

1 teaspoon sugar

1/4 teaspoon salt

2 teaspoons soy sauce

1 teaspoon Asian sesame oil

1 tablespoon finely chopped cilantro

## INSTRUCTIONS:

Blanch the corn kernels in a pot of boiling water for 3 minutes. Drain and set aside.

Toast the pine nuts in a nonstick skillet, shaking the pan occasionally, until the nuts turn light brown. Remove from heat and set aside.

Place the strips of bell pepper on a baking sheet and broil, skin side up, until charred black.

Plunge the charred peppers into ice-cold water and peel off the blackened skin. Squeeze out excess water, then dice the peppers into 1/4-inch pieces. Set aside.

Combine the chicken stock, sake, vinegar, sugar, and salt. Set aside.

Heat a nonstick skillet or oiled wok over medium-high heat.

Add the blanched corn and toasted pine nuts to the skillet and stir for 1 minute.

Add the chicken stock mixture and cook, stirring, until reduced by half.

Add the peppers and soy sauce and stir; then add the sesame oil and cilantro.

Mix well and cook for another minute before serving.

*Serves 4*

# Chapter 2

# LEARNING My PLACE

I SAT UP IN BED with a start when I heard the sound of a key unlocking the front door. It was Monday morning and Chu Ping, Eric's housekeeper, was returning to work after the week off Eric had given her following my arrival.

Eric's side of the bed was empty. I heard a gentle spray of water coming from the bathroom and realized he was in the shower. As I lay back down, my head felt thick and foggy. Eric had turned off the air conditioner when he got out of bed, and already the air was growing sticky and warm. The sip of water I took from the glass on my bedside table did little to expunge the woolly feeling from my teeth and tongue, a reminder of the wine and cigarettes I'd had the night before.

I pulled the covers up to my chin, despite the room's increasing stuffiness. Without the constant roar of the air conditioner, I could hear Chu Ping's every movement; the apartment's spare furnishings only heightened its acoustics. The living room contained an oversize, black Naugahyde sofa and matching armchair, a black plastic coffee table, and a black-veneered wall unit that housed the television and sound system. A large blue-and-white cotton rag rug and some tall potted plants were the only things that added color. In the dining room were a rectangular plastic table and four matching chairs pushed against a wall, and a large picture window that looked out over the four-building complex's treeless, concrete central grounds.

By Western standards, the rooms were spacious and sunny. With its dark parquet floors, Eric's dwelling was exceptional—the square footage and sunlight alone would have fetched a high rent in the Bay Area. It was just that the fixtures' details and quality left a lot to be desired. The walls covering the entire apartment were papered with a textured material. Once white, they had yellowed over the years and were strangely sticky to the touch, the way a kitchen's backsplash feels with cooking oil splattered across it. The draperies were the same faded yellow, and I didn't want to touch them; I was already certain that they were yet another unsatisfactory detail.

The bathroom's exposed pipes, cracked tiles, corroded fixtures, and fluorescent lighting were reminiscent of the scary public bathrooms and the shower rooms at park swimming pools that I'd visited in my youth. The spartan bedroom was huge, with a king-size, hard-as-marble slab mattress on a black-and-green plastic bed frame that was bookended by matching side tables. On the other side of the room was a dresser. In 1996 Beijing, this setup, especially compared with local Chinese accommodations, was luxurious.

*I should have gotten out of bed,* put my clothes on, and presented my-self to Chu Ping that first morning that she came back to the apartment. Instead, I lay there listening to her going about her business. I visualized what Chu Ping was doing based on the sounds she was making. Hearing the crackle of the shopping bag she carried and the jingling of her keys, I could see the faceless housekeeper, as if on a television screen, walking to the dining room table and setting down the bag and the keys. The bag rattled as she took something from it.

I concluded, based on the slamming of the refrigerator door and the rattling of the two glass vases that sat atop it, that Chu Ping was putting her lunch away. After a few seconds of silence, I heard the sound of the pots and pans I had washed over the weekend being put away. I dozed off for a little while, only to be awakened abruptly when the bedroom door opened. Chu Ping came walking in with an armful of Eric's undershirts, socks, and boxer shorts.

Totally bewildered, I bolted upright, holding the sheets to my chest indignantly, the way people in old movies do when someone walks in on them, even though I was wearing a nightgown.

I felt completely intruded upon, and as I watched Chu Ping, who continued her work without hesitating or even glancing at me, my an-ger grew. She opened each of Eric's dresser drawers carefully, putting his clothes away in their proper place.

She didn't look at all how I'd expected her to. I'd imagined her as older and thinner. Instead, a headscarf accentuated her round face, and she had the full lips that women in the States pay their cosmetic surgeons to imitate. She was short and big-boned. She wore the inexpensive pants and loose tunic with frog buttons that open-stall markets all over the place sold. I'd later find out that she was shorter than I, but she carried herself tall and straight, with composure and dignity, even though she kept her eyes downcast.

She left the room as soon as she was finished with her work. Whether it was because she'd come into the bedroom without knocking or because she'd ignored me—or maybe more because I felt that Eric should have made a point of introducing us or telling her not to enter the bedroom—I was livid.

I jumped out of bed and pulled on sweatpants and a T-shirt that had been lying on the floor next to Eric's clothes, which Chu Ping had picked up. I intended to walk out and give her a piece of my mind, and I scripted what I would say to her: *How dare you barge into the bedroom without knocking? In the future, I'd . . .* I stopped midthought, though, already partway down the hallway. I couldn't tell her any of this. I couldn't speak Mandarin, and Chu Ping didn't understand English. The adrenaline leaked out of me.

Eric emerged from the steamy bathroom in his boxer shorts and T-shirt, just as I was about to kick the wall.

"Good morning," he purred. "I was hoping you'd sleep in longer." He looked at me and changed his tone. "Is something wrong?" he asked.

"Eric, you have to talk to her and explain that you don't just open a closed door and walk in without knocking. She has no sense of respect for my privacy."

I stood between the bureau and the bed, catching a glimpse of myself in the mirror. I was aware of myself in that moment, the way I stood with one arm crossing my chest and the other flaying about as I described what had happened. My head stretched out like a turtle's. Reacting like this was bad form, I knew. Not too far inside me, I understood that Chu Ping meant no harm, but this was how I was choosing to handle the situation at that moment, a week into my time in China. The longer I lived in China, the more I would understand that my inability to convey my feelings fueled the flames of my resentment, anger, and frustration, all of which had no place to go except deeper and deeper inside me. Although I hadn't said it aloud, I had designated Eric as my guardian and advocate in my new country. And in this moment, and the several moments leading up to it, he was failing me. I was starting to realize how alone and resourceless I really was.

Eric took a pair of fresh socks from his drawer and sat down at the end of the bed.

Before he spoke, he chuckled and shook his head hard, like a dog clearing its ears. "Linda, things are different here in China. Five or six families live in one apartment. The Chinese have no concept of privacy. I'm sorry, but I don't think it's a big deal if she walks into a room without knocking. She's just trying to do her work. She knew you were coming, but maybe she forgot; I don't know."

"Well, are you still going to say something to her?" I resisted the mirror this time, already fed up with myself and Eric and the entire situation.

Eric chuckled again, and this time my stomach fluttered as I felt the full impact of its condescending tone. It was the same laugh my parents had used when I was a young girl and they thought I was being absurd.

"Well, are you?" I said, leaning forward, crossing my arms.

Eric looked me straight in the eye and said in his managerial voice, "Frankly, I think you're making too big a deal out of this."

He finished dressing and left the room. I stood there looking at myself again in the mirror, wondering what I would do next. I could feel my helplessness coursing through my body, in the very marrow of my bones. I heard Eric chatting pleasantly with Chu Ping in the kitchen, and I knew he considered the subject closed.

*Before my move to Beijing,* Eric had breezily mentioned the idea of hiring a full-time housekeeper; he'd made it seem as if it were the norm for expats. During his brief visits to San Francisco, he'd described the woman who made sure his utility bills were paid on time, cleaned the apartment, and picked up after him. She also food shopped for him every day of the week for 900 RMB, or roughly $90, per month. He told me she worked forty-hour weeks and had weekends off, but that many housekeepers lived in closet-size rooms off their employers' kitchens and worked as needed, without ever taking a day off.

Eric added matter-of-factly, "She even makes me dinner and irons my boxer shorts."

At that time in my life, I had never even used a cleaning person before. I found the idea of having a housekeeper both guilt-inducing and appealing. It was like a fantasy come true on some level, but the low wages made me feel like it was all rather exploitative. But I learned that the *ayi* (housekeepers) were an essential part of the expatriate community. Their role was not only to do housework and provide childcare, but also to deal with the necessities of living in a foreign country, which included setting up a landline account, dealing with landlords, or calling repairmen—all of which can be time-consuming in a new place. I learned just how difficult simple tasks like these could be when our electricity payment was due during a week when Chu Ping was out sick. Unlike in the States, where utility holders are issued a series of warnings before the electricity is turned off, the Chinese have little leniency and turn off the juice if payment is late by only a few days.

The payment office was within walking distance of the apartment. I knew when I had reached it, because Eric had told me that golden lightning rods were painted on the door. Judging from the mass of people clustered in the building, I gathered that everyone hand-delivered their electricity payment. Along one wall were two bank-teller windows covered with bars and glass; otherwise the room was a concrete slab, with nothing but a large plastic trash can and notices hanging on a glass-enclosed bulletin board.

Crowding in front of each window were nearly two dozen people. There was no order, queue, or even someone to supervise a system to ensure that customers were helped. A man walked into the room after I arrived and, without any hesitation, wedged and wiggled his way to the front of the line, where at least five hands were shoved under the small window slot. It was survival of the fittest, and I stood there feeling helpless as I watched an elderly woman get blocked. The teller grudgingly took whichever invoice and cash was in front of him and scribbled, stamped, and sealed various pieces of onion paper and notepads before inserting a stack of stapled, red-inked receipts into the waiting open hand and moving on to the next.

I was too intimidated to get into the swarm. The people in the front were pressed up against the teller's window from the back, yet no one said anything or seemed fazed that their bodies were being pushed and prodded.

I nibbled on my nails nervously as I waited, hoping that the horde would thin out. It was midmorning, so I decided to wait a while and see if I'd happened to come at a busy time. *Shouldn't these people be at work?* I wondered impatiently. The longer I waited, the more people arrived.

I couldn't wait forever, so I followed a Chinese man who was confidently thrusting his way to the front of the cluster. As I elbowed my way through, I said, *"Duibuqi"* ("Excuse me"), which opened up the corridor even more, as people stopped pushing to see who had spoken those words. I knew they were looking around because of my accent.

Finally, I made my way to the front. I poked my hand into the window slot and waved it around like I'd seen the others do. I could feel the pressure of bodies against me. Someone in the assembly was smoking, and I could smell sour armpit odor. I felt panic seize me as I tried to catch my breath. My slim arm was squeezed into the small area around the teller's window, but two people blocked my body, so I couldn't actually see what was going on behind the glass and bars. When I felt a tug, I ordered myself to let go of the papers I held. I held on to the counter as best I could, as people standing in the back of the pack surged forward like a shifting current.

I felt coins and bills being shoved back into my hand. Thankfully, I was finished. Like a salmon making its way upstream, I raced out of the crowd.

*"Fapiao! Fapiao! Xiaojie!"* I heard a commotion. Above all the heads, the teller stretched his neck and waved a stack of papers at me. Receipts. I hadn't gotten the receipts.

There was no way I was plunging back in. I just had to hope that our payment would be entered without a hitch, and I scurried out the door as the teller continued to yell for me to come back.

*My experience with the utility company* helped get me one step closer to accepting that Eric and I really *needed* a housekeeper, but it didn't change the fact that I was going to have to share my personal space with a complete stranger for a lot of hours during the day.

Suddenly, what Chu Ping thought of me became very important. In the aftermath of my meltdown about her barging into the bedroom, I was full of anxiety when I finally joined her and Eric in the kitchen that day. Would she take me seriously? Would she treat me as so many other Chinese had, and not know what to make of my Asian American-ness? Would I be expected to help her with her work? Would she be afraid that I would fire her? An overwhelming feeling of having to define my place to her, and to Eric and myself, struck me.

Eric introduced me to Chu Ping. I smiled and greeted her with *"Ni hao ma?"* ("How are you?"), instead of *"Ni hao"* ("Hello"). Eric corrected me and Chu Ping laughed. Her smile revealed the whitest, straightest, biggest teeth I had ever seen. My face turned persimmon red and I stood there, smiling idiotically, as Eric continued speaking Mandarin with her.

I busied myself by making a cup of black tea. During my first week in Beijing I walked to the neighborhood tea vendor almost every day, partly to acclimate myself to the area and partly to get out of the apartment. His clean store was lined with tall jars of tea, dried fruit peel, moss, and flower buds. When drinking tea, the Chinese dispensed with the formality of separating the tea leaves from the water with tea bags. Rather, they simply threw loose tea leaves into a water glass; the tea was ready to drink as soon as the leaves descended to the bottom. Although I was born and raised in the Midwest, I had a strong affinity for this organic and robust way of enjoying food. And something about this teahouse and the carefree quality of it all helped to establish the strong kinship I felt with other Asians.

The black tea leaves I'd taken from the kitchen cabinet scattered as they sank to the bottom of my porcelain cup. I dropped in a flowering-jasmine tea bulb and watched the tea leaves swell, and the ball slowly open to reveal a flower, as I leaned against the counter and watched Eric and Chu Ping talk. My newcomer feeling reminded me of the first day on a new job, only it was accentuated by my inability to understand what was being said. I listened attentively to the tongue-twisting tones in an attempt to detect whether Eric was mentioning what had happened that morning.

Chu Ping left the kitchen to make the beds, and Eric looked at me expectantly. "I bought a few things over the weekend, but we need more food. Do you mind being in charge of the grocery shopping from now on?"

"I thought you said Chu Ping did the grocery shopping," I said, wondering if she had said she didn't want to do it anymore, now that I'd arrived.

Eric looked annoyed. "I just have her buy fruits and vegetables at the outdoor markets. She can't buy Western food because she doesn't know what she should be looking for."

Before I could answer, Eric pulled a pad of paper and a pen from a pile of office stuff. He wrote instructions in pinyin, romanizing what I should say to the cab driver.

"There's a market that sells a lot of Western items right next to the Holiday Inn," he said. "Make sure you get Heinz ketchup, not the nasty Chinese stuff that's sold in a bottle that looks just like Heinz. There's a deli counter where you can buy lunch meat and cheese. The best place to buy meat is at the German butcher in Sanlitun. We'll go there sometime this week and I'll show you where it is."

He went on about which brand of white bread to choose, and told me to buy lots of fruits and vegetables.

"What should we make for dinner tonight?" he asked. Although he said "we," I had a hunch that he wasn't proposing that we cook together. I was getting the distinct impression that it was time for me to earn my keep.

I wanted to please him, but I felt put on the spot.

"How about teriyaki chicken? It's one of my specialties," I offered.

"No, I don't feel like chicken."

"What about meatloaf? I know my mom's recipe and it's delicious," I attempted again.

"I'm not a big meatloaf fan," he said, offering a weak smile and tilting his head, as if to accentuate the innocence of his responses.

He rubbed his hands together, clearly contemplating something yummy. "Steak and mashed potatoes would be good." I nodded in assent. That was what I would be preparing for dinner.

*That became the routine* for our meal planning. Eric always seemed to reject two or three choices before rubbing his hands together and announcing what he really wanted to have. As time went on, I came to accept it because he had lots of other qualities that I loved. I even became delighted and thankful on those rare occasions when he did approve of my menu recommendation.

But when this dynamic was brand new, my independent side—that sassy, vibrant part of me that couldn't believe his nerve—sprang out unexpectedly, like a warped jack-in-the-box. Only a few months earlier in San Francisco, I had thought of myself as free-spirited and opinionated.

In the short time I had been in China, I felt as if I were splitting into two different people, like the yolk and the white of an egg.

The independent side of me pointed out that if I went to the effort of making dinner, Eric should be satisfied with whatever I decided to make. The new, passive side of me retorted, *Well, he* is *paying for the groceries, and I am* living in his apartment. The complexity of this unspoken power struggle was rising to the surface like a cluster of pimples.

"Oh, can you make some broccoli, too?" Eric said, breaking me out of my daydream.

I nodded.

"I have a rice cooker and Japanese rice," he added. I sighed. I was beginning to feel like a waitress/cook combo, and I didn't like it.

He pulled a thick wad of Chinese RMB from his briefcase.

"This should be more than enough," he said, handing the crisp 100 RMB notes to me.

Now the independent side of me decided it was time to speak up. "You didn't say anything to Chu Ping about this morning, did you?"

There was a long pause. The air prickled with electricity. In a firm voice, and looking me dead in the eye, he stated, "No. I still think it's not a big deal."

My hair stood on end and my stomach muscles clinched. At the time, my mind couldn't fully comprehend what was happening, but my body knew. A collar of submission, helplessness, and dependency was being slipped around my neck, and regardless of my self-preservation instincts, I was allowing it to happen.

In Beijing, I didn't have the luxury of simply walking out like I would have if this discussion had taken place in San Francisco. I didn't know anyone in Beijing, and I couldn't speak or understand Mandarin. Airline tickets hadn't yet gone the way of e-tickets, and I couldn't just jump online and change my reservation. I thought I would stick it out. I thought I loved him. People fight. I needed to get acclimated. That was what I told myself in order to forge ahead and accommodate Eric's desires.

Eric left for work, and I stood there feeling conflicted. How could I go grocery shopping when my relationship was on the line? All morning long I stewed about how I could change my airline ticket, or at least find a hotel to stay in. Stupidly, I hadn't brought a travel guidebook or any other reference book that might direct me or orient me; I had assumed Eric would be showing me around.

By noon I had gone back and forth countless times about whether I should go through with leaving. I wouldn't have the luxury of making up with Eric and returning if I made that choice, though. Once I changed my ticket, there would be no turning back. I would be going home to my old life and a life without him.

I decided not to decide right then. It was time for lunch, and I made my way out of the apartment building in search of my favorite lamb-stick vendor. The sun was high, and smart pedestrians walked with open umbrellas to shield themselves from the sun. I walked out into the neighborhood, a maze of white-tiled apartment buildings with a labyrinth of shops selling housewares, shoes, stationery, and other everyday items. Everyone from office workers to shop owners to street cleaners ate lunch at the same time. Construction workers sat on their wicker helmets, sucking up noodles and shoveling rice into their mouths. The hair stylists at the neighborhood beauty parlor lunched at their stations while their customers in the midst of a hair treatment looked on hungrily.

On the side roads near the main thoroughfare, food vendors were attracting lunchtime crowds with sweet potatoes roasting on metal drums. These were attached to bicycles, along with caramelized crab apples and bananas, glass jars of homemade yogurt, and steamed buns.

It wasn't difficult to find the spicy lamb-kebab seller. If the delicious aroma of grilled lamb hadn't guided me, I would have easily spotted the Uighur vendor's long white robe and crocheted skullcap. The Uighurs are Turkish-speaking Muslims who largely populate China's Xinjiang Province, also known as East Turkistan. Their cooking style draws from the recipes and spices of all the surrounding regions: Afghanistan, Pakistan, India, Tibet, Russia, and Mongolia.

The vendor didn't seem bothered by the smoke and summer heat as he methodically rotated the spicy mutton skewers lined up along the shoebox-shaped grill. I paid for three skewers and was about to leave when I felt a tap on my shoulder. I turned around and saw Eric.

"What are you doing? Did you forget something?" I asked, offering him a stick. I pulled a chunk of lamb off the second stick with my mouth. I closed my eyes for a moment to savor the tender, gamy meat with just the right amount of spice. Taking the offered stick, Eric said, "Thanks. No, I didn't forget anything. Listen, I feel bad about our conversation this morning."

I felt my heart rate quicken. I still loved this man. Despite my earlier thoughts of leaving, I heard myself say, *You know, I was probably overreacting. I need to realize that I'm not in the States anymore.*

Eric was about six feet tall, and he towered over me, embracing my petite frame completely, as he pulled me to his chest. I laughed, breathing in the smells of smoke, laundry detergent, shaving cream, and bedsheets. We held each other close.

"I probably should have said something to Chu Ping, but she doesn't understand all these things and I just didn't want to get into it," he said, stroking my hair.

My head was still pressed against his chest, but I opened my eyes when he said this. *But what about the next time?* my independent side cried out. *Will you stand up for me, or stand in judgment?* I wanted to ask, but I didn't. Instead I closed my eyes, pushed my independent self aside, and allowed myself to enjoy Eric's apology.

When I called my friend Gill, she was shocked that I had forgiven him so quickly.

"What was I going to do, just hop on a plane and come back?" I said lamely.

"Uh, yeah," she replied.

"Well, I didn't," I answered. "Maybe I should have, but I can't leave Eric until I know that we really aren't meant for each other." And with that, I dug in my heels and proved to my independent self just how much sticking power I had in me.

*My fondest memories* of living in Beijing with Eric revolved around the home-cooked dinners I made. I experimented with wilted bok choy or sautéed Chinese greens from the local farmer, served with garlic mashed potatoes; or flavorful but tough local beef, lamb, or chicken served with an inexpensive bottle of Great Wall red wine, the soap-sud aftertaste of which disappeared after the first glass. I'd light candles, dim the lights, and put on Pat Metheny, John Coltrane, or the Wallflowers. For hours we'd eat, drink, and discuss everything—past relationships, family members, ambitions, and childhood experiences.

It was on one of those evenings that Eric told me a boyhood story. He remembered hiding in the back of a closet in his parents' Manhattan apartment and being deeply upset at his mother. He couldn't recall what the circumstances were or why he was mad at her, but he vividly remembered sobbing and hiccupping in the dark hall closet, where scratchy wool coats brushed his face and head. But security and calm came over him as she stood outside the closet and told him repeatedly that she would always be there for him, no matter what.

"I think I was seven or eight, but since then I've always known in the back of my mind that I could try anything and my parents would always be there," Eric said.

Maybe those encouraging words were what had injected him with wanderlust. After college, Eric headed to Russia with a high school friend; they went on to plan a motorcycle journey across that vast country. But they ended up in Taiwan instead, where Eric had landed a job. (He had studied Mandarin in high school and college.) Eric returned to the States after a few years, to take a financial analyst position at the investment bank where we ended up meeting. What I remember and admired most about him was how determined he was to be appointed to the Shanghai office. Once he got to China, he hoped to make his fortune there.

I can't speak for Eric, but my attraction to him was different from what I'd felt in other relationships. Of course I was physically attracted to him; I couldn't resist his dark, Irish American good looks, his chestnut brown hair, and his pale complexion that burned, then freckled. He was naturally thin, despite his preference for sitting and talking over a bottle of wine over working out at the gym.

Eric was the first person I'd been close to since my uncle George who told me I could do whatever I wanted if I put my mind to it. This statement is elementary and often told to children, but it was like angelic harp music to my ears. I spent my childhood being corralled into doing what everyone else wanted, particularly as I struggled to assimilate into American Midwest culture while being raised by Japanese immigrant parents. I remember vividly this sense of constant reaching and wanting, never settling, never being satisfied, that lasted well into my adulthood.

After moving to Washington, D.C., after college, I moved to San Diego and finally settled in San Francisco, where, I was certain, all my dreams and ambitions would come together. When that didn't happen, and I was instead confronted with a failed marriage at age thirty, I was crushed.

On our early dates, Eric and I got into heated arguments as he tried to convince me to pursue my dreams of quitting my job and moving to Japan, or becoming a freelance writer. He told me that I needed to conquer my fears, or I would never achieve what I wanted in life. He thought I was just making excuses when I said financial security was a major factor in taking such risks. Rather than feeling alienated by his pushing me to change my life, I envied his cavalier attitude and found myself even more drawn to the way he looked at life.

I'd learn later that Eric was fond of those "if you're unhappy, just quit your job" conversations. Friends and acquaintances often shared their reactions to his suggestions, which ranged from defensiveness to amusement to scorn. My lack of self-confidence seemed to attach itself to this man. Around Eric, the idea of living the dream became conceivable; he was providing water and sun for the tiny seed in my mind that craved more experiences. He became my guru, and I his groupie. The thought of not being with him was devastating, and I uprooted my life to prevent that from happening.

*Fall in Beijing was as beautiful* as it was cruelly fleeting. Like the sweep of a silk shawl falling from bare shoulders, the haze of pollution lifts, and blue skies and billowing clouds cap the city. The mountains surrounding the three sides of China's capital become visible and majestic, like the prongs of a crown.

In anticipation of the night when the moon is at its most brilliant and full, the Moon Festival is celebrated with feasts, dancing, and moongazing. I didn't know the importance of this holiday until Eric brought home boutique-style shopping bags full of boxes of mooncakes that his clients and coworkers had given him. In autumn, these mooncakes are as prevalent as Girl Scout cookies during fundraising season, or fruitcake at Christmastime. The cakes are sold on every corner, in malls, and in office buildings' lobbies.

I dug into Eric's mooncakes before he even set them down on the table. I love sweet red-bean paste, which is used in Japanese *okashi,* and I assumed the Chinese version must be similar.

Eric had received a fancy box containing four square treats. The thin, moist casing was embossed with leaves and a flower, and each cake had a different filling: red-bean paste (my favorite), lotus-seed paste, black-bean paste, and double yolk from salted duck eggs, which I never acquired a taste for.

*A few days after the Moon Festival,* I awoke one morning to find Eric standing by the bedside.

"Mrs. Xue wanted to stop by and do a language exchange with you," he said.

"Who? What are you talking about?" I sat up and lowered my head, letting my hair fall around my face. I hate being woken up and engaged in a conversation that has absolutely no context. I rubbed my eyes. Through the open window, morning sunlight streamed in and the sound of laughing children echoed from the sidewalk. The bedroom had that clean fall chill that made me want to snuggle back under the blanket.

"Mrs. Xue—she's our managing accountant's wife. She came into the office last week. When I told her about you, she mentioned that she'd like to do a language exchange with you." Eric sat down on the bed. "She's sitting in the dining room now."

"What?!" Was he losing his mind, or was it just that boundaries started to evaporate after a certain period of time in China? "Eric, I just woke up. I'm not going to have a language exchange this early in the morning. I can barely speak English right now." I wanted to ask him why he hadn't mentioned this to me before. The communication, or lack thereof, between us was clearly a recurring issue. "Can't you tell her to come back later?"

Eric shrugged his shoulders. "I think she works in the daytime. She's a radiologist at a hospital."

I knew that Mr. and Mrs. Xue lived in our building, and, as it turned out, Mrs. Xue's commute to our apartment was about four floors. We lived on the eighth floor of a twelve-story apartment building. In typical Chinese fashion, all the executives and their families lived in the same building. Ours was located in Yayuncun, or the Asian Games Village, in northeastern Beijing. The area was developed in 1990, when China hosted the eleventh Asian Games sporting event in Beijing. The event was considered a dress rehearsal for the Olympic Games in 2000. Beijing didn't win its bid to become the host city, but in honor of its candidacy, the city built hotels, arenas, and a stadium. In 2008, the area would hold the summer Olympic games.

"I guess this is one of the disadvantages of living in the same building as your coworkers," Eric said. I knew he was joking, but I wasn't amused. My desire for alone time and privacy was unusual in close-knit Chinese culture, particularly business culture. Every morning, the executives of Eric's company met at the apartment building's curb, where a driver in a Cedric, a Crown Victoria knockoff, waited. Five people, including the CEO's wife, would stuff themselves into the car. The need for a bit of personal downtime before or after work to read, think, or be alone was completely foreign to the Chinese. Eric's initial insistence on taking a cab on his own was considered odd, a response that was not surprising in a country where several families occupy one apartment, and several siblings share a bed. I admired how the Chinese could zone out and find their own mental space in a crowd. I remember talking with a group of affluent Chinese who had grown up poor, and who spoke with great affection about the good old days, when they'd slept four to a bed and shared a kitchen and a bathroom with six other families.

"Didn't you say you wanted to learn Chinese?" Eric insisted. "She's eager to practice English." I was caught up in a now familiar standoff between my two sides. I was finding myself getting sucked into my obligations more readily than I could ever have imagined before I'd moved here to be with Eric.

"Yeah, I said I wanted to learn Chinese, but someone showing up at seven in the morning isn't what I had in mind." Eric was silent.

"Oh, all right!" I said, giving in. I put my clothes on and washed my face. I had pinkish circles under my eyes. The night before—as usually happened when we stayed in for dinner—we'd polished off a couple of martinis and shared a bottle of wine. I needed coffee desperately.

Mrs. Xue was sitting at the dining room table with a small note-book, a pen, and a Chinese-English dictionary in front of her. She was probably in her early fifties, but the vitality of her skin and her thick, wavy hair gave her the look of someone much younger. She had the high cheekbones and jawline of a cover girl, and her deep-set eyes were as shiny as polished chestnuts. I was taken aback and intimidated by her beauty.

"*Ni hao,*" she said, giving me a smile. Her teeth were straight and white, of course.

"*Ni hao,*" I said, not sure what to say next.

"Excuse me for just a second. I need to make some coffee," I said abruptly. Mrs. Xue frowned, perhaps trying to process what I had said.

"*Hao,*" she said with a little smile.

Chu Ping was wiping dishes in the kitchen. I saw her look up, and felt a flash of resentment at being left alone with two Chinese women.

"I gotta run," Eric said, giving me a quick peck on the cheek. "Thanks for stepping up."

I made my coffee, which was a French roast I'd bought at a coffee shop called Johnny's Coffee. It was some brand I'd never heard of, but it did the trick. I added milk and sugar, took a sip, and felt the magic happen almost instantly.

I sat down opposite Mrs. Xue and noticed her looking at my coffee cup.

Chu Ping had her feather duster and was dusting the entertainment center in the living room.

"Oh, I'm sorry," I said, embarrassed. "Would you like something to drink?" I motioned with my hand, like I was drinking from a cup.

"*Wo bu yao kafe,*" she said, shaking her head and enunciating every syllable for my benefit.

"*Kafe*." Sounds like coffee. "*Bu yao*." She doesn't want any coffee. I knew what *bu yao* meant. I'd say it when hawkers of scarves, kitchen utensils, and umbrellas approached me with their wares. Chu Ping said something to Mrs. Xue from the living room. Mrs. Xue laughed and said something back. I wished I knew how to say, "Go find somewhere else to dust" in Chinese.

"Would you like something to drink?" I asked, speaking slowly and motioning again with my hand.

"*Yao*," she answered. Yes. Okay, maybe this could be fun.

"What would you like to drink?"

"*Wo yao he yibei chashui*," she responded.

"*Chashui? Chashui?*" I asked myself repeatedly, hoping it would ring a bell. "*Cha*. Tea? You want some tea?" I asked out loud in English.

"That's right," she said, in very good English. It startled me, the way hearing a mime suddenly speak would.

"Do you speak English?" I asked.

"A little," she said shyly. I knew that when my parents' modest Japanese friends said they knew a little English, it meant they knew quite a bit. Mrs. Xue was a radiologist, a doctor, educated. Of course she knew English.

I paused. I felt stupid in the aftermath of the toddler-level exchange we'd just had.

Mrs. Xue sat there and smiled at me. "It's better for you to learn Mandarin if you don't know I speak English."

She was right. I was working hard and struggling to decipher what she was saying because there was no alternative to communicating. But when I learned that she spoke some English, that urge to try simply disappeared. I was doing Eric a favor, but I wasn't at all eager to learn Mandarin yet.

Mrs. Xue started coming to our apartment three mornings a week at the glaring hour of seven. The arrangement in the Xue household was that Mr. Xue was responsible for getting their son off to school so that Mrs. Xue could make it to the radiology department by nine. Most of the doctors I knew in the States were often tired and overworked, but Mrs. Xue always arrived looking fresh as a flower, like she'd had a good night's rest. She told me that she got up at five every morning to do qigong with a group in the nearby park.

We devised the language exchange so that we'd have equal time speaking Mandarin and English, but after a couple of meetings I noticed that we spent most mornings practicing English. I didn't know the grammar structure or enough words to form a sentence; we could work on eating and drinking for only a few minutes.

After a month, I began looking forward to these visits. Mrs. Xue was always warm toward me, and asked many questions about my life in America. She was eager to share information about new restaurants, and we actually had a fair amount in common. I never got out of bed until I heard Chu Ping let her in. Sometimes she'd arrive at the same time as Chu Ping. Oftentimes they were chatting pleasantly when I walked into the dining room.

One morning, Mrs. Xue arrived with a big shopping bag of packaged Chinese sweets, items that I'd mentioned I'd seen but was too afraid to try. The cartons contained cartoonish zoo animals grinning from colorful boxes; a cookie with red-bean filling and a funky, waxy chocolate coating; and a sponge cake–like cookie with whitish pastry icing on it.

That morning, I told Mrs. Xue how Eric and I had met in San Francisco, and she shared how she'd met her husband at the university.

As Mrs. Xue bit into a sweet red-bean paste–filled sponge cake, I asked, "Was this after the Cultural Revolution?"

"Of course. No one attended college during that time. We were just trying to find something to eat," she said with a chuckle. Laughing at misfortune and sorrow was familiar to me: My parents often tried to lessen the gravity of their own personal history with laughter. But it had always seemed to enhance the unspeakable, rather than lightening the mood.

"My husband and I went to university late, married late, and had our son late," she explained.

For her, going to college during that time was exceptional. As in many cultures, Chinese children often pursued their parents' careers, and the educated often educated their offspring. The Cultural Revolution under Mao, however, had attempted to destroy all social classes. Educators and doctors went into hiding or were sent away for reeducation, and the heritage and passing along of knowledge had therefore been abruptly cut off.

"Were your parents doctors also?" I asked, the cookies now forgotten.

"*Wo bu zhidao ni de yisi.*" ("I don't understand your meaning.") I knew what that meant; I heard and said it constantly. I couldn't imagine that she didn't understand me, so I tried a different approach: "What was it like for your family during the Cultural Revolution?" I asked in English, feeling suddenly stimulated by the conversation.

"*Bu zhidao, bu zhidao,*" she said, shaking her head and looking away. Suddenly, Mrs. Xue seemed to have lost her ability to speak English.

I dropped the subject and we moved on to movies. When she left, I realized she'd forgotten the bag of sweets, but I didn't go after her. She'd get them back the next time she came over.

But Mrs. Xue didn't show up for our next meeting. She didn't call or come down to explain. When she didn't appear for the third morning in a row, I took the elevator upstairs to the Xues' apartment, using the bag of sweets as an excuse.

I rang the doorbell. Mrs. Xue answered the door. As usual, she was classically dressed, in a fawn-colored V-neck and form-fitting black pants. There was some movement in the background and the television was on, with the volume blaring.

"Good morning, Linda," she said. I tried to detect some resentment or embarrassment in her flawless face, but I saw none.

"Are we no longer doing the language exchange?" I asked.

"Oh," she said, as if my question brought back some long-forgotten association. "I'm too busy now with my son and work at the hospital. *Wo tai mang,*" she added, smiling.

"I understand; that's fine." I hesitated before adding, "You never came downstairs to tell me you weren't coming, so I've been waiting for you."

"I'm sorry," she said. She looked over her shoulder in a way that indicated I was keeping her.

"Okay, maybe I'll see you again sometime," I said.

She nodded her head. As she was about to shut the door, I pushed the bag I was holding forward. "You forgot these the other day. I want to return them to you," I said, handing her the bag.

She backed away from it as if it were some foreign object. "*Wo gei ni.*" ("I give to you.") "Keep them, please. Goodbye."

"Bye." I stood there in disbelief, my face just inches from her wooden door and the number 1204. I walked down the hall and pushed the button to call the elevator. Before stepping inside, I tossed the bag of sweets into a nearby trash can.

During the elevator ride back to my apartment, I realized that Mrs. Xue hadn't invited me into her apartment. Rather than feeling annoyed by her blatant rudeness, I smarted, like a grade school kid spurned by the pretty, popular girl. Had I offended her, or had my usefulness to her run dry? I felt petty, yet I wanted an explanation about what had happened.

Later, when Eric asked how the language exchange was going, I made him believe that we had decided mutually to quit the early morning meetings.

*The time I spent with Mrs. Xue* did little to help my Mandarin. When I tried to communicate, I felt just as frustrated as I had before. I didn't want to accept the fact that my neighbor had had only her own interests in mind when she'd shown up. And the way things ended with her had the effect of decreasing my motivation. There was no point in practicing Mandarin when I had no foundation to draw from.

Meanwhile, the situation with Chu Ping had come to a standstill. I wasn't leaving and neither was she. When I needed something, I asked Eric to relay the request to her. During the first few weeks, we exchanged only two words: "hello" and "goodbye."

My initial jealousy and feelings of being excluded ebbed, however, and I became accustomed to hearing Eric and Chu Ping carry on their chummy banter in the mornings. And despite my resistance to learning the language, I was determined not to abandon my book, and I felt more motivated than ever to drum up freelance work.

On a bright, invigorating Sunday morning with a snap in the fall air, Eric and I took a cab to the west side of town, to a small dim sum place located in a courtyard house. It was within walking distance of Ritan Park, the park where we had taken the crickets just a couple of months earlier, during the heat of summer.

It was still warm enough that day to eat outside, but it was going to be one of the last. The whole city seemed to sense this, and the entire populace was outside strolling, sitting in chairs, and flying kites. The hostess found us one of the few empty tables in the courtyard. I was feeling a bit sluggish after a late night of bar hopping with Eric in Sanlitun.

Our waitress was a tall, surly-looking, young Chinese girl wearing black Vans high-tops, a faded black T-shirt, and a thick studded belt. Her scowl indicated to me that she had waited on one too many of the expat customers who frequented the restaurant.

She threw down two Chinese menus and took her pen and pad out of her back pocket. Eric asked for English menus and she returned with just one, at which point Eric asked if she might bring another one for me. I was in a good mood that morning. It had been some time since I had eaten dim sum at my favorite restaurant in San Francisco's Sunset district, and I was looking forward to the real thing.

She scowled again, looking at me. She said something that sounded hostile.

I looked at her and said nothing, not understanding a word she had said.

Eric said something to her, to which she replied haughtily. Eric laughed and shook his head before replying. At that point, the waitress stormed off.

"What was that all about?" I asked.

Eric laughed again before telling me that she'd been incredulous that I couldn't read Chinese.

"So I told her you were American, not Chinese. And she accused you of pretending."

"You're kidding, right?" I said. I couldn't believe it. "She doesn't even know me." I was feeling very worked up; I was nearly out of my chair by that point.

Eric sat back, looking bemused by my reaction. "I know, but there are some women who do this when they're dating foreigners."

"But I'm not Chinese."

"I know, but she thinks you are."

I was speechless with anger. My thoughts were racing a million miles a minute, but no words were coming out.

"It's not a big deal," Eric said calmly.

"Of course it's not a big deal to you—you know Mandarin. And you don't get mistaken for being Chinese! Besides, she's a waitress and I'm the customer," I said, enraged.

"But you didn't understand what she was saying," he added.

"Well, now I do and it pisses me off. I'm sick and tired of being treated like shit because these people assume I'm trying to trick them!" I blurted out. "I'm Japanese American. Not Japanese *Japanese*—Japanese *American*."

I don't know why I felt compelled to say all this to Eric. He didn't need to hear my rant, but I had to say aloud what I had been feeling for weeks. I felt my anger deepening as the old unfairness of being prejudged washed over me.

I mustered my meanest, most powerful glare when the waitress came back with my drink. It was a petty, small-minded thing to do, but I looked her straight in the eye and said in English, "You know what? You need to mind your own damn business."

I searched her face for a reaction, but it was blank. She didn't give me the satisfaction I sought. She looked at Eric, but he told her only what we wanted to order, and they exchanged no further words about me or my heritage.

I kept to myself on the cab ride home while Eric read his *Economist.* I looked out the open window. Even though the air was polluted enough to leave soot marks at the base of my nostrils, I liked the wildness of having the windows wide open. When I saw the sign for the Fatted Calf Chafing Dish Restaurant, right off Third Ring Road, I knew we were near the Asian Games Village. I couldn't handle another helpless episode like the one I'd had at the restaurant that morning. Even if I didn't master the language, it was time to arm myself with knowledge.

"Hey, Eric," I said, turning away from the window. He looked up from his magazine. I looked at him with determination and asked, "How do I find out about taking Mandarin classes?"

# LAMB KEBABS

*This recipe has been adapted from one in* Chinese Home-Style Cooking, *by Wang Jinhuai and Xue Yuan. The Uighurs don't use a dipping sauce, but I think it makes a refreshing accompaniment, especially if you serve the kebabs as an appetizer.*

INGREDIENTS:

1/2 pound boneless lamb loin

1/2 teaspoon salt

1/4 teaspoon pepper

2 teaspoons soy sauce

1 tablespoon chopped green onion

1 tablespoon minced fresh ginger

Dash cayenne pepper (optional)

1 teaspoon Asian sesame oil

1 tablespoon water

12 (12-inch) bamboo or metal skewers

Mint Dipping Sauce (see recipe)

## INSTRUCTIONS:

The meat is easier to slice if it has been partially frozen. Trim any fat from the meat and slice it lengthwise into 10-inch strips that are about 1/2 x 1/2-inch thick.

Mix together the salt, pepper, soy sauce, onion, ginger, cayenne, sesame oil, and water in a bowl.

Mix in the lamb with your fingers until the meat is thoroughly coated.

Let marinate for 30 minutes or longer.

Preheat an oven broiler, or light a charcoal grill.

Starting at one end of a strip of meat, carefully thread the meat onto a skewer. Spread the strip evenly along the skewer, not too loosely or too closely, to ensure even cooking. Repeat with the remaining meat.

If using bamboo skewers, cover the exposed ends with aluminum foil. Broil or grill for 5–7 minutes, rotating every 2 minutes.

Serve with the Mint Dipping Sauce.

*Yield: 12 skewers*

# MINT DIPPING SAUCE

INGREDIENTS:

1/4 cup chopped mint leaves

3 tablespoons white vinegar

2 teaspoons sugar

1 tablespoon water

1 teaspoon white sesame seeds, toasted

INSTRUCTIONS:

Put the chopped mint leaves into a bowl. Add the white vinegar, sugar, water, and toasted sesame seeds. Stir until the sugar dissolves.

Let sit at least 20 minutes before serving.

*Yield: about 1/2 cup*

# Chapter 3

# WANING
## Blossoms

WHEN I WAS GROWING UP, Chinese dishes were as prevalent at my house as Japanese ones. I vividly remember my mother preparing delicacies such as juicy steamed meat buns, Hainan chicken soaked in an oily star anise-and-soy sauce dressing, and bok choy, grown in my father's garden and stir-fried with shiitake mushrooms airmailed from my uncle's rice store in Tokyo.

On the first of the year, we'd celebrate Japanese New Year with the special meals my mother toiled over for the occasion; then, depending on when the lunar new year fell, my parents would observe the Chinese holiday by taking my two older brothers and me to Dayton, Ohio, to eat at a real Chinese restaurant. It was such a special occasion that I had to wear a dress, and my brothers, their clip-on ties.

As a young girl, I was familiar with the food, but Chinese culture was as foreign to me as South America's or Africa's. I knew about Japan because my parents were Japanese, and the America I knew—in the small town of Versailles, Indiana—was 100 percent Midwestern.

I'd browsed through books illustrated with drawings of Chinese people in my school library, focusing on the ones that featured long-braided, slanted-eyed men pulling rickshaws, portraying Chinese servitude under colonialism. I knew these drawings were from the late 1800s, but I found them disturbing because I was often teased about having different-shaped eyes. The only other images I saw of China during my youth were the ones in my fifth-grade history book, of Chinese men building the railroad system across the American West, and some scratchy courtroom footage of Mao's widow, Jiang Qing, and the Gang of Four after the downfall of the Cultural Revolution in the 1970s.

Since my peers called me a chink as early as grade school, I developed a negative association with Chinese culture at a pretty young age. The first time someone launched this racist epithet at me, I didn't know what it meant. I asked Keven, my oldest brother, and he soberly told me it was a racist name for Chinese people. He only shook his head in response to my plaintive reply, "But we're Japanese."

By the time I was a teenager, this mistaken nationality became a pet peeve of mine. Even when I was being provoked, the fact that the person teasing me was incorrect seemed more offensive than the fact that they were using racial slurs. I became more fixated on pointing out this error, and on magnifying the perpetrator's stupidity and ignorance, than on the graveness of their verbal attack.

I never thought I would end up living in China. When the opportunity to visit Eric came along, I didn't bother to see where Beijing was located. I knew it was in China, and that China was huge, and that seemed like enough. My plans included spending time with Eric and working on my book. I had no intention of studying Mandarin or anything else related to Chinese culture.

Throughout college and my postcollege years, working in Washington, D.C., I was at odds with my Japanese identity. I felt that I had to be either Japanese or American, and that there wasn't room for both. During those conflicted years, I quit cooking Japanese food at home.

It wasn't until I moved to San Francisco, the city that showed me what Asian America was, that I came to realize that I could proudly and beautifully be both Japanese *and* American. Every weekend I went food shopping in Japantown, then hurried home to call my mother in Indiana and tell her what I'd bought.

The easy availability of Japanese grocery stores, bookstores, bakeries, and restaurants in San Francisco was staggering to me. Throughout my childhood, we'd had such poor access to these same things, and my parents had mounted such elaborate excursions in search of Japanese food and ingredients, that basic necessities—white rice, green tea, miso paste, and soy sauce—had adopted dire importance. In San Francisco, I took advantage of the opportunity to study Japanese and to become active in the Japanese American community there. Not only did I come to terms with my Japanese side, but, for the first time, my experience of growing up in the rural Midwest piqued the interest of people who had spent their entire lives on the West Coast.

For several years, I attended a Japanese language school and became a board member of the Japanese American Citizens League. My parents and I became closer as my Japanese fluency increased. Since I was studying kanji (Japanese written characters), I regularly wrote my mother letters detailing what I was doing. I asked her to correct my correspondence and send it back to me.

Right around the time I left for Beijing, I felt that I had finally fulfilled my longtime wish to feel proud and contented about my dual nationality.

My decision to quit my job in San Francisco and stay on with Eric in Beijing indefinitely altered all my original ideas about what going to China would be like. Suddenly, my need to communicate became vital, and I had to reckon with the culture and people that I'd viewed so negatively in my youth.

I had come to terms with my Japanese heritage in America, but not in China. In Beijing I was struggling in a different way: Not only did I want to push away that old Chinese association, but I also wanted to be seen as American. I had the startling realization—one that I kept to myself for a long time—that in China, I wished I were white.

*I arrived early for my* enrollment appointment at the Taipei Language Institute. The school was tucked away on the fourth floor of a conventional white-tiled office building on the east side of town, within walking distance of the Beijing Lufthansa Center, a landmark plaza with a five-star hotel and a Western grocery store.

I sat in one of the stained, slipcovered armchairs in the small student lounge. Scattered atop a scratched wooden coffee table were the morning *China Daily* newspaper and a glossy tourism newsletter featuring an iconic photo of Tiantan Gongyuan, the Temple of Heaven, on a spring afternoon.

Peeking down the pale yellow corridor, I saw groups of students and teachers disappearing into their assigned classrooms. The doors shut behind them and the hallway was soon empty and still, except for a sole cleaning woman whose shoes squeaked as she wiped down the floor.

When I'd finished enrolling in Mandarin classes, I had an appointment with an American woman named Susan, the publisher of a weekly English-language lifestyle and culture newspaper called *City Edition*. Since I was staying on in Beijing, I didn't want to abandon my plan of completing my novel and breaking into freelance writing, but I knew my only option was writing in English. My decision to learn Mandarin was far more about my yearning for basic communication than it was about hoping that I'd ever master it well enough to be able to write for a Chinese-language anything.

I was deep in thought when a petite woman with a short haircut and a pretty face, like a wood sprite's, stopped in front of me and asked me a question in Mandarin.

"Oh, um, I'm here to sign up for class," I said in English.

*"Ni xing Linda ma?"* she asked, holding her hand out for me to shake it.

I understood only the Linda part. "My name is Linda," I answered, taking her hand.

*"Shuo, 'Wo xing Linda'"* ("Say, 'My name is Linda'"), she said in a slow, measured voice.

I still didn't know what she was saying, though it was clear enough that she was trying to get me to speak Mandarin. I played along and repeated her. The same impatience and restlessness—about reciting the equivalent of a first-grade "see Dick and Jane run" primer—that I'd felt on my first morning with Mrs. Xue washed over me.

Beaming, the woman continued to speak to me in Mandarin until I blurted out in a desperate voice, "I'm sorry, but please, I just need to sign up for class."

The woman laughed and guided me to her office. "My name is Li Laoshi (Teacher). We spoke on the phone. I'm the administrator and teacher here. *Ni naguoren?*"

*Oh no, not again,* I thought. I looked at her quizzically. I was prepared to endure the frustration of learning a new language in class, just not at that particular moment.

"What country are you from?"

"America. I'm American," I said, bracing myself for the nationality discussion.

"Are you American-born Chinese?" she asked, as she scribbled in her receipt book before pounding it with red ink.

I sighed. "No, my parents are Japanese and I was born in the States."

We stood in silence as I signed some papers and she finished writing out and stapling my receipts. I dug through my bag for the envelope holding cash, and Li Laoshi handed me a thick red workbook from a neat stack behind her desk.

"Your English is really good," I said.

"Thank you."

"Did you study English here in Beijing?" I asked.

"No, in Taiwan," she replied.

"Oh, so you went to school there?"

"No, I'm Taiwanese," she said in a crisp, decisive way. I realized that her brevity and clear annoyance were much like my own. She'd been born in Taiwan, not in mainland China, and she was evidently tired of being asked this question. At the time, I didn't know the full history of the Chinese who'd fled to Taiwan with Chiang Kai-shek in 1949, when Mao Zedong and communism took over China. Although Taiwan and China have a financial relationship, China's insistence that the small island is part of its whole, not a separate state, creates strain between the two regions.

As we wrapped up the enrollment transaction, I was surprised at the impression Li Laoshi's answer made on me. I saw my own defensiveness and irritation mirrored back at me, and, like seeing a ghost, the reflection stayed with me longer than I would have liked.

*Outside the school,* the cold air, clear skies, and warm sun recharged me for my meeting with Susan. There was no trace of wind, just a caressing breeze from the north.

I had been in the school's stuffy rooms all morning, so I decided to wait for Susan outside the hotel where she'd asked me to meet her. Though I had spoken to her only briefly on the phone, I was surprised when I saw her coming my way, pedaling up the hotel driveway on a black-and-white Flying Pigeon bicycle. She was a Caucasian woman in her early forties, dressed in a well-worn navy blue Mao suit and looking very much like a young girl except for her chin-length, prematurely gray hair, which was covered by a jaunty cap.

As she leaned her bike against one of the tall potted plants flanking the hotel entrance, a uniformed doorman said something to her and she turned around to retrieve her bike.

"Susan," I yelled, waving to her.

"Hi, Linda," she said, as if we were old friends. "Let's go to the hot pot restaurant down the road. Do you like hot pot?"

I walked alongside her, and she alongside her bike. I liked Susan instantly. For the first time since I'd arrived in Beijing, I felt at ease, as if I were meeting a girlfriend back home for lunch or a drink.

"What was that all about?" I asked, looking behind us at the guard.

"He didn't want my junky-looking bike messing up the front of their hotel. Plus, I was wearing this." She gestured at her suit. "He thought I was a peasant, someone he can mess with."

"But you're clearly not Chinese."

"I know, I know, but that's how things have become lately, since there's been more prosperity. They just see the designer handbags and clothes, not underneath," she explained.

This was the first time it sunk in why the young construction workers from the countryside wore double-breasted suits with the designer label stitched onto the sleeve as they dug ditches, and why the young farm girls selling garden vegetables on the sidewalk wore knockoff Burberry plaid dresses and toted fake Louis Vuitton handbags. I had assumed they wore these items for fashion's sake, but now I realized that they were very likely hoping to gain respect by trying to look prosperous.

Susan's Mandarin fluency whisked us right to a good table in the hot pot restaurant during the lunchtime rush. At first, the hostess made an excuse about not being able to seat us, but Susan just started talking to her and pointing at some open tables. With an expressionless face, the hostess nodded her head and showed us to an empty table in the back.

As if in a choreographed routine, half a dozen waitresses gathered around our table. One switched on the gas tank that heated the hot pot, while another lit the burner in the middle of our table. Another waitress began pouring hot stock, mixed with the chef's secret combination of herbs and spices, into the metal vat she placed over the burner opening; yet another took our drink orders.

Two hand trolleys came rattling down the aisle and came to a halt beside us. One was loaded with sliced mutton, beef, shrimp, napa cabbage, lotus root, noodles, enoki and shiitake mushrooms, spinach, an assortment of Chinese green vegetables, tofu, and other items I couldn't recognize; the other displayed peanut sauce, soy sauce, chili oil, chopped garlic, minced cilantro, and rice vinegar.

Once our table was so covered with plates of meat and vegetables that we couldn't see its surface anymore, Susan and I were finally left to cook everything ourselves in the boiling stock.

Susan recounted how she'd come to Beijing as I slipped some marbled, lace-thin beef, spinach, and lotus root into the bubbling-hot stock.

"Back in the mid-'80s, I was working in New York City as a freelance journalist and decided to apply for a writing position for various Chinese publications. I got an offer from one and was off to Beijing."

I couldn't help letting out an "mmmm" when I tasted the cooked meat and vegetables coated in my dipping sauce mixture of chopped cilantro, soy sauce and peanut sauce, a heaping spoonful of minced garlic, and a drizzle of chili oil. The key to the hot pot's flavor wasn't in the dipping sauce, but in its broth foundation, similar to a fondue. Each restaurant had its own interpretation and secret ingredients or technique, whether it was its beef marrow or how liberally it used *mala* peppercorns, a unique and memorable spice from Sichuan Province whose name literally means "numbing" and "hot."

"My husband is Chinese, and we have two kids," Susan told me, as she checked the doneness of her shrimp with a small wire-mesh ladle.

Thinking about the students I'd seen earlier that morning at the Mandarin school, I asked Susan, "So, did you study Mandarin before you came here?"

"No," she laughed. "I'm not like a lot of people who come here thinking they have a Chinese soul. I was looking for some adventure, not to assume a new identity."

We both looked down at her outfit, then at each other, and shared a good laugh.

The lunch rush dwindled, and we continued eating and talking. The waitresses had bused and cleaned the vacant tables, and several were resting across their folded arms where they sat. The kitchen crew was sprawled out across the restaurant, eating and playing cards as the overhead television blared.

"I'm looking for the usual city-lifestyle articles, but Asia related, of course," Susan told me. "Travel pieces, but Lonely Planet/off-the-beaten-trail stuff, not fancy spa- or hotel-related travelogues. The feature stories can be profiles on a local, quirky personality or any investigative reporting. You get it, right?" she asked, putting money on the little tray the waitress had left with the lunch check.

I got it, but I couldn't think of anything I might write about. As we left the restaurant, I could tell that Susan was waiting for me to shoot her ideas. Stalling, I told her about an article I had written but hadn't yet published, about a trip Eric and I had taken to Lijiang in Yunnan Province. Located at the base of the Himalayas in southwest China, the charming village of ethnic minorities and rugged mountain vistas frozen in time was the ideal travel destination. Climbing onto her bike, Susan asked me to bring the story to her office the next day.

On the way home, I thought about what else I might pitch. Carving out a feature story seemed daunting and impossible, since I didn't speak or understand Mandarin. Here was my chance to land a writing gig in

Beijing, and I couldn't even come up with anything to write. "Write about what you know," I said aloud to myself. But I knew nothing about Beijing, except the things every newcomer does: Visit the Great Wall and the Forbidden City, walk in the *hutong*.

I was still full from the hot pot, but it was already time to start making dinner. I marinated the pork loin I'd bought at the German butcher. In the refrigerator was fresh, flaky baklava that I'd purchased from a Middle Eastern bakery next to the meat shop.

Eric came home. Preoccupied with what stories I could write, I half listened to him and nodded at the right moments as he described his day of training a new assistant. On autopilot, I pieced together the meal. Then two column ideas popped into my head: restaurant reviews aimed at Mandarin illiterate expatriates, and articles that would be all about tracking down hard-to-find items that expats take for granted in their native countries, complete with a list of where those things are sold in Beijing.

The next morning, after Mandarin classes, I stopped by Susan's office to drop off a hard copy of the Lijiang travel story. Her office was on the top floor of an eight-story, green-tiled building.

I gave Susan my article, which she threw on the pile of other paperwork heaped on her desk. Instead of sporting the Mao uniform she'd worn at our previous meeting, Susan was perfectly coiffed this time, in a tailored sheath dress with matching jacket, heels, and briefcase. There was no stalling with her, so I plunged into my story ideas.

She tapped her chin, not saying anything. "Let me toss it around, and I'll get back to you."

On my way out, Susan steered me toward the open office area. "Linda, I've been dying for you to meet Gina, our advertising manager," she said.

"Susan tells me you're from San Francisco," Gina said. "I'm from the Bay Area, too."

Half-Chinese, half-Caucasian, Gina was one of those geek-chic women I saw all over San Francisco. She was thirty-one, the same age as me, and had also just moved from San Francisco to Beijing. She wore tailored, stylish clothes and her hair was long and naturally curly. Her signature glasses added a studious edge to her sexy femininity.

Susan drifted away to her office as I stood and talked at Gina's desk. Soon we were in the stairwell, smoking cigarettes. I learned that Gina's Korean American husband had brought her to Beijing when he'd decided he wanted to master the language. He was studying full-time and she needed to work, which was why she'd come onboard to help Susan.

Before Gina got back to work, we promised to get together again. By the time I got home, a phone message from Susan was already waiting for me. She wanted to use my Lijiang article, and she was giving my two column ideas the go-ahead.

*I learned from some* finicky students at my school that Taipei was the most desirable location in which to study Mandarin because of its people's pure-sounding speech, devoid of the local intonations found in many Chinese cities where local dialects are spoken. To me, however, Beijing—the capital of the People's Republic of China, and the epicenter of Chinese history and culture—was the ideal place to learn the language. Unlike the flawless Mandarin the Taiwanese spoke, I liked the Beijing locals' noticeable accent: Words ending in "n" were punctuated with an "r" sound. For example, the word *yidian* (a little) was pronounced *yidiar.*

I learned this information and more a few weeks into the program, during the two fifteen-minute breaks we had every morning. We'd gather around the entrance to the small break room and the kitchenette, where the familiar *ping* sound of dried tea leaves falling into porcelain cups immediately conjured the taste of green tea in my mouth.

As is generally the case, people gathered according to nationality. Brigette, Jacques, Jean, and Paul, from France, were an inseparable group. The Germans, Johanna, Anna, and Freda, never left one another's side. Kimiko, Tetsuo, and Hiroshi were from Japan, and were quick to find each other as soon as our break started.

Joe and Julie were the only Americans besides me. Joe was an older businessman from Pittsburgh, where he owned a hand tool manufacturing company. I frowned at him when he told me he had mistaken me for one of the new teachers. Joe had been taking classes full-time for the past three weeks. He was living at the expensive Kempinski Hotel, just down the street in the Lufthansa Center.

Julie was a no-nonsense, thirty-eight-year-old attorney from Portland, Oregon. I heard from our teacher, Ding Laoshi, that she had left her husband, a copyright attorney, at home in Portland so that she could study in Beijing. Julie was carrying a full eight-hour-a-day class load. She raved about living in the student dorms. She told us how she'd roam the streets in the evenings after class, striking up a conversation with anyone who would talk to her.

I was intensely curious about Joe's and Julie's attraction to China, which was so strong that they'd left their livelihoods and loved ones. As I got to know each of them better, I learned that they were trying to figure out a way to live in China for a year or two. I hoped that perhaps something would click for me as well—maybe my own feelings toward China would change if I could grasp someone else's determination to live there. Was it based on a desire to make money, like it was for Eric, or was the incentive more emotional?

When I asked Julie about it, she responded, "I know, it's the weirdest thing." When she talked about China, she sounded like a youthful adventurous woman, rather than the formal, conservative lawyer persona that she presented. "My husband doesn't like to travel, especially overseas," she said. "I haven't been married long, and I just saw some show on television about China and I knew I had to get here." She paused, looking thoughtful, before continuing, "I don't have a plan, but I love it here—the people, learning the language." She drifted off. "My husband is coming for a visit. I hope he likes it, because I don't want to go back."

Joe's story was similar, only he had a plan in the works.

"I came here last year for a work conference. It was very informational, and I learned about how the Chinese manufacture their tools. Maybe I was in a rut, but when I got back to the States, I applied for a visa and decided that studying Mandarin would be an interesting thing to do. Like Julie here, I think I've got the fever too."

"So you plan on moving here?" I asked. He had already taken quite a bit of time off from his responsibilities at his company.

"I don't know if it's possible," he said, scratching his balding head. "Actually, it's impossible. In two weeks I go home, and I plan on staying there for about two months. Then I'll return, hopefully for another month. We'll see."

I envied the "fever" that Joe and Julie radiated. Their enthusiasm and all-consuming sense of purpose felt like the honeymoon stage of a romance, in which even little annoyances are charming.

Not having China fever made me feel like an alien at the school. Because I hadn't come to Beijing for the love of China, I didn't have anything to add when people spoke about everything they loved here. In class, I began to notice how good a particular student's Chinese was becoming. I started to wonder if perhaps their desire to be here was what was helping them to advance. It's true that I didn't know anything about the other students—how long they'd been in China, if they'd studied in their native country before coming here—but everything about my own disinterest seemed to point toward my shortcomings. Luckily, I wasn't the only one who complained about the hardships of living in a country that didn't offer many of the amenities that most of us were used to.

The poster child for suffering was Inga. Inga and her fiancé, Rudi, were Chinese who had grown up in Indonesia, both of them children of wealthy families. They were in their mid-twenties, taking a year to live and study in China.

When I first started taking classes, I signed up for a group lesson; the two of them and I were the only students. They both spoke English, but they were not very talkative. Rudi's hair was thick and parted perfectly on one side, very much like an Asian Ken doll's. His face was soft, and transitioned easily into a smile and laughter, but he exuded a seriousness that made him seem emotionally distant.

Inga was sweet and engaging, but also reserved. I asked her a lot of questions, which she politely answered with short, finite statements that stopped me from pursing further conversation. Both of them were recent college grads, and Inga explained that they'd known each other since childhood. I felt a kinship with them. Like me, they'd grown up in a culture that was foreign to their parents. Just as I'd spoken English while my parents spoke Japanese, Inga and Rudi spoke Indonesian and English outside the home. The Mandarin they spoke at home was rudimentary, not proper, and only enough to communicate with their parents.

They were in Beijing, Inga asserted, to learn the language correctly. Inga glanced over at Rudi, who nodded his head in agreement. It was as if she was confirming that she was conveying a shared message.

Inga, Rudi, and I spent the first week repeating the four Mandarin tones with different consonants. By the end of the week, my mouth, tongue, and jaw felt as if they were unhinging.

The classrooms at the school were small—about the size of an office cubicle. Each was equipped with a chalkboard, a small table, and a couple of metal folding chairs with red vinyl–padded seats. The height of the table varied from room to room. In one classroom, the tabletop reached my knees when I sat. In another, it came up to my chin, making me feel like a child. Each hour we changed classrooms and teachers; the new setting and person protected us from the boredom that sets in with the same teacher day after day.

Ding Laoshi was the teacher I had most often. Small-boned, she concealed her delicate facial features behind studious wire-rimmed glasses. But her natural beauty and long, lustrous hair refused to hide. Throughout the season, she wore the same style of conservative dress: a Mandarin-collared, frog-buttoned garment with a long skirt and long sleeves in the colder weather, and a slightly shorter, sleeveless version when it was warmer.

At first, I found her giggle and the way she always laughed at her own jokes quite annoying, but as I got to know her I looked forward to her lightheartedness and goofy sense of humor.

Ding Laoshi had a persistent gurgling cough, and it was hard for me not to visualize mucus working its way up her throat, since she'd always end her fits with an *uh-oh* noise before spitting into a tissue.

Every morning for a month, Inga, Rudi, and I sat next to each other on the same side of the table, facing the teacher. Rudi had a constant cough, too, and cleared his throat habitually. Between him and the teacher, I just sipped my tea and tried not to think about getting sick.

After spending an hour repeating what the teacher said, like macaws, we'd bumble through the rest of the lesson. I once asked Inga during a break if she and Rudi found our lessons together unbearable. It was nerve-racking for me to know that they already spoke Chinese, yet were going through the tedious basic exercises as if they had never uttered a word of the language before; I couldn't help but think that it was on my account.

Inga assured me in her sweet, lilting voice that there was no problem, that of course Mandarin was easier for them, since they'd grown up with their parents speaking it to them. But she insisted that they didn't mind going through the basics again. She felt that they needed to start from the very beginning.

One cold, rainy afternoon more than a month after we'd started our class, Inga asked me to join her for lunch. Rudi had other plans after school, so Inga offered me his lunch ticket to the dorm cafeteria. I was a bit surprised at the invitation—although I felt a connection with their youth, we didn't have much else in common. I had never been in the cafeteria, which was located across the glass walkway in the other wing of the school building. At every meal except breakfast, the students and teachers who lived in the dorms lined up to pick up one big Styrofoam box and one smaller one. Today's big box held vinagered vegetables in one slot, stir-fried pork strips in another, and some noodles. The smaller one held rice.

"So, you eat here every day?" I asked, as I broke apart my disposable chopsticks. The cafeteria looked more like a conference room than any school lunchroom I'd ever seen.

Inga sighed and said in her slight accent, "Yes, every day. I'm so tired of it." Inga's hands were so small that her chopsticks looked like drumsticks between her fingers.

I took a bite of the fatty pork strips, cooked with onions and snow peas. It was surprisingly good, especially the sliced celery with lily bloom. But I could see how eating this kind of food every day would get old very quickly.

To make conversation, I asked her where Rudi was.

"He's having lunch at the Kempinski Hotel," she said dramatically, suddenly bursting into tears. "I love him, but he's so bourgeois. He thinks only about material things and comforts."

She and Rudi were together constantly, so she knew no other students except me. It turned out that Inga's motivation for asking me to lunch was simple: She was looking for someone to talk to.

I understood what she was going through, because I had my own reservations about Eric. Over lunch, I listened as Inga unloaded about all her unhappiness. She told me that Rudi complained incessantly about how awful the living conditions here were. I had peeked into one of the rooms during a tour I'd taken early on; it was slightly bigger than a farmhouse pantry and much too small for two people, even for a couple. I couldn't picture how they managed to sleep together in such a short, narrow bed.

"The rooms are a decent size for one person, but they do look a little tight for two," I said, trying to be honest without seeming like I was trying to take sides.

Inga explained that they were living on a stipend and eating only Chinese food to save money.

"Why?" I asked. Everyone knew that their families were affluent, but I left it at that. This was by far the longest conversation I'd ever had with Inga, and the amount of personal information she was revealing was overwhelming—part of me didn't even want to hear so many intimate details. I was growing uncomfortable with how desperately forthcoming she seemed.

"Before we get married next year, I wanted us to connect with our Chinese heritage. In Indonesia we are treated badly and our rights are limited."

"What do you mean, you're treated badly?" I asked, now genuinely curious and concerned.

"The Chinese are the minority population there." Inga went on to explain the tense situation for them in a predominantly Muslim country. Inga was ethnically Chinese, born in Indonesia. She and her family were discriminated against because of their ethnicity, and often the target of violence because of their privilege.

I had eaten the last grain of rice from my smaller box, and found myself fidgeting with my chopsticks, looking for something to do with my hands. Trying to leave her on a positive note, I said, "It's hard enough being away from home. I know that. It must be difficult with him complaining and all, but he seems to be trying. At least you have each other." As I spoke, I found myself poking my chopsticks through my foam lunch box, a practice I'd been told prevented the boxes from being reused.

She looked at me blankly.

"Are you going to eat your sliced meat?" I asked.

"No, please take it," she said, sliding her untouched food toward my side of the table.

"He didn't want to come here and study Mandarin in the first place," she said quietly. "He thought it was a waste of time, actually."

She looked at me with eyes like shiny maple drops. I should have stopped talking at that point, but I was feeling more comfortable, apparently, now that I had more food in front of me to distract me. I said, "Gosh, you're only in your twenties; you've got your whole life ahead of you." I realized instantly how clichèd that statement was, and how I'd hated it when people had said the same thing to me when I was her age.

She dabbed her eyes with her napkin and smiled slightly.

"Inga, honestly, you can't make Rudi see the importance of doing this. I don't know—maybe you're better off doing this on your own."

I watched as her smile suddenly faded.

*Our group class continued* as usual the following week. The week after that I heard from Julie, the woman from Portland, that Rudi was going back to Indonesia. I felt a quick jolt, something like the feeling of being out and realizing that you've left the iron on at home. The sinking feeling got worse when I learned from Ding Laoshi that Inga had decided to switch to private classes in the afternoon.

Ding Laoshi apparently thought my worried look had to do with my feeling bad about having kept Inga and Rudi back. She told me in Mandarin, "You're where you're supposed to be."

My compassionate side wanted to talk to Inga, to find out how she was doing and what had happened. I tried a couple of times to speak to her. I read her reaction, when I approached her, as friendly and polite but guarded. It was such a striking shift from her previous candor that I was overrun with guilt over what I'd advised her to do. When the opportunity to apologize arose, my good intentions fell short when she gave me what felt like an obligatory smile and said everything was fine, as if we'd never had our lunchroom talk. As noble as it would have been, I'm not very good at facing up to my errors—I'd rather be told off. I rationalized that I didn't know Inga well enough to invest more energy in something she obviously didn't want to discuss.

*With Rudi back in Indonesia* and Inga in one-on-one classes, there were no other students in my group class. Until other students at my level enrolled, I was getting a private education and receiving more than my money's worth, but the learning felt twice as long and twice as exhausting. I was improving my vocabulary and memorizing new words every night, and it was exciting to be able to assemble simple, useful sentences, but when I got to class all my hard work crumbled when I attempted to speak. What I said was garbled and unintelligible, and the same was true where my comprehension was concerned. I was cross about being corrected constantly and not understanding what the teacher was saying.

On one occasion I argued fiercely with Ding Laoshi, claiming it was impossible to memorize the numbers required of us in two hours. Another time, she grew impatient with me and demanded, "What is the point of this lesson?" I knew it had something to do with place words or applying possessives, but I got flustered and my eyes welled up with hot tears. "I'm not stupid," I sobbed.

Since I'd begun to study Mandarin, I was listening harder than I ever had to native speakers. Ding Laoshi suggested that I eavesdrop on conversations in Mandarin; I listened so attentively that I could detect the click of a tongue against front teeth, and the hiss of expelled air. During cab rides and at home, I listened to radio talk shows. It was challenging to force myself to listen when it would have been easy to let the words pass as meaningless noise, the way I once had. But I was persistent; I was on a mission to learn Mandarin. Even so, the language continued to be as elusive to me as China fever.

*In the States,* I'd always associated colder weather with carved pumpkins on porches and Halloween decorations in doorways and windows. In Beijing, the transition was marked by the servicemen who came to every home, office, and store at the end of October to switch on the radiators with the crank of a wrench.

Our apartment had become freezing by the time they showed up one October morning. Chu Ping was starting to resemble the Michelin man, so thick was the padded underclothing she wore each day. I took many hot baths and took to walking around the apartment with a blanket wrapped around me. Chu Ping suggested that I turn on the air-conditioning for a few minutes, claiming that the cold air would make the room feel warmer once it was turned off. I gave her the benefit of the doubt, but it didn't work.

Once the radiator was on, the dry heat ran nonstop until the same servicemen returned the following spring to turn it back off. There were no thermostats to control the heat, so when it started to feel too hot, the only recourse was to crack open a window.

In mid-autumn, before the air became choked with the smoke rising from coal blocks burned by locals for heat and cooking, I reached my first learning plateau. I could count, ask for directions, state simple observations and opinions, give out information about myself, and, most important, order food in Mandarin.

One morning, I noticed that Ding Laoshi was sipping something tasty looking and frothy white. When she saw me staring, she offered me a sip. It was milk thickened with oatmeal, with green tea added for flavor. I loved it, and from that day on it became my morning drink of choice.

During another class, I noticed a beautiful assortment of red wolf-berry seeds, flower buds, and nuts floating in Ding Laoshi's mug. It was a kind of medicinal flower tea that's good for the throat and lungs. She gave me a packet to try.

The following week, Ding Laoshi brought Chinese cookies that tasted like English tea biscuits, but sweeter, to accompany our drinks.

At times I was lazy during my lessons, particularly on mornings when I'd had too much to drink the night before. Many times I longed to talk to Ding Laoshi outside the parameters of my limited Mandarin vocabulary. Our conversations usually turned from the incidental, like the latest pirated movies the vendors were selling in Sanlitun, to the deep and personal aspects of our lives.

I told her about my youth in middle America, and I learned that she'd grown up in Shanghai. She and her sister had been born before 1979, when the one-child policy was enacted. Her father was a professor who encouraged academics and scholarly vocations. She talked fondly about the weekend lunches she'd shared with her parents and sister, when her mother would prepare a feast and the family would engage in discussions about politics and culture.

She shared with me the details of her conflicted relationship with her boyfriend. He'd been a monk for three years and was now a religious scholar working at a Buddhist publishing house. On the side, he sold religious statues and other supplies.

I didn't have any girlfriends to talk to about my relationship with Eric, so I welcomed these conversations.

One particularly cold, gray morning, I arrived late for class. Ding Laoshi was sitting in the classroom, reading a book while she waited for me. I was flustered when I sat down, in part from rushing to class, but she could tell that there was more to my preoccupation than my tardiness. When she asked me what was going on, I felt that I really did have a friend in her. I told her about a fight I'd had with Eric the previous night.

I had painstakingly made vocabulary flashcards since the beginning of my language program. I had been adding and practicing new words with each lesson. After dinner two nights earlier, I'd asked Eric to go through the cards with me to see if I had memorized them correctly. I thought he would enjoy sharing in my learning experience, since he was fluent and seemed genuinely supportive of my learning the language.

He flashed a card to me with the word "tomorrow" on it.

"*Mingtian*," I said.

"No, it's *ming-tian*," he said, correcting me by enunciating the first syllable like a question, and repeating the second in a higher pitch.

"Okay, *mingtian*," I said, imitating him.

The second card was the word "happy."

"*Gaoxing*."

"No, *gao–xing*," he said, repeating the first syllable again in a higher pitch, then dropping it sharply for the second syllable.

"Isn't that what I said?"

"No, you're using no tones whatsoever."

"Okay, I'll try," I said feeling self-consciousness creep into my initial breeziness.

As we went through each card, Eric became quieter. After a few more cards, Eric said he was tired and we stopped. The next evening I asked him to go through the flashcards with me again.

"I can't," he said.

"Why not?" I asked, even though I had a nagging feeling that he was going to tell me something I didn't want to hear.

"You're not using the right tones. It's wrong," he said with finality.

I felt like an imbecile. The independent side of me was already long gone by that point. She would have spoken up and countered with: "Then why do all the local people talk to me and understand what I'm saying?" Instead, I decided that I couldn't speak a word of Mandarin in front of Eric. Years after I became better at the language and could get around confidently in various situations, I would slide silently into a cab next to Eric and let him instruct the driver. At restaurants, I let him order. If I had to speak in his presence, it was as if all the years I'd spoken Chinese melted away, and I found myself sitting across the table from Eric that evening with the flashcards, the cards slipping from my fingers and scattering across the table and onto the floor.

I still believe he didn't hurt my feelings intentionally, but rather because he was a perfectionist—with himself and with me. But my putting up with this kind of behavior from him, which I wouldn't have tolerated from anyone else, reflected both how much I loved him at the time and how much I depended on him while I was living in China. And Eric's refusal to help me with my Mandarin flashcards was only the beginning of this type of display from him. As the years crept by, I'd see that same look of discomfort when I gingerly tried to engage him in a discussion about politics or economics. There were things that seemed to be simply off-limits, and rather than assert myself, I allowed my own confidence to erode again and again.

As I retold the story to Ding Laoshi, I wondered out loud whether Eric and I should stay together. All this talk must have sparked Ding Laoshi to examine her doubts about her former-monk boyfriend.

"A similar situation happened to me last year," she said, "a situation that tested my feelings for him." Tears started running down her face, and she couldn't speak. I didn't say a word as she tried to regain her composure.

The words that followed were difficult to comprehend, but I didn't want to ask her to repeat herself. I gathered that the year before she'd been very sick, so sick that she'd been bedridden. Ding Laoshi was very thin and frail, and her appearance, plus her constant coughing, made it easy to imagine that she could have been that ill.

At the time, Ding Laoshi and her boyfriend had been living together, and he'd had to take care of her. At one point, he did the unthinkable, telling her that she was making up her illness, and that nothing was wrong with her.

As if she were speaking to herself, she said, "I should have just filled his thermos with hot water, as he wanted. It was a simple thing to do, but I was so weak. All he wanted was the hot water for tea by his desk. I saw that he was selfish. He thought only about what made him happy."

I felt that familiar panicky jolt, and an overwhelming urgency to talk to Inga came over me. Who was I to give her relationship advice when I was allowing Eric's superiority to gnaw away at my self-esteem, all in the name of love? I felt myself get misty eyed. I didn't know if I was crying for Ding Laoshi and Inga, or for my lack of assertiveness when it came to Eric.

As if reading my mind, Ding Laoshi said with a tragic smile, "I guess everywhere the woman's lot is a difficult one. We start off hopeful and beautiful, then fade away like waning blossoms."

Ding Laoshi was digging through her book bag, looking for a packet of tissues, when the bell clanged, announcing the end of class.

*Money was stolen from* Li Laoshi's office on a Friday afternoon. On Monday morning, Ding Laoshi informed me about what had happened. Apparently, someone had walked into the administrators' office while Li Laoshi was in the ladies' room.

The Beijing police had been called in to investigate the crime. According to Ding Laoshi, the Beijing teachers were all under suspicion and had been brought in over the weekend for questioning. Their bank accounts were checked, and their dorm rooms searched without a warrant.

Neither the students nor the Taiwanese teachers were questioned. Ding Laoshi and the other Beijing teachers believed this treatment was unfair. She only shook her head, though.

"That doesn't make sense," I protested. "Shouldn't every one of us be a suspect? Why just the Beijing teachers?" I asked.

"If you are a foreigner, the authorities think you are rich and therefore untouchable," she replied, stone-faced.

"Isn't it obvious that a student is the likely suspect? None of the students I know have a lot of money! And why would an educated teacher risk their job and face criminal punishment for a couple hundred bucks?" My head reeled from how ludicrous it all was. They'd checked the teachers' bank accounts? Would a thief really be that shortsighted?

"It's because the police can do these things," Ding Laoshi told me, "to show their power as an example. Sometimes I think it's so unfair. I try to live like a model Chinese woman because I'm proud of being Chinese. I dress traditionally. The Western students sometimes ask me out. I pretend they are teasing me and laugh. I would not change my stature to date a white man. Yet the citizens of the Republic are distrustful of one another. The uneducated rule—whether it is the local police or the local district leaders. Decisions are based on money and face."

The mood at the school deteriorated further as rioting and unrest in Indonesia mounted: Citizens were protesting hikes on fuel prices and taxes, and demanding that the president step down. I wondered how much the political upheaval and economic problems had affected Inga.

Before the final class of my first session, I'd seen the students saying their goodbyes to her. I asked Ding Laoshi where Inga was going. Was she going back to Indonesia? Soberly, she steered me into the student lounge, away from the cake where everyone was gathered. She told me in a low voice that the political unrest in Indonesia had caused Inga to have to transfer downstairs.

"Downstairs?" I asked Ding Laoshi.

She nodded. "Yes, Inga has transferred to the International Youth University. It's a Chinese-run language school. It's much less expensive than TLI," she added, looking me directly in the eye. It seemed that Inga couldn't go home, and finances were tight.

I joined the group eating the farewell cake, a cloyingly sweet concoction of yellow sponge cake, not unlike Twinkies held together with whipped cream.

I finally had an opportunity to speak to Inga when she went to cut more cake. "Inga, I'm sorry you're leaving the school," I began.

"It's for the best for now," she said, with her usual grace.

"Um, I hope I didn't say anything when we had lunch to break things up between you and Rudi. It was wrong of me to give you advice like that," I said, thinking to myself, *That wasn't so bad.*

"Don't blame yourself, Linda," she said, touching my arm. "Rudi and I are just separating for a while."

I nodded, saying nothing.

"I couldn't go home now, even if I wanted to," she said wistfully. Inga had let me off the hook, and while I felt relieved to have been forgiven, I was still ashamed for having advised her to move on from Rudi when I certainly couldn't move on from Eric.

The students grouped around Inga, and she promised to come upstairs and visit us from time to time. But we knew that this was goodbye, and that Inga, like Julie and Joe, and eventually even us, would become just another casualty of the transient Beijing expatriate culture.

# MOON CAKES

*No fancy equipment is necessary to make this*
*delicious pastry. I used a well-greased metal 1/3-cup*
*measuring cup as a mold. If you have a wooden mold for*
*moon cakes, soak it overnight in vegetable oil.*

INGREDIENTS:

DOUGH:

2 cups flour

1/4 teaspoon salt

2 tablespoons brown sugar

4 tablespoons chilled margarine

1/4 cup water

FILLING:

2 tablespoons chopped nuts (your choice)

2 tablespoons toasted sesame seeds

2 tablespoons pine nuts

4 boiled chestnuts, peeled

2 tablespoons finely chopped apricots or dates

4 tablespoons brown sugar

2 tablespoons margarine

1 tablespoon flour

GLAZE:

1 egg plus

1 teaspoon sesame oil

INSTRUCTIONS:

DOUGH: Sift flour and salt together into a bowl. Whisk in brown sugar. Cut margarine into 1/2-inch cubes; quickly mix into dry ingredients with a pastry cutter until it forms pea-sized crumbs. Sprinkle dough with half of the water, lifting it with a fork to distribute liquid. Add remaining water. Quickly gather dough into a ball, handling it as minimally as possible. Put dough in an oiled bowl, cover with a towel, and set aside.

FILLING: Combine nuts, sesame seeds, pine nuts, and chestnuts in a food processor; process until finely ground. Mix in dried fruit and remaining filling ingredients.

TO FORM CAKES: Preheat oven to 400°. Grease a baking sheet. Roll out dough as thinly as possible on a floured board. Cut out 6 circles big enough to line your mold. Grease inside of mold and line with 1 circle of dough. Spoon in 1/6 of the filling, and wet the dough along rim. Cut out 6 circles of dough just big enough to cover filling. Place 1 circle over filled cake and press down firmly to seal. Unmold cake onto baking sheet. Continue forming and filling remaining cakes.

Beat together egg and sesame oil. Brush tops and sides of moon cakes with the glaze. Bake for 30 minutes, or until golden brown.

*Yield:*

*6 (2-inch-diameter) cakes*

*Chapter 4*

# Home for the
## HOLIDAYS

ALMOST EVERY CHANCE WE GOT, Eric and I entertained at home, whether we were having one friend over for a full dinner, or a big group for drinks and appetizers. I found myself feeling most secure and whole in my relationship when I was surrounded by guests, listening to Morcheeba, Beck, or Dave Matthews, enjoying the egg rolls and little quiches Eric and I made together.

When we went to a party or met up with a large group of friends at a restaurant, nothing was more blissful and exciting than having my gaze fall on the handsome man across the room or table and realizing that he was mine.

As much as we enjoyed entertaining, going out, and being with our social circle, we truly were homebodies. We spent many weekends without answering our phone, as we didn't want it to intrude on our precious time together. Something about living in this vast Chinese ocean, far away from our old friends and families, brought us closer together. Without the distractions of television, movies, and social obligations, time had a special magic. We read in bed for hours; Eric propped up his head on all of our pillows, and I rested my head on his chest. We had nothing urgent to do, other than enjoying cooking and eating.

This isolation from the rest of the world benefited our relationship. Going against the grain by ditching our jobs and security in the States and testing our fortitude in the wild East unified us in a highly romantic and adventurous way. I saw us as two wolves breaking from the pack to live life in the harshness of the mountains. This fantasy storyline made me think we were special: We were visionary and unconquerable, among other self-inflating qualities.

At the same time, the fact that I'd moved to Beijing to be with Eric made the consequences of breaking up much more explicit, and that was both good and bad for the relationship—good in that we would have to be extra certain that we wanted to end it, and bad because we stayed together during times when we should have parted.

*One of our favorite snack runs* on nippy autumn weekend mornings was for *shuijiao* (boiled dumplings). Eric would hurry down to the neighborhood dumpling restaurant and return out of breath from running with plastic bags filled with steaming pork, beef, and vegetable Chinese ravioli fresh out of a hot-water bath. In other bags he carried whatever seasonal fruit had inundated the market that day. We often ate these simple, filling breakfasts as we read tattered *New Yorker* magazines and mystery novels.

We loved experimenting with the vegetables we found in the market. Using spices, soy sauce, and broth, we tried to make the dishes we'd sampled at the local restaurants. There was an incredible selection of cabbages: Chinese flowering cabbage, with tiny yellow flowers among the green leaves; bluish-green flat cabbage; and kale. We made stir-fried feasts with garlic shoots, foot-long long beans, water spinach, fresh water chestnuts, and bamboo shoots, and ate them over steamed white rice.

I was fortunate to taste an exquisite variety of Chinese dishes and styles of cooking during my years in China, but Eric and I also gravitated toward the American foods we missed. Plenty of hotel lobbies housed high-end Western restaurants, and some decent places in Sanlitun served pub-style food. But it was in our kitchen that we could best re-create the dishes we craved.

In the summertime I made light yet filling niçoise salads, Greek salads, and mixed-green salads. Fall and winter meant meatloaf, osso buco, leg of lamb studded with garlic and coated in oil, and beef tenderloin. Our favorite meal, though, no matter what the season, was a classic cheeseburger, built just the way we liked it.

Good, fatty ground sirloin was easy to obtain in Beijing, and the problem of the Chinese version of a hamburger bun, sweet and unable to hold up to the burger juices, was resolved with a new breadmaker. A hamburger is incomplete without hot, golden french fries, of course, and that presented yet another challenge. Once, we tried coordinating a McDonald's french fry pickup in conjunction with our hamburger preparation. While I got the hamburgers ready, Eric raced to the McDonald's down the street. We timed it so that everything would come together just right: As I was slipping the patties onto the buns, Eric would be stepping through the door with the fries. Unfortunately, the fries didn't stay warm for the trip home, and reheating them in the microwave wasn't an appetizing option, as they'd come out greasy and soggy. Then, by sheer luck, I happened to find bags of frozen shoestring fries in a hole-in-the-wall Chinese market, of all places.

*Few things brought us* as much joy as our homemade hamburgers and fries, washed down with icy Cokes. One weekend afternoon, after we'd enjoyed one of these perfect meals, we got into a discussion about going to visit my parents in Indiana for the holidays.

For me, it was perfect timing. My Mandarin was improving tremendously. I was speaking to Chu Ping almost daily, and confidently initiating conversations with strangers. My daily frustration surrounding communicating information had decreased considerably. Understanding what people were saying to me, without having to use Eric as a translator, was intensely gratifying. I knew I had to admit that Craig, the fellow who'd given the grandiose speech at the dinner in Uighurville my first week in Beijing, was right: My connection with the people and the culture was growing with my command of the language.

Even my freelance writing was progressing. I had published a restaurant review in a women's magazine in Hong Kong, but I still devoted most of my writing efforts to the restaurant and shopping columns that I'd pitched to Susan after our first meeting. Both columns were fun to write. I used the pseudonym Miss Xiaojie for the restaurant column; I decided that the best way to entice readers into going outside their comfort zone was to create a dominatrix character who commanded them where to go and what to order, and told them that they'd be punished if they didn't enjoy it. Each column was accompanied with a sidebar providing the address and recommended dishes written in *hanzi*; this helpful technique was popular with readers.

Writing the shopping column familiarized me with Beijing's quirky side. I wrote an article about "sex health" sections of department stores and boutiques, in which middle-aged women wearing lab coats sold vibrators, penis enlargers, dildos, and condoms in a sterile, pharmacy-like environment. The column also helped expats like me who needed to buy a turkey and all the fixings for Thanksgiving, or hard-to-find cookie cutters and decorations to make Christmas treats.

In addition to freelance writing, I worked on my novel, and within a few months I had a finished manuscript.

I felt like my life in China was getting better, particularly compared with how I'd felt the summer I arrived. Eric's and my relationship was growing stronger, too—our love no longer felt wobbly. We were making a go of it as a new couple in a foreign country, and we were doing okay.

That being the case, there seemed to be no better time to introduce Eric to my parents in Versailles, Indiana. As wonderful as my life was in Beijing, my relationship with Mom and Dad had soured over the previous two years, since my first divorce. It wasn't the failure of my marriage that disappointed my parents, but its effect on me afterward. My move to China was, to them, the equivalent of my being taken over by some stranger they'd never met.

In some ways, I can understand why they felt the way they did. For as long as I could remember, I'd followed the "good girl" path. And my traditional Japanese upbringing in conservative Indiana was the perfect breeding ground for my fantasies of home, husband, and children, complete with pets and a freshly painted white picket fence—ideals that I carried into my early adulthood, as I developed a fascination with Martha

Stewart and decorated and organized my apartment to magazine-worthy perfection—for what, exactly, I can't say.

When I moved to Washington, D.C., after college, I couldn't choose between living in a slightly more expensive studio in upper Georgetown or a less expensive place in the then rougher Adams Morgan neighborhood. My aunt Milly was the one who advised me to choose a place I would feel confident bringing my parents to. Being as young and indecisive as I was, I found that this question could apply to almost any situation, and from that point forward it became the gold standard by which I judged many dilemmas I encountered. Though it helped me make decisions, I wasn't exactly making them for myself.

But when I got divorced, I spent the six months afterward dissecting my failed marriage and analyzing my past, and in the process I decided that I needed to lead my life differently. As when a cub first ventures out into the world, I decided that I had to detach myself from the fear that had always prevented me from taking risks. I would instead pursue the things I'd always wanted to do—like learning to ride a motorcycle. I enrolled in a training class and bought a used café racer-style motorcycle that I rode to work. I went to the Chinatown YMCA and learned how to swim, then joined the Dolphin Club at Fisherman's Wharf's Aquatic Park and swam in the San Francisco Bay.

My parents couldn't identify with what I was going through, and their vocal protests only pushed me further away from them. They believed in sticking with a job no matter how much you disliked it. Misery, in their minds, was better than not having the security of a regular paycheck and medical insurance.

It wasn't just my rebellious behavior that strained our relationship;

it was how they felt about my writing, too. My writing was fueled by the questions I fielded when I moved to San Francisco, particularly around the experience of growing up in a Japanese family in the Midwest. I submitted stories to various Japanese American and Canadian newspapers. I was getting published, being noticed for my words, yet my parents were never supportive.

My dream was to be able to support myself full-time as a writer, but I was doing all I could to work toward it, and it didn't seem like a tenable way to make a living. Before I left for China, Mom asked me what I was going to do once I got there.

I decided to tell the truth. My stomach flip-flopped and I felt like a ten-year-old.

"I'm planning on working on my book and freelance writing," I said, noticing the palpable nervousness in my voice.

"Writing is a hobby for you, right? Not a job," she said cheerfully. I could hear her low chuckle over the receiver.

"I'd like to make a living from it someday," I said.

"What are you talking about? What kind of job is that?" she exclaimed.

"It's freelance. I work for myself," I tried to explain.

"Oh no," she moaned, not letting me finish.

Why did I even bother? Deep down, I wanted her to support me and encourage me to give it a try, not to scare me away with her own monstrous fears. Our communication had been difficult enough when I was growing up, but as I'd gotten older, gone away to college, and lived my own life, I'd realized that my parents and I got along only when I agreed with what they wanted for me.

I put off telling my parents what I had planned for my future far longer than I should have. During a visit home over Mother's Day weekend, I announced that I was going to Beijing for three months to be with a man they'd never met. Mom waved her hands and turned her head away, saying, "No, no!" as if I were tormenting her. Looking down, Dad shook his head. His ironic smile hit home more than Mom's hysterics, because he usually sat and listened in the background, giving Mom the role of handling the proceedings.

"Your job," Mom wailed, "your job! What about your job? Do you have medical insurance? Why *China?!*"

When Mom got worked up, she became very physical. Her energy filled the air and she seemed to grow bigger. I felt as if I were losing my footing on slippery rocks, so I sat up straight and reminded myself that I was a grown woman and not nine years old.

That Mother's Day weekend, I silently let them voice their fears and I tried my best to deflect their worries. All I could say was that I wouldn't stay in China forever, and the idea that I would be returning after three months eventually seemed to offer them some solace.

As it turned out, that three-month stay turned into an indefinite period almost immediately. Once I'd made my decision, I didn't have the nerve to call Mom and tell her that I had quit my job in San Francisco and was staying in Beijing.

When I mustered the courage to make the phone call, Mom didn't say much, but I could feel her disapproval over the phone, emanating like shock waves. I was hoping that my visit home, and introducing Eric to my parents, would bring us all back together.

*Our flight from Beijing* to San Francisco was thirteen hours. Eric and I decided to stay overnight in the Bay Area, rather than get on another flight to the Midwest straight away. The next morning we flew out of the Bay Area and arrived in Cincinnati in the afternoon, where we rented a car for the additional one-hour drive to my parents' home. I felt giddy and nervous. I knew that Eric loved me for who I was, but I couldn't help worrying about what he would think when he saw the house where I grew up.

As we pulled into the gravel driveway, my mother and father came out to greet us. It was surprisingly sunny and bright for December—no snow on the ground, but the tips of the grass were dusted with frost. Mom was wearing a sweater I recognized as the one I'd worn in my 1984 high school yearbook photo. Dad had on his fleece-lined denim jacket.

"Here we go," I muttered to myself as I opened the car door.

As I introduced Eric to my parents in the cold driveway, I sensed the usual stiff formality that they reserved for people they didn't know.

Despite my embarrassment about the house—its claustrophobic smallness, its one tiny bathroom with no shower, its even smaller half bath on the second floor, and its aged wood-paneled walls, like the ones you see in 1970s dens—it was my home. Every piece of furniture had history: the heavy wood colonial dining room set that my brothers and I had chased each other around, the glass-cased cabinet containing *kokeshi* dolls and Japanese knickknacks, and the sofa where my brothers and I used to pile on Mom as we watched *Emergency, Adam-12, Cannon,* and *Mannix.*

I helped Eric drag our luggage up the narrow staircase that led to Alvin's old bedroom, where pieces of cellophane tape marked the spots where a *Star Wars* movie poster and pin-ups of Cheryl Tiegs and Jaclyn

Smith had hung. Except for some cosmetic improvements, the house hadn't changed much since I was a kid. In fact, it had changed so little that the entire space felt miniaturized, and Eric's height—almost six feet—only enhanced that perception. He must have felt like a giant.

Despite my feelings and the way I was taking it all in, as if through new eyes, I felt grateful for being able to come home to the house where I'd grown up. I wouldn't be able to truly define this sense of pride, or the strength it gave me, until having a child of my own made me want to try to emulate the same circumstances for him; returning to the same home that I'd lived in since infancy provided me with a priceless, secure foundation.

By the time Eric and I got settled and cleaned up, the sun was fading like burning embers, leaving thick streaks of begonia pink and violet before settling into a winter blue.

The dining room was festively lit, and in the center of the table was a burner heating a skillet of sukiyaki. White cubes of tofu, transparent cellophane noodles, bright green spinach, shiitake mushrooms, green onions, thinly sliced meat, and Japanese cabbage bubbled in a brown sauce of sake, sugar, and soy sauce in the very same *sukiyaki nabe* (cast-iron vessel) my mother had cooked my parents' first Japanese meal in when they were newlyweds.

The table was set Japanese-style, with individual bowls of vinagered vegetables, chopsticks, and extra bowls for soup and rice. At each place setting was an egg for us to break and beat in a small bowl. The cooked meat and thick noodles were then dipped into the beaten raw egg. The lightly cooked egg coating on the sukiyaki ingredients gave them a velvety creaminess.

Dad was seated at the head of the table; Mom was at the other end, near the kitchen. A carafe of warmed sake waited on the table. Dad motioned for Eric to take the seat on his right, the seat I'd sat in throughout my entire youth. I ignored a flicker of jealousy, telling myself that Eric was a guest.

Dad and Eric immediately started eating and talking as Mom dashed around in her usual way between the dining room and the kitchen. I excused myself to help her and began bringing out dishes of fish broth with egg and green onions; shrimp and vegetable tempura; stir-fried tofu, shiitake mushrooms, carrots, and asparagus; and salmon sashimi, as well as all the fixings for the sukiyaki.

Eric gave me a big smile, indicating that everything was going well, as I moved some dishes to make room for the beef slices. I smiled back when Dad asked where the wasabi was. He gave Eric's arm a friendly nudge and asked, "Do you drink beer?"

"Sure!" Eric said. Dad looked up at me expectantly.

"Yeah, I'll get it," I replied almost robotically. I was shocked at how quickly the words spilled from my mouth. I watched as Eric and Dad raised their square cypress-wood sake cups for a toast between bites, then looked into the kitchen at a cloud of steam rising over Mom's head as she added rinsed vegetables to a hot wok. I had been home for less than three hours, and already I was falling into the submissive role of my youth.

*All right,* I told myself, *don't make a big deal about this.* I reminded myself again that Eric was a guest, and that his getting along so well with Dad was a good thing. But my resentment bubbled as furiously as the sukiyaki cooking on the dining room table. I wanted to be showered with attention. I wanted Dad to invite me to sit beside him and ask me questions about my impressions of living in China. I didn't want to be looked at as just an extra pair of helping hands.

Finally, once all was delivered and in its proper place, Mom and I were able to sit down and start our meal. The flavors of the savory sukiyaki dipped in the raw egg wash overrode all the meals I'd had since I'd been home last. The good food pacified me enough to put my anger aside and enjoy the red wine and fixings that accompanied this traditional Japanese meal, as well as the festive family atmosphere I'd missed when I was in China.

Dad retold stories about coming to Indiana; Mom recalled arriving with no understanding of English. They both laughed off the challenges and pitfalls fondly, and credited good fortune for their having made it.

Eric paralleled their experience with our new life in Beijing. I listened with pride as he described his constant struggle to master Mandarin, and how I'd taken it upon myself to learn the language.

There was a lull in the conversation as Mom brought out teacups and green tea to conclude the meal.

Red-faced from the sake and beer and smiling, my father asked Eric, "Do you think Linda is a good writer?"

Eric looked at me uncomfortably. I was sitting right there, but being talked about as if I weren't present. He cleared his throat and said that yes, he thought I was.

Dad replied, "Okay," as if that were the only confirmation he needed.

But my thought that the discussion might be left at that was far too optimistic, because as soon as Mom sat down with her tea, Eric turned to her and asked cheerfully, "So, what do you think about your daughter being a writer?"

Mom looked around for a moment, as if trying to get her bearings, and then said, with no hesitation whatsoever, "Writer? Linda's not a writer."

A strained and awkward silence followed. I got up from the table without excusing myself, walked into the kitchen, and started running the faucet. Eric came in and said, "Go back out there. I'll wash the dishes."

"No," I said, fighting to keep from crying, "I think my dad wants to keep talking to you."

I was so distracted that I was just going through the motions. I couldn't focus on anything except the movements of my hands—picking up, scraping, washing, and rinsing the dishes—in the sink full of hot, sudsy water, and my tears dripping into it.

Later that night, Eric and I snuggled into the deep sag in the middle of my brother's old bed. He held and comforted me as I sniffled and cried about my parents' insensitivity.

Eric stroked my hair and soothed me, whispering that my parents loved me, that they were just confused about showing it.

I knew this on some level, of course, but my own ideas about how their support and affection should look were so deep-rooted that I couldn't see their love, and I didn't have the patience to tolerate their inadequacies. It had been a long time since I'd had that old, guilty wish that my parents could be all-American cheerleader types who thought anything their daughter did was great. I thought I'd accepted that they were never going to change, but here was my shame, rearing its head again, so many years later.

*The next morning* I showed Eric around town: the courthouse square my friends and I had driven circles around on weekend nights, the elementary school I'd walked to, the store where I'd bought candy after school, and the post office where my brothers and I had hung out during long, hot summers. We had lunch at the Colonial Cottage Restaurant, where I'd been a waitress. And we visited the state park whose gatehouse I'd worked at during summers off from college.

After so many months of breathing sooty air and walking around the congested streets of urban Beijing, strolling outside and showing Eric the highlights of my life in Versailles was refreshing and exhilarating. The country air was cold and clean and tasted sweet, like apple cider. Even though winter had stripped the trees of their leaves and left the grass frozen, the blue skies and pine trees were a feast for my eyes. It all looked so vibrant and alive compared with the drab charcoal gray of Beijing's sky and landscape.

Over a lunch of *chashu* (sliced pork) ramen noodle soup, Eric suggested that he and Dad catch the Cincinnati Bengals' home game. Dad loved spontaneity and was immediately up for it. The game was outdoors, so they bundled up in heavy parkas and hats that covered their ears. Dad siphoned some Chivas Regal into a plastic water bottle to take to the game, and Mom and I saw them off as they loaded themselves, loud and boisterous, into Dad's white Cadillac.

*Mom decided to make ochazuke* (rice soaked with tea) for supper for the two of us. It was one of my favorite childhood comfort foods—homey, simple, and uniquely Japanese. She used to make it at times like these, evenings when Dad took Keven and Alvin to a baseball game, or after my older brothers moved out and my mom and I were often alone at dinnertime.

I watched silently as she rinsed the rice. I took comfort in the familiarity of her movements, as I had watched her go through this ritual hundreds of times before. She swirled the rice with her hand in a whirl-pool motion, producing a pleasant *swish* sound as the grains hit the rice cooker's metal bowl. I could have gone off somewhere in the house and done something else, but there was an unsettled feeling between us that I hoped we could resolve.

As she set up the rice cooker, Mom asked me to get the tall canister of green tea from the cabinet. I saw containers there that I hadn't seen in years. There were Howard Johnson and Holiday Inn plastic ice buckets holding open sacks of confectioner's sugar, brown sugar, and gravy flour. In the drawers were ashtrays used to store rubber bands and twist ties. As survivors of the Depression, and having experienced great loss in their lives, my parents kept and recycled everything. My mother always surprised me by wearing my old clothes that I had long forgotten, including the sweater she'd had on when I arrived for this visit.

We had some time before the rice would be done, so we went into the living room with our cups of hot tea. Usually Mom turned on the television to watch CNN, but she didn't reach for the remote control. Instead she pulled a package of *osembe* (rice crackers) from the bottom shelf of her china cabinet. Each golden-brown disk, shiny with a soy sauce glaze, was individually wrapped to retain its freshness. The crackers were mouthwatering and crunchy, delicious with the green tea. We munched in silence.

"I have to talk to you about something important," Mom announced gravely. She walked over to Dad's desk and took out an envelope from the top drawer. She placed it on the coffee table and slid it across to me. As I opened it she said, "Dad and I made a living will. We decided that when we die, we will donate our bodies to science."

I didn't know what to say. I had barely spoken to her all day, and now this. She must have taken my silence for disinterest or my acting out, because when she spoke again her voice was tinged with hurt and anger. "There will be no funeral, so you don't have to worry about coming home. There will be no viewing. Our bodies will be taken away. Did you want to see us before we're taken away?"

I knew that Mom was trying, in her own unusual way, to gauge how much I cared about her and Dad. While she was testing the waters, her assertion that I didn't need to come home was true. My parents' plan for the disposal of their bodies was intended to create as little nuisance as possible for my brothers and me.

"Mom, of course I'm coming home, and . . . I don't know . . . of course I'd like to see your bodies before they're removed. Who knows what the situation will be then?" I answered haphazardly, flustered by the subject of my parents' hypothetical death and the poor timing of the whole conversation. Even though Dad was seventy-four and Mom was sixty-eight, they were both in great health, and Dad hadn't changed at all since the last time I'd seen him. He was fond of making a muscle with both arms and announcing that he was going to live to be ninety-nine. Mom complained of aches and pains, but she moved as fast as a striking snake.

So here we were, on our night alone, Mom wanting to discuss the scenario of their possible death, and I wanting nothing to do with it. There was a Chinese saying that discussing death invited it.

"Put that in a safe place," Mom said. "We have a little bit of money, but not much to leave you." She laughed at this.

"Mom, don't worry about it. I don't need any money. You and Dad paid for my college education. That was plenty. In fact, you should spend it now and enjoy it."

When my two brothers and I had all been in college at the same time, Dad had worked double shifts and overtime at Cummins Engine and sold his vacation time. He'd made so much during those years that we weren't eligible for financial aid.

"Eric is a nice man," Mom said.

"Yeah, I think so too," I answered.

"Linda, why are you so mad?" she asked.

"I'm not mad," I lied. "I'm tired from the traveling. I think I'm jet-lagged, that's all."

On the one hand, I longed to talk to her about my feeling that she and Dad didn't offer the support and encouragement that I needed; their inability to show their love for me openly, and their lack of respect for and pride in what I was trying to do, saddened me. Yet I couldn't bear what I truly believed: that discussing it with her wouldn't make a difference. I knew from past experience that it would only sadden her and make her feel like she had failed.

Less than ten years earlier, a year after I graduated from college, I was driving Mom home from a day of shopping. It was the type of rainy autumn afternoon when colorful wet leaves fall and plaster themselves on the car windshield, like papier-mâché. The sky was getting darker earlier each evening, and it was pitch black on the roads as we headed home.

Mom made a comment about how she had never allowed spanking to play a part in her and my father's child rearing. I had been paying close attention to the road, but I snapped out of my driver's trance when she made this declaration.

"But Mom, you slapped us across the head when we didn't behave," I said accusingly.

"Did I?" she replied, genuinely surprised by my assertion.

I brought up other incidents, which she also claimed she couldn't remember. The more I recalled, the more the pain resurfaced. "Mom, you used to say things to me that made me feel very bad. You got mad at me once because I didn't have a boyfriend like my other friends did."

On the windshield, the incident played out like a movie: I must have been thirteen or fourteen. It was a weekend. Mom was sewing at the dining room table while Dad enjoyed his pipe before leaving for work. I told Mom that my best friend, Tracy, had been asked to the prom. Mom asked me why I hadn't been asked. I didn't answer. "Why do your friends have boyfriends and you don't?" she asked, with a disapproving gleam in her eye. I don't remember if I said anything, but I recall hearing Dad reprimanding her as I left the room.

"I don't remember that," Mom said quietly.

People harboring negative feelings about past grievances with someone are encouraged to confront the other person in order to move on. Gripping the steering wheel that night, I felt my own anger, but I also felt anguish for my mother. She'd done these things without understanding the consequences of her actions. I believed that until that moment, she'd believed that she had raised me without the burden of physical pain. I couldn't be vindicated by dumping the anger I had carried all this time. The weight of her own emotional burden in the car that night felt like more than I could handle, and I vowed to never again make a big deal of the past.

Back in the living room, Mom attempted to pursue the conversation about my attitude just as the rice cooker clicked off.

Wearily, she got up off the sofa and I followed her into the kitchen, where she began assembling our supper. She usually used leftover rice for this dish, but we had eaten all the rice the night before. She put the new rice in a deep bowl, added some of the leftover meat flavored with sukiyaki broth, and put chopped green onions and pickled daikon on top. Over that she sprinkled *arare* (rice cracker pellets), bonito flakes, toasted sesame seeds, and a dab of wasabi. Last, she snipped thin strips of nori with a pair of shears.

She put hot water in the teapot and poured the green tea over the rice and toppings. With our bowls of rice before us, I left the discussion of my anger unresolved, letting it drift away like milkweed fluff on a breezy day. I felt I owed my mother some nonsensical chatter; she nodded and listened gratefully.

*Christmas came and went,* and I was back in Beijing to experience the first snow accumulation in years. It wasn't much, but it was enough to turn the stark, sprawling concrete setting into a temporary winter wonderland.

The morning after the snowfall, I happened to be lucky enough to be near the Forbidden City. I had just finished a very early meeting with a state-operated tourist magazine that was looking for English writers. Their office was located in a compound of several beautifully preserved *siheyuan*.

The meeting with the magazine editor took less than half an hour. It was midmorning, and there was no chance of the sun's penetrating the smoggy clouds. As my cab passed the Forbidden City, its tall red walls and moat coming into full view, I acted on impulse: I stopped my cab and paid my fare. Outside the gates, not a soul was in sight besides the lone person manning the ticket counter. In the vast main courtyard inside the city were just a handful of people, including one lucky photographer who was capturing images of the buildings cloaked in snow.

I separated from the rest of the people and found my way down a path where the only sound was the crunch of snow under my boots. Along a side passage away from the main palaces, large red lanterns dusted with white snow lined a building's corridors; their color blazed through the gray morning. It reminded me of a scene in the Zhang Yimou–directed movie *Raise the Red Lantern*, in which a lord signaled his arrival to one of his wives' houses by ordering that rows of large red lanterns be hung.

In my solitude, the present melted away. The romantic, extraordinary setting, with the red lanterns glowing and the snow blanketing the black-tiled roofs of the red buildings, seemed to whisper imaginary tales and forgotten intrigues. The story the cricket peddler had recounted to Eric and me on that hot summer day not so long ago came to mind as I imagined the way these surroundings must have appeared to a lonely, anonymous concubine, one of thousands, who kept as her sole comfort and companion a cricket, warm and fed.

# OCHAZUKE

Ochazuke *means "tea and pickles," but as long as you include
the bonito flakes, rice crackers, nori, and pickles, you'll create
the essential seasoning base. The Japanese tea is a key ingredient,
not an option. I prefer* hoji-cha *or* genmaicha. *If you want
to make more of a meal, you can add cooked egg, scrambled
with a drop or two of soy sauce and mirin (seasoned rice wine).*

INGREDIENTS:

4 cups cooked rice (fresh or leftover)

6 cups hot green tea

TOPPINGS:

1/4 cup bonito flakes

1/2 cup *arare* (rice cracker pellets) or crumbled rice crackers

1/2 cup nori (cut into 2 x 1/4-inch strips or purchased preshredded)

4 pickled plums

1/4 cup chopped *takuen* (pickled daikon)

1/4 cup chopped green onions

1/4 cup toasted sesame seeds

2 cups bean sprouts

Wasabi – to taste

Leftover salmon (cut into small bits) or beef (sliced thin)

INSTRUCTIONS:

Divide the cooked rice among 4 bowls. Arrange the assortment of toppings in individual bowls. Create your own flavors by adding the toppings and seasonings to your liking. Pour hot tea over rice and toppings, enough to cover the rice. Allow the rice and tea to sit for about a minute so that the flavors will meld (and will warm up the rice if it has been refrigerated).

*Serves 4*

*Chapter 5*

# Face
# VALUE

BECAUSE I DIDN'T SPEAK MANDARIN and she didn't speak English, Chu Ping had made it clear from the very beginning that she answered to Eric and Eric only. Chu Ping tidied and dusted Eric's nightstand, straightening his books and papers, throwing away his used tissues, and taking away his water glass. She picked up after him, took his shirts to the cleaner, and pressed all his clothes, including his blue jeans, T-shirts, and boxers, to brand-new crispness. But when it came to doing things pertaining to my space and things, she completed them only up to a point. She didn't dust or clear off my bedside table. The water glass remained there until I went to refill it or replace it the next night. She left my clothes and undergarments on the bed folded but wrinkled, hard and stiff as stale bread from hanging out on the *yangti* (enclosed porch).

I felt a spark of annoyance in the beginning, toward her and toward

Eric. I believed that many of our original misunderstandings could have been prevented if he had been willing to support my desire to have things done the way I wanted. Over time, as my Mandarin improved and I got to know Chu Ping better, she and I developed a rapport and a relationship apart from Eric. From her, I learned about the plight of the *ayi*, which translates to "auntie" and is the word the Chinese use for "housekeeper."

But long before Chu Ping and I got to a place where we were comfortable with each other, I was trying to figure out how to make the best of the situation I was in. We had to have a housekeeper, but Eric was dedicated to Chu Ping, and I didn't enjoy being ignored and disliked. I told a handful of my friends about my situation: Susan, my editor at *City Edition,* and Gina, the head of advertising, both of whom I liked and now enjoyed socializing with; and Miranda, Eric's friend Tulley's Shanghainese girlfriend.

Alert and jittery from coffee and cigarettes at a little café near their office, Susan and Gina mutually agreed that if I were Caucasian, Chu Ping would treat me with respect and go out of her way to help me. However, because I looked Chinese but spoke no Mandarin, I made her uneasy. I didn't want to believe that the friction between Chu Ping and me could be about race, particularly since it smacked of discrimination toward one's own race. I felt like no matter where I went, my Asian-ness influenced other people's ideas about the treatment I deserved as an individual.

Talking to a Chinese-born national like Miranda offered me a firsthand glimpse of Chinese housekeepers' disposability. I explained my situation to Miranda over cocktails one night, and found her attitude strikingly similar to the ideas about "the help" that I was not fond of in the West.

I recalled how the first night I'd met her, at the Hidden Tree Bar, she'd been dressed up like Daisy Duke. This particular evening Miranda seemed to be channeling Princess Leia with her midlength white dress, white boots, and silver lipstick. Sipping her gin and tonic, Miranda was outraged by Chu Ping's attitude; she offered to set things straight on my behalf. Her authoritarian air put me off and made me feel protective. I declined her offer.

"If you're not happy with her, just fire her, hire another one, and train her to do what you want," Miranda said. I shuddered inside, feeling guilty about talking about another human being as if she were a circus monkey.

"That's not really an option," I responded, treading lightly on this subject. "Eric hired her and he's really fond of her. I don't really have a say."

"Ahh," Miranda said, with a knowing look in her chestnut-brown eyes.

"What?" I asked.

"If you have no say, she will never show you respect." She cast her face downward dramatically before driving home the message: "She sees you as her equal."

I didn't know what to make of this comment, exactly, because I believed Chu Ping *was* my equal as a fellow human being. In the States I'd known housekeeping as merely a job, but here it designated a person as inferior, socially and otherwise. I was becoming increasingly uncomfortable with the conversation.

"How much do you pay her a month?" Miranda began questioning me like a gumshoe on the trail of a criminal.

"A little more than average," I replied, looking away and trying to figure out how to change the subject. "Do you know if they serve food here?"

"Like, how much more?" she pressed.

"A thousand yuan a month," I blurted out. "Hey, I see someone eating french fries!"

"That's too much!" Miranda shrieked. I covered my ears. I knew she would react this way.

"Well, it's a little more than a hundred dollars a month," I explained. "Eric believes that she'll appreciate her job and go out of her way."

"You mean he *hopes* that. Does she at least live with you?"

"No. . . . "

"*What?*"

"Well, she works regular hours and has the weekends off." I felt defensive and frustrated. There was no escaping her line of questioning.

"You give her the weekends off?!"

At this point, I felt shriveled in my chair. I thought that any additional information might give Miranda an aneurysm.

"Don't tell me she gets paid vacations," Miranda said pointedly.

I didn't answer.

Miranda muttered something to herself in Mandarin.

"You know what?" I countered. "It doesn't matter. We're just paying her a little more than average, and she just doesn't know what to make of me right now."

"You foreigners are ruining it for the rest of us," Miranda sighed, clearly resigned to the information I'd just laid on her. "I pay my *ayi* 750 a month, and she comes in on the weekends. Three hundred yuan more is nothing for you, but it's a lot of money to us. What do we do if our *ayi* come to us demanding more money and less days working?" Miranda was worked up again, and her question was clearly intended to scold me.

"Would it be so bad? Maybe you would treat her better and appreciate her more," I responded, feeling my own dander rising.

Miranda scowled at me. "The next thing you'll tell me is that you two are best friends."

I kept to myself that I thought being friends with Chu Ping wouldn't be such a terrible thing.

*Despite my honorable intentions* and defense of Chu Ping, I looked like a slave driver compared with Eric. Gina referred to Eric's way of compensating for his request that someone iron his boxers, by offering them more money and more freedom, as "the white man's burden." There were times when I felt spoiled, and other times when I felt like I wasn't showing my appreciation for having an *ayi*, but I also often felt angry when I had to pick up the slack for Chu Ping.

I resented being made to feel bad because Eric, in his usual grandiose way, initially told me that the *ayi* was there to help me, to free up my time, and I then found out that that wasn't actually the case. Eric frequently overrode my authority, claiming that he didn't want Chu Ping to work more than forty hours or on the weekends. So I inevitably felt some dissatisfaction when I cleaned up alone the morning after a dinner party, or some hesitation when Eric suggested cooking for friends on the weekends. On this teeter-totter of power, he had the final say.

Would it have been so awful to have Chu Ping come one Saturday a month to help clean up after a get-together? In hindsight I see that the whole idea of having a housekeeper, one who was dirt-cheap and who could do practically any task, made us both uncomfortable. But we never admitted this to each other, so we each struggled with our own ways of dealing with the ramifications.

Ultimately, Eric was a big softy, and I was distressed by the dark side of the way the housekeepers were treated by their own people. When I expressed this disparity to Miranda, she said dismissively, "All the *ayi* are from Anhui Province."

"They're still Chinese, even if they're from Anhui Province," I argued. "Would you hire a Shanghainese housekeeper?"

"No Shanghai-*ren* would work as a housekeeper," she refuted.

"Well, if one was looking for work, would you hire them?" I pressed.

"No, I would offer them another job," she said haughtily. By this point, I wanted to bang my head against the wall.

It took me some time to fully comprehend the way the Chinese saw themselves. Their pride wasn't so nationalistic as it was regional; they saw themselves as a whole, but chopped up into pieces, like a cabbage. People from Shanghai, like Miranda, saw themselves as the tender, delicious leaves. The Chu Pings, from the provinces, were seen as the tough, expendable stems.

*As I became closer* to Chu Ping over time, Gina, Susan, and Miranda continued to tsk-tsk and roll their eyes whenever we discussed her. But in the end, the relationships I developed with Chu Ping and my future *ayi*, Sally, were among the most cherished, memorable, and inspiring ones I had during my time in China. I also came to understand that expatriates and Chinese nationals alike created their own boundaries with their *ayis* because they didn't want to feel responsible for them, get too involved, or potentially get hurt. But sometimes I spent an entire day with Chu Ping, and it just wasn't in my nature to simply ignore her.

At times I wondered in the back of my mind what Chu Ping really thought about her situation. Did she appreciate what great employers we were, as Eric and I believed, or did she actually think we were a couple of suckers? Maybe her attitude changed, too, as she got to know us better. Certainly, that was true for me. As I watched her help him put his coat on, or leave his shoes out in the foyer, I longed to be doted on too. But, as in any relationship, it takes time to get comfortable with someone, and in time I learned to appreciate that Chu Ping didn't owe me that level of service just because I was Eric's girlfriend. In fact, it was quite the opposite: I had to earn her respect, and then her love.

Before I started learning Mandarin, my pitiful vocabulary was limited to greeting Chu Ping with "*Ni hao*" in the morning, "*Zajian*" at the end of the day, and, before she left for the weekend, "*Zhoumo kuai le*" ("Have a good weekend").

I spent my mornings tapping away on my laptop while she dusted around the piles of CDs in the living room or scrubbed the kitchen floor. From my office, I listened to Chu Ping sing, unfettered by any sense of self-consciousness. I later learned that they were Cultural Revolution songs; Ding Laoshi told me how they were pounded into the collective memory, and how people were required to sing them daily as they worked.

When the sun was out and the air was clear, Chu Ping opened the windows to freshen the rooms and hung our duvets on the *yangti*. She often watched television as she folded laundry. Occasionally I found myself studying her while she watched her shows; the way she freely and often burst out laughing with such abandon left me curious to know what was so hilarious.

These were the few times I saw her girlish, carefree side. As soon as she clicked off the television, she was her reserved, stoic self again, which seemed to me to be accompanied by a whiff of sadness that surrounded her like soft cologne.

*At noon I'd make my lunch:* a grilled cheese sandwich and tomato soup. I'd craved this all-American combination since I'd moved to China. I often saw Chu Ping watching me as I spread butter on white bread before throwing it on the hot skillet. As I added cheese and waited for both sides of the bread to turn golden brown, I realized how difficult it felt to be around Chu Ping so much of the time and not be able to hold a conversation with her. I longed to have the random, casual chats I'd had back home that I'd never thought I would miss: talking to an attendant while paying for gas, chatting with a fellow customer at a convenience store, or making small talk with someone while waiting at a bus stop.

In Beijing, my interactions were limited to a single response—"*Shenme?*" ("What?")—when someone tried to talk to me. And that was if things were going well. "*Shenme?*" was my knee-jerk reaction when I was spoken to in Mandarin—it gave me a few moments to get my bearings. A clerk would generally repeat himself and look at me strangely. If I didn't respond, the person behind me in line often repeated what the clerk had said. Then I'd back away slowly, muttering, "*Wo bu hui shuo Putonghua*" ("I don't speak Chinese"), and hurry out of the store. I'm sure the poor store clerks were commenting about the weather or asking me if I wanted a straw for my drink. But my inability to interact made Beijing a lonely place for me.

One afternoon I noticed that Chu Ping was staring down at my sandwich in the pan, her hands clasped behind her back. Normally she was a bit more subtle, but this time she leaned in and said something I didn't understand.

"*Shenme?*" I asked.

She waved her fingers across her face with her eyes half-closed dreamily.

"*Xiexie* (thank you)," I replied, feeling pleased that her gesture indicated that she thought the sandwich smelled appetizing. I placed the toasted cheese sandwich on a small salad plate.

I stood near her in the kitchen while I ate my lunch, noticing how short she actually was. From a distance she looked taller—she had a noble pride that elevated her. As she wrung out her mop in a bucket, I could make out the muscles of her upper back and shoulders knotted under the knitted material of her traditional Mandarin tunic, like a burly tree with layers of wood rings inside its thick bark. She worked with the ease and brute strength of a power lifter.

Some days we ended up eating lunch at the same time. The two of us sat at the table, facing each other in silence, like two monks in a monastery dining room.

Most often, Chu Ping brought lunch from home. Her staples were an old Tang jar with tea leaves, to which she added hot water throughout the day, and a serving of rice in a plastic container stowed in a navy blue cloth bag. The rest of her meal varied. Some days she brought a big tub of noodles or some homemade winter-melon soup. Other days she cracked a one-thousand-year-old egg, a Chinese delicacy formed from a duck egg or chicken egg preserved in a coating of red earth, garden lime, salt, wood ash, and tea. After the egg is wrapped in rice husks, it is traditionally kept in a large crock filled with garden soil for three months.

I often caught myself staring as Chu Ping chewed the dark green yolk and the egg white, now a deep amber. The ammonia-and-sulfur smell turned my stomach, but when I finally tasted an egg, it turned out that its odor was more potent than its flavor—similar to the rich, earthy taste and creamy texture of artisan cheese. Occasionally Chu Ping would cook up some ubiquitous Chinese staple like fried rice. Whenever I smelled and heard her preparing it, it reminded me of what delicious leftovers this dish made.

Chu Ping finished every lunch with a piece of fruit. One day I was watching her handle the fruit when I noticed how beautiful her hands were. Despite the toll housecleaning takes, Chu Ping had the naturally tapered fingers of a hand model: fleshy, padded palms and white fingernail tips. The skin covering those strong fingers looked as smooth as lambskin gloves. She later told me it was the green tea that made her teeth strong, and rubbing her hands with cooking oil that kept them supple. I tried the cooking-oil trick and found that I simply ended up smelling like french fries.

She kept her fruit in her dark blue bag. Every day, the fruit she brought out was a surprise; if I hadn't been in the apartment for lunch, I'd peek in the trash bin for seed, core, or peel remnants to see what she'd eaten that day.

Like her lunches, the finale fruit was seasonal. In the fall she ate Asian pears and large, grapefruit-like citrus fruits; in the winter, she had apples and nuts. Before eating her fruit, she'd always spread a piece of newspaper on the table. If she had a pear, she'd eat sections of it while holding both the knife and the fruit. She chewed thoughtfully and with intent, her gaze cast downward, as if she were attending to the taste of the fruit with all her being.

Before wadding the newspaper into a ball, she'd pull out a tooth-pick, modestly covering her mouth with one hand while she cleaned her teeth with the other. If it weren't for the occasional sucking noise she made as she loosened bits of food, she might have been mistaken for playing the harmonica.

*As my Mandarin improved,* Chu Ping and I shared stilted, broken conversations that started with good intentions and died out midway through. I made it a point to have my English-Chinese dictionary handy so I could look up a word if I got stuck.

Only a couple of months after I started my language classes, I was able to put together bits and pieces of her history based on what Eric told me and what I was able to understand from Chu Ping herself. She was born and raised in Anhui Province, southeast of Beijing, near Nanjing. She and her husband lived an hour and half by bus from Beijing, where they had a pig farm. They had a son—a blessing in China. Her pride was evident in the way she beamed when she took out a picture from a worn leather billfold.

He looked to be about eight or nine years old. "Does he go away to school?" I asked. I knew that some children were taken from their homes and raised in academies that set them up for life in a particular area.

No, she responded. I was thrilled that she understood my meaning, and that we were moving along fairly smoothly in this conversation.

But that didn't last long, and I was soon confused by what she was saying. It seemed that her son lived on her parents' farm in Anhui Province while she and her husband worked, but I couldn't understand the circumstances or the reason, though she seemed to be explaining them.

"Isn't it hard," I asked, "being without your son?"

Chu Ping looked at me questioningly. I knew I'd used the wrong word—"hard" as in "hard surface," rather than "difficult." I quickly thumbed through my red dictionary and showed her the word I'd meant. She nodded and told me that she saw him during the national holiday in October and the new year. It didn't make sense to me, exactly; I didn't make the connection that she and her husband couldn't support themselves in Anhui, nor did I understand how common it was for a couple to not have relatives who could take care of their children while the parents worked near Beijing.

For one second I was startled by a raw, haunted look in Chu Ping's eyes. It was a look I'd seen on a man's face one night during my first summer in Beijing, along Qianmen Road, when our cab was following a cyclist hauling garbage in a wagon. The traffic was heavy and the cars and cabs slowed alongside the cyclist, honking, beeping, and yelling out their windows as they passed him. In the headlights I could see that he was dripping with sweat. His tank top was soaked through and his legs shone with perspiration. Then several bags of garbage came loose from the rope that tied them to the wagon; they tumbled out and spilled out onto the road.

The cyclist stopped his bike and attempted to scrape up the trash with his hands. I felt miserable for him, and Eric took out his wallet, pulled out a 100 yuan bill, and told me to give it to the guy. I understood that Eric meant well by doing this, but it rubbed me the wrong way. The better solution, to my mind, was to get out of the cab and help him clean up, but I didn't know how this gesture would be interpreted either, and in the end I wasn't willing to dirty my own hands to help.

Eric ordered the cab driver to pull over, and I took the money and ran up to the man. The day's heat still rose from the pavement, and the air was heavy with humidity and car fumes. I knelt next to the man as he bent over, gathering the loose garbage. The smell of rotting cabbage and fish, and a sweet, fermenting odor, blew up into my nostrils.

Lit by the car headlights, the man's face glistened with sweat. I handed him the bill, but he just looked at it. I pushed it out again, but he still didn't take it. A flash of recognition, perhaps the realization that I was giving him money, crossed his face a moment later. And then he looked up at me with flat, dull eyes and that same haunted look I saw now in Chu Ping's eyes that said, *You know absolutely nothing about life.* I was immediately taken aback and ashamed that evening as I, clean and privileged, hunched over the bicyclist and offered him probably more money than he earned in two weeks. Who was I to give him money like this? I put it on the ground and ran back to the cab.

And now, at the dining room table, I felt that I'd learned something new about Chu Ping. And about the vast disparity between her world and mine.

*One weekend on the cusp of spring,* almost a year after I arrived in Beijing, Eric and I explored a market near our apartment building. The meat and fish sections were housed in a concrete shelter where the air was cold and wet. Even in the summertime, the vendors wore parkas.

Except at the entrances, there were no windows and no light other than a row of hanging bulbs casting an eerie yellow glow. Fresh vegetables and fruit created bright splashes of color in the cavernous surroundings.

There were garlic shoots and real bamboo shoots. Displayed along planks of wood set across sawhorses were some cabbages and greens that we had seen and tasted before, and just as many that we hadn't. On another table was a variety of homemade tofu: hard and soft; webby looking and freeze-dried; puffy, golden, and fried. Nearby was a metal vat full of unpressed tofu. Seeing it reminded me of my dad, who told me the best way to eat this exceptionally fresh tofu was with a squirt of lemon juice and a dribble of soy sauce. In China, homesickness and hunger went hand in hand for me.

We walked to the meat section, which was part slaughterhouse, part petting zoo. The large room was divided equally into a dead-animal side and a living-animal side. The former was lined with racks of whole cow and pig carcasses swinging from hooks, their innards piled on ice in Styrofoam iceboxes. Another part of the room featured a variety of caught fish and crabfish–lined tanks.

The living-animal side was the more sickening for me. Live animals—rabbits, fowl of every variety, and sheep—sat in wire cages. In a tank of turtles and frogs, the water was so high that the turtles stretched their necks out of their shells, straining to keep their heads above water, and the poor frogs stood on tiptoe. In small, stacked cages, snakes defecated on one another.

The smell was revolting, and the stressed animals' noises were deafening. The air smelled of raw meat, dank basements, wet animal fur, and cigarette smoke.

A vendor carving half a cow carcass with a handsaw looked up and acknowledged Eric. Another man stood next to him, holding the animal's chest cavity. The fresh meat was bright red and moist looking. Big, pearly bits of fat swirled through the meat like oil beading on the surface of water.

Eric stood there in a trance. He enjoyed his steak and liked to have it at least once a week. He'd taught me how to make a red-wine marinade of French mustard, olive oil, and fresh garlic, in which we'd immerse the meat all day before cooking it in a skillet. Eric was the type who liked his meat accompanied by a vegetable, usually broccoli, and a starch: mashed potatoes or steamed rice. We clashed on this issue; I didn't mind making the mashed potatoes, but he insisted that his rice be served with butter, salt, and pepper. Coming from a Japanese family meant that I had very strong opinions about how rice was meant to be served and eaten. Mom used to forbid my brothers and me to sprinkle soy sauce on our rice. I could have let it go, allowing Eric to add those ingredients to his own rice and eating mine the way I liked it, but he was adamant about mixing the butter, salt, and pepper into the rice. He seemed to relish the idea of it, too: He'd rub his hands together in his prayerlike way, which I found incredibly annoying and simultaneously hard to resist. It was the way Eric beamed to himself that generally sold me on his requests. I had seen that look of gleeful anticipation on my father's face when he planned his annual trip to Florida to buy fresh fish.

The men stopped sawing when Eric started speaking in Chinese. I could make out only some of what was being said. There was lots of agreeing and nodding of heads. One of the men wiped the blood from his hand across his white lab coat, leaving a stark handprint like a child's finger painting. As he spoke, Eric motioned to me.

"Eric, what are you telling them?" I asked. I didn't like being left out of a conversation, especially when it was obvious that I had some sort of role in it.

The men then glanced at me. Eric handed them some cash and

turned to me. "Wow, this is great!" he exclaimed. "I bought an entire side of beef for 700 RMB. I can cut up the meat myself, and we won't have to buy beef from the German butcher." Eric explained that he was pointing me out to the meat-market men because I would return next week with Chu Ping to pick up our side of beef and pay them the remaining amount.

I usually didn't argue with him when he went off on his culinary adventures. I thought about the time he'd decided to make homemade ravioli. We didn't have a recipe book, so he'd just experimented with water, flour, and egg to make the pasta skin. We didn't have a rolling pin, so he'd used a soup can to roll out the dough, and a water glass to cut out the circular shapes. After all his hard work, the end result, filled with sautéed shiitake mushrooms, had been scrumptious.

But this wasn't ravioli. As we left the immense building, a sudden blast of heat and fresh air flushed the smells of the meat market from my nose. I held my tongue as I wondered how Chu Ping and I were supposed to get the cow carcass home, and where we would store all the meat.

In the meantime, Eric went to the hardware store to buy a handsaw.

*On the morning of* the beef carcass pickup, Andrew, Eric's friend from prep school whom I'd met in Uighurville my first week in Beijing, came by the apartment to get some back issues of *The New Yorker* that I'd told him he could have.

I told him about the meat pickup, and he volunteered to come along. I led Chu Ping and Andrew to the stall where Eric had closed the deal. The two men from the previous week were there, along with a masculine woman who turned out to be the *laoban* (shopkeeper). Chu

Ping explained what we were there to pick up as she handed the *laoban* the purchase receipt. The *laoban* looked carefully at Chu Ping, then at the receipt.

She nodded to the two men, who obliged her silent command by going into a nearby freezer and bringing out a side of beef. The carcass they threw on the butcher table wasn't the brilliant red, muscular cow laced with veins of fat that Eric and I had seen, but a considerably smaller and mangier animal that looked as if it had been sitting in the back of the freezer for a while.

Even though Chu Ping hadn't seen the meat the week before, she knew this was a bad piece. She spoke to them politely, with her hands folded in front of her.

Andrew listened silently to Chu Ping, then elbowed me. "Things aren't looking good."

The *laoban* stepped forward and let out a string of phrases in rapid, loud Mandarin. Spittle flew from her mouth as she yelled. The two men didn't say anything, but glared at Chu Ping and took a few steps forward.

"They think Chu Ping is accusing them of trying to cheat you," Andrew translated.

The two men soon joined in the shouting. Now all three were screaming, yelling, and pointing at Chu Ping in an obvious attempt to draw attention to her. She remained calm, still standing with her hands folded across her chest. The reddening of her face and neck was the only sign that she was angry. A crowd of customers was beginning to gather.

"They're calling her a whore and insulting her mother," Andrew whispered to me.

"Andrew, do something," I said.

"I can't. If I interfere, they'll really rip into her." So we stood there silently.

Chu Ping slowly backed away from the stall. Like wild dogs, the three circled around her, yelling in her face. On display in this relentless way, she straightened her back and squared her shoulders like a soldier, and walked out with her head held stiff and high. The other vendors stood back and stared as we passed. Customers walked past us slowly, some whispering amongst themselves and looking us over suspiciously. Andrew and I followed her out. When I turned around to look at the vendors, I saw them laughing and turning back to their stall.

Once we were away from the building, Chu Ping started shaking. Her breath was shallow, and perspiration dotted her upper lip. I could tell she was about to cry. I wanted to touch her shoulder, but my sympathy would only confirm that she had lost face.

She began wringing her hands and fretting about finding another meat vendor to replace the side of beef. She said she would pay for the meat, which was almost equivalent to a month's paycheck. When I told her she absolutely would not be doing that, she kept insisting she would find another good vendor. She was afraid she was going to lose her job, even though I reassured her that I would tell Eric what had happened, and that he'd appreciate how she'd handled the situation. She looked both hesitant and relieved.

I phoned Eric's office from a nearby kiosk. Eric was understanding, and he asked me to tell Chu Ping to end her search. I think he was thankful, in a way, that the deal hadn't gone through, as I'd witnessed him in the kitchen, opening and closing the freezer, perhaps realizing only in retrospect that we didn't have enough space to store all that meat.

Eric spoke to Chu Ping the following morning. I never asked him what he said to her, and Chu Ping and I never discussed what had happened. She had lost face, which in Chinese terms means losing your dignity in front of other people. The butchers had tried to take advantage of Eric because he was a foreigner, and when she called them out on their attempt to present inferior-quality meat, they made a public spectacle of her in the market where she shopped. She had failed to complete what her employer had asked of her, and she had to depend on me, an outsider, to explain to Eric what had happened.

The day after the incident, we sat at the dining room table with our lunches. After we'd finished, I got up to return to my writing when she told me to wait a minute. Surprised, I sat back down. She wore a coy smile that showed off her perfectly white, straight teeth. She pulled two bunches of lychees from her bag and set one in front of me.

I smiled, accepted the fruit, and began eating it with a relish that matched hers.

# FRIED RICE

*This is a great dish for using up any leftover*
*meat and vegetables you may have in your refrigerator.*

INGREDIENTS:

1 teaspoon plus 1 tablespoon vegetable oil

2 eggs, beaten

5 green onions, trimmed and chopped

1 cup diced ham

1 tablespoon minced fresh ginger

4 shiitake mushrooms, diced

1/2 cup frozen peas

1 green, yellow, or red sweet pepper, stemmed, deribbed, and diced

4 cups cooked rice (fresh or leftover)

Salt and pepper to taste

1 tablespoon soy sauce, or to taste

INSTRUCTIONS:

Heat a nonstick wok over medium heat. Add 1 teaspoon vegetable oil. Add the eggs and scramble in the hot wok until they separate into small pieces. Remove and set aside.

Add the remaining tablespoon of oil to the wok and place over high heat. Add the green onions and ham; stir-fry for 2 minutes.

Add the ginger, mushrooms, peas, and peppers; stir-fry for 2 minutes.

Add the rice, salt, and pepper; stir-fry for 2 minutes, using the spatula to break up the rice.

Mix in the reserved cooked egg. Drizzle the soy sauce along the outer edge of the wok; stir-fry for 30 seconds, or until the color and ingredients look evenly distributed throughout the rice. Serve hot.

*Serves 4*

# Chapter 6

# Awakening the SLEEPING DRAGON

ON A COLD, SUNNY SUNDAY MORNING in early March, Eric announced that we were moving to an apartment closer to Haidian District, the Silicon Valley of China, where he worked. The week before, we'd looked at a new apartment building on the west side of town. Wei Zhou, who was Eric's boss's wife and the company's human-resources manager, and another woman, who was the leasing agent for the new building, met us for lunch before we viewed the apartment.

I didn't particularly enjoy being around Wei Zhou. She was the type of person who refused to listen to anyone whose language was not up to her standards. I often caught her staring at me and then quickly looking away when I met her eyes. Sometimes she seemed to forget my limited Mandarin skills and would start talking to me. Flustered by my inability to comprehend her or by my slow response, she'd wave her hands like a bathing pigeon, her eyes bulging out, and stammer as she asked Eric to translate. I imagined that she thought I was mentally impaired.

It didn't help matters when Eric told me that she'd mentioned how impossible it was to understand a word I said when I tried to speak Mandarin. Having grown up with parents who spoke English as a second language, I firmly believe that there are two groups of listeners: The first group tries their best, using the context of the conversation and listening intently to make sense of what's being said; the second type of person just doesn't want to exert any energy, seems to become frustrated by the notion that someone would attempt to speak their language, and gives up right away. My mother, in particular, struggled with being understood in English. My father had been in the States much longer, and had studied English while training to be a chick sexer on an American farm and waiting for his U.S. citizenship to be reinstated. His English was choppy and broken, but understandable. Within my parents' marriage, the responsibility for communicating rested mostly on his shoulders. As a result, I became a good and conscientious listener.

Although my Mandarin speaking ability was improving, my comprehension left a lot to be desired. Some days I interpreted the words I heard as those of the grownups in *Peanuts* cartoons—"wah, wah, wah, wah"—while other days it all seemed to click, and the language flowed between speaking and understanding.

Even before I understood a single word of Mandarin, I really tried to listen to what was being said, thinking that maybe I could pick up on some reference that would give me insight into the conversation topic. When everyone laughed at a joke, I'd look from face to smiling face, trying to figure out what was so funny and wanting to be a part of it. By the time Eric translated whatever had been said, the rest of the group had moved on, or it simply wasn't funny because I hadn't been involved in the momentum and energy of the original dialogue.

I often felt vulnerable, and many times I thought of Mom's struggle to participate in conversations in which she always felt she was two sentences behind. By the time her mind had translated what was being said and she'd readied her response, the conversation had moved on to the next topic.

The feelings of isolation and awkwardness that not being able to participate evoked in me didn't do much for my self-esteem. I began dreading the work functions that Eric insisted I accompany him to, where I had to endure a table full of non-English speakers. Of course, given my appearance, new acquaintances always assumed I was a Mandarin speaker. They'd start up a friendly conversation that would then end abruptly when they realized I wasn't what I appeared to be.

Eric got to a point where he told me what was being said only if I asked. Meanwhile, I stopped trying to understand and participate— conversations moved much too fast. When all the sentences snowballed into a bundle of gibberish, I switched off the discussion around me like the volume knob on a radio, allowing it to play like background noise. Usually by the middle of a meal, I was like a ghost at the table. Mentally, I was miles away, working on a scene in my book or planning an article I wanted to write.

Even after I expressed my feelings of inadequacy, Eric continued demanding that I attend these events with him. He just laughed off my discomfort, saying it didn't matter what other people thought, and that my presence meant I supported him. The only thing that kept me going was my love of food and eating out. It was the one ace he held; he knew he could always entice me with a place we'd never been to.

"We're meeting at a seafood restaurant," Eric would say. Then he'd add something that would seal the deal: "Zhu Yin will be ordering" was a sure bet.

"I'm going," I'd answer without hesitation.

Zhu Yin was Eric's boss and Wei Zhou's husband. He had a particular gift when it came to ordering, which is no easy task when food is served family-style, as it is in China. Ordering food skillfully is similar to ordering the wine for an entire table: Someone must act as the leader and decide on the various courses everyone will be sharing. Disorder can ruin a meal when multiple diners start to express what they want to eat. Taking into consideration every request in a large party, or knowing which dishes complement each other, is difficult. A person who orders well is able to field all these requests, is familiar with the signature dishes and the texture, color, and presentation of the courses, and knows the best order in which to eat them.

Wei Zhou wasn't as good at ordering as her husband, but together they worked like a seasoned comedy team: Wei Zhou's suspicious nature played foil to Zhu Yin's earnest attempts to order well.

"Let's start with the mung bean sprouts and leeks," Zhu Yin might tell the waitress.

The waitress would nod.

"We can't get that; I saw the dish at a table when we came in, and the bean sprouts were limp from being cooked in too much oil," Wei Zhou would interject.

"Okay, then the fragrant soybean sprouts. How are the shrimp today? Fresh?" Zhu Yin would ask.

Before she could respond, Wei Zhou would interrupt, "Why are you asking her? Look at the dirt under her fingernails. She wouldn't know fresh from rotten."

The waitress invariably kept a straight face despite the insult, holding her pen to her order pad.

"All right, let's just get the spicy shredded pork."

"Didn't you hear that Wei Li's uncle died the night he had that dish?"

"Was it spoiled? At this restaurant?" Zhu Yin would ask with genuine concern.

"No," she'd say, annoyed by his slowness. "He died of a heart attack, but this is not a lucky dish to order."

It would go on like this unless someone distracted Wei Zhou into another conversation.

I found these types of conversations amusing, and would work to piece together what I could understand with what Eric recounted after meals like this. Zhu Yin and Wei Zhou always seemed to have some version of this conversation in restaurant after restaurant, but the payoff was extraordinary: The meal was always perfectly balanced and delicious.

*By late winter, my second in Beijing,* even the idea of appetizing food or a new restaurant wasn't enough to get me to endure an entire dinner at which I couldn't understand a word. Having to depend on Eric to translate a conversation became equivalent to relying on someone to spoon-feed me. The only reason Eric was able to drag me into our lunch date with Wei Zhou was that we were viewing the new Haidian District apartment afterward.

The development was five minutes from Eric's office in Haidian

District, and about a forty-five-minute drive to my Mandarin class. Rising up from the basket weave–patterned tiled roofs of the *hutongs* were two buildings, thirty-two stories each, for living and working. The developers' original plan had been to build a third structure in an area marked by a block-long hole.

Despite its sticky walls and unfinished bathroom, I had become attached to our quirky apartment in the Asian Games Village. I was a creature of habit and enjoyed the conveniences I had found in the area, like the Olympic pool open to the public, and the beauty salon where I could get an hour-long head massage for 30 RMB. But I changed my mind almost immediately when I saw the new wood floors and openness of the living and dining rooms in the new apartment.

In less than two months we were moved in, during the season when the great winds from the Gobi Desert begin stirring the fluff from the cottonwood trees. I'm not sure if it was the change in my living space or the fact that I'd been in Beijing for more than a year and a half now, but around that time, my feelings of low self-esteem and resentment, combined with my constant low-grade frustration with the culture, awakened in me a sleeping dragon that emerged when I drank.

My history with drinking makes me think of my father, who loved his wine, his beer, and, on occasion, his whiskey. When Dad drank he grew reflective, counted his blessings, and wore a big smile. He never became mean or abusive. Mom occasionally indulged in an alcoholic beverage, but she usually regretted it. Without fail, after one drink, her face turned scarlet and she felt disoriented. When I drank, on the other hand, my emotions bubbled right up to the surface. There had been times, particularly in San Francisco, when I'd experienced heightened affection or self-confidence, but in Beijing insecurity and resentment were my most prevalent feelings.

I had my first drink when I was thirteen, sipping from a Wild Turkey whiskey bottle, listening to Lynyrd Skynyrd in the middle of a cornfield with my best friend and a group of girlfriends. I hated the stomach-turning taste of it, but I kept it down. Growing up in a town where there was nothing to do, I had plenty of time to acquire a taste for alcohol. At the time, it was a weak excuse to let go of my inhibitions, and I drank a fair amount during my high school years.

When I started to get serious about leaving Versailles, I sobered up. I didn't miss the strong, bitter taste of alcohol, or the hangovers. It wasn't long before the college social scene thrust me back into drinking, though. And that was weekend binge drinking that involved saturating myself with the cheapest beer I could find, or splurging on the high alcohol content of Long Island iced teas.

After I graduated from college, I stopped drinking altogether for about seven years. One night I'd caught a glimpse of myself in the mirror, chugging a bottle of Pop's homemade elderberry wine. Alcohol was no longer a social lubricant; it was a temporary escape from the loneliness of living in a new city and the reality of my first job. It was then that I realized I needed to pull myself together.

After my divorce in San Francisco, I was single, dating, and living near wine country, and I started drinking again, but in moderation. Still, only one glass too many could send me plummeting into despair about my failed marriage.

When I began dating Eric, I quickly immersed myself in his fast-paced lifestyle, and alcohol played a big part in that. Shakers of martinis, highball glasses filled with gin and tonic, fifths of bourbon, and bottles of wine were the fiber of Eric's social life, all part of the excitement of his visits and our dinners at restaurants.

Foolishly, when I lived in Beijing, I tried to match Eric drink for drink. I could have one martini to Eric's two, and held my own when we split a bottle of wine over dinner. I tried, but I often couldn't join him in the beer or two that sometimes followed.

In the beginning, our drinking was merry and bright. But not long after our visit to my parents', my previously amiable drinking demeanor became bristly and unpredictable. A simple evening often turned into a yelling match, followed by reconciliations stained with tears and filled with regret.

One memorable liquor-fueled evening that I would love to forget exemplified the messy, drunken affairs our nights had become. It started out badly and only got worse. As Eric and I walked out onto Kunming Road, the major thoroughfare outside our building, I saw a large group of people gathered. No one was saying anything; they were just staring downward. The crowd parted, maybe because Eric was the only Caucasian in the group, and I saw that they were looking at a body lying on the sidewalk. The man was lying face down, with his hands under his torso in front of him. The oddest thing about this scene was that his pants were around his ankles and his white underwear was peeking out from under his jacket.

There were no sirens from an approaching ambulance. No one was checking the man's vitals or trying to wake him up. Everyone, including us, just stood there for a few minutes, looked at one another, and moved on. We had had a drink or two before leaving the apartment. It was one of those hazy experiences in which I assumed the situation was being handled, that the authorities were on their way, but, in retrospect, I'm not sure they were. I should have taken this as a sign to stay home, but we hailed a cab. As we drove down Kunming Road, the body attracted more onlookers, like tombstones in a cemetery; like us, they had been ensnared by the sight of the anonymous man lying face down in the dirt.

The scene outside our apartment had faded in my mind by the time we arrived at the cigar event, held at the only swanky restaurant in Beijing at the time. Located in the shadow of the Forbidden City, a *siheyuan* (courthouse) had been converted into a fusion restaurant with a contemporary Chinese art gallery and a cigar room. The event was being held in honor of a visiting Cuban cigar roller, a former employee of Fidel Castro.

The guests assembled in the lower-level art gallery against a backdrop that included wall-size modern Chinese paintings and various sculptures. We sipped wine and nibbled on shrimp and crab canapés as cigars were rolled before our eyes. It was one of those splendid and surreal occasions that I had to credit Eric for—he was always finding amazing events for us to go to, like the night we saw Puccini's *Turandot* performed in the Forbidden City.

We were talking with friends of Eric's—an Englishman he played squash with, a wine importer, and an orange juice distributor. When we'd all finished our first glass of wine, Eric bought another round for everyone except me. The first drink had already roused the dragon, but I took this gesture as a snub or, worse, as his being condescending and controlling, telling me to pace myself without his actually saying so.

*I'll show him,* I said to myself as the dragon stretched, not fully awake. I stomped off to the bar and got myself another glass. I returned, smiling and cheerful, to the group. *Ha!* I thought when I saw Eric glancing at me uncomfortably.

Armed with our hand-rolled cigars, we retired to our tables for a four-course dinner at which I drank four more glasses of wine. I felt wonderful, fabulous. The dragon was rested and raring to go. Dessert was accompanied by cognac and the lighting of our cigars.

My cheeks burned like two embers. I felt thick with a smug sense of satisfaction when I put my cigar between my lips for Eric to light. I took a few short puffs without inhaling. I had smoked a few cigars during a recent visa-renewal trip to Hong Kong, so I believed I knew what I was doing. I could tell Eric didn't want me to smoke it, but he wouldn't dare say so in front of everyone, particularly because of the volatile state I was in.

I swished the cognac around in my mouth a couple of times to enhance the cigar's rich flavor. And then, like a cloud passing over the sun, the energy in the room suddenly shifted. I felt shaky and unbalanced and very hot, and the voices around me sounded muffled and loud. I excused myself to the ladies' room. As I stood up, all the alcohol swept over me like an avalanche. I made it to the bathroom uneasily. Eric was too angry with me at this point to help me out. I stood at the washbasin and splashed cold water on my face, not caring that I had raccoon eyes from my running mascara and eyeliner. Just when I thought it was safe to return to the dining room, I experienced a head rush and needed to sit down. There was nowhere to sit except for on the commode lid, so I stayed there for a few minutes, riding out waves of nausea.

I don't know how long I sat there—only that I got up at some point because I figured out that I needed to get some fresh air before I passed out.

A security guard stood near the entrance, opening and closing the door for patrons. When he saw me staggering toward the door without my coat, I felt self-conscious. *Here's another drunk* xiaojie *who's going to throw up on the sidewalk and I'll have to clean it up,* I imagined him thinking.

Although the days felt like spring, the night refused to surrender to it. The crisp air seemed to clear my nose, throat, and lungs of cigar smoke. My face and neck felt cooled, caressed, and revived, as if I were standing under a gentle waterfall.

There was residential housing around the restaurant, and nearby, along a sidewalk leading to another courthouse, was a cement pedestal—the kind statues are displayed on. As I walked closer, I saw that there was a wooden armchair with a blue velvet cushion on the pedestal. I climbed up the platform and sat in the chair.

It was a clear night, with enough moonlight that I could make out the red walls of the Forbidden City just a few feet away. I was thinking about the ancient city and the people who'd dwelled in it when I nodded off for a moment. When I came to, I was still drunk, but at least the queasiness was gone.

I was experiencing the morning-after sheepishness I often felt after I knew I'd gone too far. I collected myself and slowly went back inside the restaurant. When I saw Eric deep in conversation with the people at our table, I felt even more guilty and ashamed about how I'd behaved. I wondered how long I'd been gone.

Eric looked up at me when I touched his shoulder. I didn't sit down, because someone I didn't know was sitting in my seat. I felt like I was intruding. I leaned in toward Eric's ear and said, "I don't feel well. I'd like to go home."

Eric flashed me an annoyed look that said, *Oh no, here we go again.* I felt sick to my stomach, but the feeling was different from the alcohol-induced queasiness.

"I'm going outside," I said to him, and left quickly.

Outside, I looked for the chair, but someone had removed it already. I couldn't help wondering if maybe I'd imagined its presence in the first place. I thought a little walk would help me clear my head, so I headed several yards in the direction of the Forbidden City's gate. I turned when I heard someone approaching me from behind. It was Eric.

"I—" I started.

"What now?!" he screamed, before I could get another word out. His body was curled up and over, like a big wave. His eyes were slightly glassy, and a deep reddish-pink crept up and along his neckline, like a bad sunburn.

I shrank back. "I, I d-don't feel good. I thought I was g-going to throw up in t-there," I stammered, suddenly feeling the cold that had seemed refreshing just moments earlier.

He spun around without a word and stormed back into the restaurant. I followed him slowly.

I got my coat and said goodbye to everyone at the table, acting as if everything were perfectly normal. I reassured the people at our table that I was all right when they asked how I was feeling. Eric and I made our way back outside and stood silently on the corner of a deserted street, waiting for a passing cab.

We finally waved one down. After we took our seats in the back and Eric gave the driver our destination, our silence and civility snapped, and we yelled at each other all the things we'd been holding back.

"Why do you have to drink until you get sick?" Eric yelled.

"You didn't even know I was gone until a whole hour had passed!" I screamed back.

"It's so selfish of you to get upset whenever we go out! I work all week long and I just want to relax!"

"You're so self-centered!" I screamed. "You have no idea what it's like to not understand a word that's being said. Then you go off and abandon me for hours."

The cabbie took the scenic way home, weaving through the tree-lined streets to the broad boulevards that ran past the lit Palace Museum and Tiananmen Square. We didn't even notice the circuitous, half-hour-long trip because we were too busy howling at each other—Eric at me for getting drunk and belligerent, and I at him for treating me insensitively.

Even though the driver didn't know what we were saying, he expressed his solidarity with Eric by opening Eric's door for him. Eric, of course, gave the guy a huge tip.

Eric was the first man with whom I'd ever experienced such relationship drama. When I dated, I usually steered clear of personalities that thrived on the excitement of volatile last-minute departures, tearful ultimatums, and endless rounds of breaking and making up. But even as my independence and self-confidence crumbled as slowly and surely as the Roman Colosseum, I truly believed that Eric and I were compatible. It didn't seem apparent at the time, but it's clear now that the strong feeling growing between us wasn't closeness—it was codependency. My reliance on him to communicate and my deteriorating self-worth were the glue that adhered me to him.

I reasoned that all our hysterics and volatility must be because we loved each other so. Because I'd shied away from such fireworks in all my other relationships, this dynamic fanned the flames of sexual tension with Eric, and made the everyday details more exciting. All I knew then was that I would do and become whatever I had to in order to stay with him. And unless he asked me to leave, I couldn't.

That night after the cigar party, our arguments and accusations exhausted, we made up by the time the elevator arrived at our floor. The next morning, we talked and decided it was up to me to figure out how to handle my drinking.

*One weekend in May,* my period didn't start when it should have. I was thirty-two years old, and like most women at that age, I'd experienced plenty of missed periods. Stress was usually to blame; a few times it was due to too much exercise or an abrupt change in diet.

In the past, I'd been struck with panic upon missing my period. My mind would race through the possibilities: a birth control pill forgotten, or a contraceptive malfunction? But then a patch of cranberry-red blood would appear on my panties one day, setting my life back in gear. Another crisis averted.

That didn't happen this time. My period was a few meager dots of dark brown blood, not the deep crimson splashes that usually appeared every twenty-eight days. Also, I was experiencing inexplicable queasiness, which I'd previously felt only during bumpy plane rides. I didn't mention a word about my suspicions to Eric. I told myself there was no need to get worked up. What if it was nothing? I had a feeling in my gut that this time my hope was fleeting.

Without a pregnancy test, I decided to find out for sure by making an appointment with a gynecologist at the International Medical Center, located in the Beijing Lufthansa Center.

My mind was buzzing and preoccupied the entire morning before my appointment. Ding Laoshi did her best to keep the lesson moving forward, despite my repeated mistakes.

When I asked her to repeat a drill question a third time, she asked with an understanding smile, "Your mind is not here today, is it?"

"No, it's not," I said sheepishly, drumming my fingers impatiently on my teacup. "I've got something important I need to take care of after class. Sorry, I'll try to concentrate."

She nodded and continued.

Outside, it was a stunning spring day. I could almost smell the mountain air surrounding three sides of the city. Unhindered by smog and clouds, the bare sun shone white rays that brightened and bleached out the previous months of winter gray. Along the curb, farmers from the outskirts of town peddled ducklings, chicks, and baby rabbits. Couples walked away cuddling small wire boxes holding the hatchlings.

Most days I would have delighted in the quality of the afternoon and loitered my way down the avenue, but I neither felt the sun nor paid any attention to the baby animals.

When I got to the medical center, a nurse took me into a large room that served as both examining room and office, and I sat on the crinkly paper-lined examining table. A general practitioner could have administered the pregnancy test, but I'd been told when I made the appointment that the clinic had a Romanian ob-gyn on staff. I didn't give much thought to the physician's gender at the time, and though I've always felt more comfortable having a female gynecologist, I realized where I was and that I couldn't be picky.

The nurse had not asked me to remove any of my clothes, so I sat there waiting, looking around the sizable room. Beside me were a medicine cabinet and a metal trolley for medical instruments. A screen partition blocked my view of the desk and two chairs on the other side of the room. I heard the happy sounds of a little girl laughing through the thin walls.

Suddenly the door swung open without a knock and the doctor strode into the room. I expected an old doctor, someone whose career was on its last legs and who had sought an easy practice in Beijing. Instead, the Romanian doctor was young and handsome, and seemingly fully aware of it.

He introduced himself and extended his hand. I shook it as I took in his appearance. How strange and sloppy looking it was to see a physician wearing a lab coat that barely concealed his unbuttoned shirt, which displayed a couple of strands of gold against a woolly thatch of black chest hair. I felt him trying to be relaxed and easy, but his mannerisms were cold and stiff.

He led me from the examining table to one of the chairs by his desk. I saw a desk calendar with pin-up girlie pictures; then my eyes tracked up to a similar wall calendar, not unlike the smutty kind you'd find hanging in a teenage boy's bedroom.

That was when the screaming started. The gurgling laughter from the little girl next door turned into ear-piercing wails. "No, I don't want it! Mama, I don't want it!" she wailed in English. She sounded to be about six years old. As her fear heightened, she screamed over and over in Mandarin, as if the devil were in the room with her, *"Wo bu yao de!"* The sound was nerve-racking enough to make me break a sweat.

"What do you need?" the Romanian doctor asked calmly, not acknowledging the child's screaming.

Trying to appear unshaken, I told him I needed a pregnancy test.

He opened the medicine cabinet, reached inside, and produced a plastic cup. He pointed to a door that led out into the hallway, where the ladies' room was.

After I provided some urine for him, he left the room for a couple of minutes, then returned and sat back down at his desk. "The test came out positive. I could perform another test, but the strip reacted immediately." He paused, then said, "Well, that's all."

"Okay," I said slowly, trying to figure out what to do next.

"I suggest you have a pelvic examination as a starting point," he added. "I have time now to do this."

I looked at the girlie calendar and then back at him. "Thank you, but I need to discuss this with my significant other first," I said.

"All right, but you must start taking prenatal vitamins right away," he said, scratching a triangle of chest hair as if it were the belly of a cat.

"Yes, of course," I answered absently. The screaming in the other room had become exhausted, muffled whimpers. I felt as woeful and gripped with fear as the little girl next door, but I knew it was important to tell Eric about the situation as soon as I could.

*I took a cab straight from* the medical center to Eric's office. By this time the skies were dark and spring rain showers were falling. I didn't know if he would be free to talk; all I knew was that I needed to see him before I went crazy.

By the time the cab pulled up to the white tile–topped pagoda building where Eric's office was, every imaginable insecurity and fear about our relationship was thrashing around inside me like fluttering moths.

Questions streamed through my head with alarming intensity: Would Eric want to keep the baby? Did I want to keep the baby? Would he think I expected him to marry me because I was pregnant? Would he think I'd done this as a way to get him to marry me? If he asked me to marry him, would it be because he wanted to or because he felt he had to?

I found Eric on the phone in his office, making dinner plans with Andrew while trying to fax a document. He smiled and waved when I walked in.

Eric put his hand over the receiver and asked, "How about having Andrew over for dinner tonight?"

"I don't know, can we talk—" I walked across the room and sat down in one of his chairs. There was a loud *beep* as the fax machine jammed.

"Darn it! Andrew, let me ask my other half and call you back," Eric said, trying to open the fax machine with his free hand. "This machine is driving me nuts!"

"Eric, I have to talk to you about something."

"Hey, can you bring me the roll of paper towels over there? I have ink all over my hands."

I stood up and took the paper towels from the credenza to him, then closed his office door.

He looked at me quizzically as he wiped his hands and sat behind his desk.

I sat back down and said calmly, "Eric, I went to the clinic today and had a pregnancy test. It turned out positive. I'm pregnant."

I studied him carefully. His first reaction was crucial to me.

He tilted his head back against his chair and rubbed his face with both hands, then sat forward to rest his face in his hands and his elbows on the desk.

He looked at me and said, "Fuck."

I felt as if I were sitting in the principal's office or in front of my parents, admitting to a mistake and waiting to hear what my punishment would be.

I knew this wasn't a fair way of approaching the situation. My being pregnant was a surprise, an accident, and I was springing it on him. I couldn't know what was going on in his mind.

I kept telling myself that we were both responsible for this. We were here, it had happened, and we would make a joint decision about what to do.

Eric took his face out of his hands and just looked at me—not accusingly or judgmentally or tenderly. He just looked at me.

I felt like I had to say something, but all that came out was "I guess this answers your question about dinner with Andrew tonight."

Eric smiled at me, and I knew we were going to be all right.

*There was a two-week wait* to schedule an abortion.

We'd talked through our situation at length later that evening. I would be lying if I said I wasn't disappointed that Eric didn't want to take a leap of faith and have the baby. But as hard as it was for me to admit, I knew we weren't ready to start a family.

A wistful side of me—propped up by romantic movies in which rich men marry hookers and lieutenants sweep factory girls off their feet— wanted Eric to propose to me and tell me that having this baby together would make him the happiest man in the world. Getting married because I was pregnant, I told myself, was idealistic, not realistic. Eric and I proclaimed our love for each other, but I kept my ideas about commitment to myself, knowing that Eric was uncertain. An innocent child shouldn't be the deciding factor in whether we would remain a couple.

I was already feeling doubtful about our decision not to have the child. And then, to make matters worse, we flew to Shanghai to attend Eric's friend's wedding a week before the procedure. I tried not to punish myself by comparing my hidden desire to get married with the bride's happy moment. I wouldn't find out until months later that she was pregnant when she walked down the aisle.

I can't speak for Eric about what he was thinking during that time, but my nausea and fatigue during those two weeks were constant reminders of the cells dividing and growing in my body. Still, I kept my mind in check, dashing any thoughts of what my dream child, who would never exist, might look like or be like.

I hadn't made friends close enough to share this information with, and not having a girlfriend's shoulder to cry on was difficult. A couple of times I tried to engage Eric on the topic of the child, but then I'd feel him get quiet and I'd quickly change the subject. I knew that even if he wanted to, Eric wouldn't allow himself to discuss something that was never going to happen. Right or wrong, it was his way of coping.

I chose a Hong Kong–managed clinic in one of the nice Western hotels to perform the procedure. Dr. Zhi was my doctor; she was in her mid-fifties and spoke decent English. Her bedside manner was brisk and businesslike, stern but not uncompassionate. I thought she would make a great attorney.

I decided to go to class the morning of my appointment, to keep my mind occupied. It felt like the longest morning of my life. After class, I walked to the main road outside the school to wave down a passing cab.

It was a gorgeous spring-going-on-summer day; the sun's warmth was getting stronger, but the air wasn't yet saturated with humidity—it felt like feathery strokes on my skin. But my mind was elsewhere.

Before I knew it, my cab had pulled up to the fancy entrance of the hotel. Some sort of pageant or fashion show was going on in several of the hotel's banquet rooms near the clinic. Thin, attractive Chinese women, tall in their platform shoes, were floating about the halls like ethereal goldfish.

I was early for my appointment, so I sat in the waiting room and watched three women from the event come into the clinic. They were gathered tightly together; the middle one was hunched over her thumb, carrying it like a delicate corsage. As she was led from the waiting room into an examining room, the other two women stood in front of the long mirror near the entrance, brushing their hair, checking their teeth, and moving their bodies every which way.

Dr. Zhi came out and took me into a small room the size of a New York City kitchenette. Eric had arrived, and when he joined us in the room it was a very tight fit. I wanted him to stay, but Dr. Zhi said it would be too crowded. Before he went to the waiting room, Eric asked the doctor how long the procedure would take. "Ten or fifteen minutes," she replied. He gave me a caring look before closing the door.

An old, wizened woman who looked to be in her nineties rolled a machine into the room. She said hello to me in Mandarin.

Startled, I asked, "Who is she?"

"This is Dr. Ma. She will be performing the procedure."

"Wait a minute. I thought you were doing it," I said, sitting up on one elbow.

"Oh, no," Dr. Zhi said matter-of-factly. "But don't worry, Dr. Ma does three hundred of these a week."

When it was over, Eric came in and sat with me for about ten minutes as the cramps subsided.

Dr. Zhi came in, handed me a packet of antibiotics, and said I could go home. There was no post-procedure literature about things I needed to do over the next twenty-four hours. There were no reassuring words.

The doctors cleaned up the equipment and restored order to the room. I was left to clean up after myself, wiping the blood from my legs and stomach.

I straightened my dress. There was one tiny drop of blood on the hem. I dabbed it with a wet paper towel and walked gingerly out of the room.

*When we got home,* Eric fixed me up in front of the television with a hot-water bottle. I was craving a grilled cheese sandwich. I had lost my appetite over the past weeks, and the gooey cheese between two slices of crunchy, butter-grilled bread was the most delicious, comforting food I had eaten in a long time.

Not long after I wolfed down the sandwich, I fell asleep. I woke up in the middle of the night to the sound of clanging metal echoing outside our building. Eric was snoring beside me.

That gaping hole where the third apartment building was supposed to be built had become an active construction site. We had asked about its status before we moved in, knowing that the dust, noise, and overall inconvenience of having a building erected right next to ours would be a deal breaker. The leasing manager had explained that the development company had run out of money. She had assured us that it would be some time—maybe years—before they could resume building.

Now a metal fence and tall wooden barriers surrounded the hole. Truckloads of metal rods were hauled in, and day after day a wiry-looking spine, like the stem of a gigantic metal plant, emerged ever higher from the ground.

Twenty-four hours a day, seven days a week, a crew of more than a hundred workers hammered and welded. Construction cranes filled our view, like oil drills across a Texas plain.

That night after my abortion, I was awakened from a black sleep by what sounded like a tray of silverware being dropped on a marble floor, only amplified a thousand times. I sat up and felt my left breast. My nipple was swollen and tingling. When I touched it, it was wet with milk.

The contractions caused by the abortion had tricked my body in thinking it had delivered a baby, and it was producing milk. Realizing that my body was experiencing what it was naturally meant to do filled me with a gut-wrenching, heart-wringing sadness that there was no baby to satisfy my physical instincts.

I held myself and let my mind slip into a place I hadn't allowed myself to go before now. I gave myself permission to imagine what that baby might have looked like, smelled like, and felt like. Eric woke up and didn't say a word; he just rocked me and stroked my hair. He didn't ask me any questions, and I didn't tell him what I was thinking about or going through as we each mourned, in our own way, what would never be.

Back then, I couldn't handle the idea of walking out on Eric and going back to the States on my own when I was expecting a child. The idea of choosing a life of uncertainty and financial hardship, and of the responsibility I'd have for the life of an innocent child, was too great. Only now am I confident that everything would have been fine, and that taking such action might have gotten me what I really wanted at that time. I wish I had trusted myself. I wish I had believed in my judgment and my ability to take care of myself and a child.

Eric and I stayed together for years after that. After all we had been through, I don't regret that decision. I only regret my feelings of unworthiness and my inability to stand up for myself. I was doing what I'd said I wouldn't—relying on someone, in the same way I'd relied on my parents, to make the hard decisions for me.

In the years that followed, it was impossible for me to forget about what happened that spring afternoon at the hotel clinic. It was permanently imprinted on me like a tattoo. I felt consumed by fears that I'd be seen differently, that people would know I'd had an abortion, that it would be obvious to casual observers. Trapped by these feelings and by my secret, I smothered the memory of the child even more. Still, even though I have a child today, the one I didn't have is very much alive. I continue to roll over in my mind what might have been. Releasing the secret now, I feel like that baby's memory has taken on wings.

# TENDER CHICKEN BREASTS WITH FIRECRACKER SAUCE

*This is my version of* gong bao ji ding, *or kung pao chicken.
I decided to alter the recipe by using whole chicken breasts,
rather than cutting them into pieces for a stir-fry. I've also
substituted pecans and almonds for the usual peanuts. This version,
served with rice and vegetables, makes a complete dinner.*

INGREDIENTS:

MARINADE:

1 tablespoon soy sauce

Dash of salt

1 tablespoon dry sherry

3 tablespoons cornstarch

3 tablespoons water

SAUCE:

2 tablespoons soy sauce

3 teaspoons sugar

2 teaspoons rice wine

1 tablespoon Chinese vinegar

2 teaspoons Asian sesame oil

1 teaspoon water

1 teaspoon cornstarch

## CHICKEN:

2 boneless, skinless chicken breasts

4 tablespoons vegetable oil

4–10 (depending on desired spiciness) dried red chili peppers, seeded and cut into 1-inch-long pieces

2 garlic cloves, minced

2-inch piece of fresh ginger, peeled and minced

3 green onions (white part only), chopped

1/3 cup chopped almonds

1/3 cup chopped pecans

## INSTRUCTIONS:

To prepare the marinade: Combine the soy sauce, salt, dry sherry, cornstarch, and water in a bowl; stir to blend. Set aside.

To prepare the sauce: Combine the soy sauce, sugar, rice wine, Chinese vinegar, sesame oil, water, and cornstarch in another bowl; stir to blend. Set aside.

To prepare the chicken: Beat the chicken breasts on both sides with a mallet to tenderize the meat, but not flatten it. Place the chicken in a bowl and add the marinade, making sure that each piece is well coated. Let marinate for at least 15 minutes—the longer, the better.

Heat 1 tablespoon oil in a skillet over high heat. Reduce the heat to medium, add the chicken, and fry until cooked through. Transfer the chicken to a plate, cover with aluminum foil, and put in a low (180°) oven.

Rinse out the skillet and heat the remaining 3 tablespoons oil in it over high heat.

Add the chilies to the hot oil. Turn the fan on and stand away from the skillet, as the cooking chilies may irritate your eyes. Reduce heat to medium and stir the chilies until fragrant and reddish-brown in color. Be careful not to burn them.

Increase the heat to medium-high and add the garlic, ginger, and green onions; stir to combine. Add the nuts and stir well.

Increase the heat to high and add the sauce mixture; stir quickly and cook until the sauce thickens. (Add a trickle of water to the pan if sauce becomes too thick.) Remove from heat.

Slice the cooked chicken and arrange the pieces side by side, like an open fan, on a serving platter or individual plates. Spoon the sauce over the meat.

*Serves 2*

# Chapter 7

# Gone Before
# SUNRISE

IN DECEMBER 1998, the week before Christmas, on my last night in Beijing before I moved back to San Francisco, Susan, Gina, and I met for a work/farewell dinner. I was writing a round-up article about Beijing's courtyard restaurants for United Airlines' in-flight magazine. It was my first glossy-magazine assignment. I'd invited Susan and Gina to join me in my research that night, and, as it turned out, we had to work for our meal. I had been to the unmarked restaurant—a tiny, delicious place that served Beijing roast duck, hidden somewhere in a *hutong* neighborhood near Tiananmen Square—only once before. One of Eric's China-hand friends had taken us there, so I had only a general sense of where it was. The challenge of finding it made it that much more unique.

It was already dark by the time I met Susan and Gina at their office. Susan had recently bought a car, stating that she and her husband couldn't haul their two children around in cabs forever, so she offered to drive the three of us to the *hutong* where the restaurant was. I climbed into the back seat; it felt strangely natural, which I attributed to the fact that I'd been riding around in cabs my entire time in Beijing.

"Linda, do you want to get behind the wheel on the way home?" Susan asked, looking at me in the rearview mirror as we motored down Chaoyang Lu.

I thought about it for a second. "I think I'll pass this time, but thanks for asking," I said, raising my voice to make myself heard over the soulful Chinese-pop love song playing on the radio. "The last thing I need the night before I leave is to hit some guy on a pedicab."

Susan nodded in agreement. "That's actually what I love about driving here. It's like a video game where all these different challenges come racing across the road—pedestrians, a mother carrying a baby, a construction worker pulling a wagon holding lumber, bicyclists with a passenger, an old man in a wheelchair. . . . You never know what's going to jump out."

Susan circled around the wide boulevard of Tiananmen Square and past the Palace Museum. "Just look at these drivers in front of us!" Susan exclaimed impatiently. "They're going so slow!"

"Well, Susan, we *are* driving through the Capitol Hill of Beijing," Gina responded.

"I know, but look how I can speed up and whip around them like a Formula One racer," Susan said, pressing the gas pedal and weaving through the line of cars.

"So, Linda, did you ever imagine that on your last night in Beijing, you'd be joyriding around Tiananmen Square with a middle-aged woman?" Gina joked, eliciting a slap from Susan.

"Oh, I love this song," Susan said, moving on good-humoredly and singing along to a cheerful Chinese pop tune.

*I loved winter evenings in Beijing.* During the day, the pale sun struggled to peek through the soupy, gunmetal haze formed by the burning coal of factories and the outdoor burners people cooked on. At night, though, the dark smog obscured city views. Restaurants glimmered under neon signs and strings of white and colored lights. Warmth glowed from the windows of old-style Chinese homes and gave them the charming aura of illustrations from children's fairytale books. The city felt festive; people walked excitedly, whether they were going to a warm restaurant or being welcomed home. Traces of soot in the air and different tones of grays and blacks imparted a Dickensian quality to the surroundings.

Susan found parking near the *hutong* entrance.

"So how are we supposed to find this place?" Gina asked, jumping in place to keep warm.

Directions to the Beijing roast duck house, Eric's friend had told me, were painted on the walls leading into the *hutong*. We scanned them, looking for writing.

Unmarked restaurants, bars, and stores are quite common in Beijing. I'd been to restaurants that were so hard to find that it was easier just to rendezvous on a familiar corner with the person I was meeting (usually a local or a friend who knew exactly how to get there), and have them escort me. The *hutongs* are especially hard to navigate, as the street names and building numbers are often not marked.

"I found it!" Gina shouted, squinting to make out the faded, chipped red block letters. "It says, 'Go straight until path opens.'"

"That's what I love about living here," Susan said cheerfully as we entered the *hutong* maze. "There's still so much to be discovered. I've been here for a decade and I didn't even know this place existed."

After we'd walked about a hundred yards, the route we were on opened and split into three different directions. We stopped and studied the walls for another painted message. We wandered around for a while, then backtracked.

Finally, we found the weathered, dark green–painted gate I'd been told to look out for. The doorway opened into a spacious, dark, smoky courtyard. We followed a string of hanging lightbulbs and the sounds of Chinese cooking as spatulas chimed against metal woks.

In one section of the house was a roasting room. Through the misty windows, we saw a rack where two dozen ducks hung, ready to be roasted. A chef was throwing wood into a blazing brick oven.

"I made a reservation, so we'll have duck tonight," I said, more for my own benefit than for Susan's or Gina's—I am a self-confessed duck aficionado. Because of the restaurant's small size, duck had to be reserved a day ahead of time. Walk-in customers were welcome to order anything off the menu—except this specialty. How disappointing it would have been to go to all the trouble of finding this place, only to discover that we couldn't partake in it.

The smoky-sweet aroma of roasting meat and burning applewood lingered in the air both inside and outside the building, reminding me of bonfires crackling in an open field. Across the courtyard I could see the dining room, crowded with tables and people. We were feeling the cold now, and the smells were making my mouth water.

We walked through the dining room's narrow doorway and found an empty table against a wall amid a mishmash of flimsy furniture. The dining room was unheated, and the floor was bare concrete. Some of the diners had put newspaper under their feet to retain warmth, and almost everyone had their coat on. The shadeless lightbulbs cast a yellow tint on the walls, which were decorated with a ubiquitous Chinese cartoon poster featuring a cherubic boy and girl in good-fortune red attire, and a promotional poster of a sweaty beer bottle.

As we settled ourselves in our seats, the waitress noisily set down water glasses, teacups, chopsticks encased in thin plastic, packets of towelettes, and a pot of jasmine tea. As she poured the tea, Susan ordered us two tall bottles of Tiger beer.

I ordered the traditional Beijing roast duck, which would come with all the fixings: pancakes, plum sauce, and scallions; hot-and-sour cabbage; cubes of bean curd in sesame paste; and duck soup.

The hearty food and the beer took off the chill, and we soon felt warm enough to shed our coats. We laughed and talked about boyfriends and husbands. As Gina and I listened intently to Susan's story about how she'd met her husband, it hit me strongly and suddenly that I would be on a plane to San Francisco the following morning.

I realized, as I sank my teeth into a succulent duck-meat roll with sharp green onion and savory-sweet plum sauce, that this was the same dish I'd eaten on my first night out with Eric in Beijing. Was it merely a year and a half ago that I'd had my first Beijing roast duck in an expensive, touristy restaurant? And now I was tracking down unique hole-in-the-wall eateries. I couldn't help the feeling of self-satisfaction that washed over me, but it was short-lived. I wished Eric could have been there with us, to see me engaged and immersed in my Beijing life.

*I felt like everything about living* in Beijing finally started coming together the summer and fall after my pregnancy. When I stopped taking learning Mandarin so seriously, the pressure seemed to lift and I began to understand the language. And though they were still rudimentary, the words started flowing out of me. I was having conversations and dreaming in Chinese!

My best Mandarin practice came from my cab rides. There was no better way for seasoned cab drivers to kill time than by trying to find out what my story was.

In the beginning, I always sat in the back seat, but then one morning on the way to school, I decided to sit in the passenger seat so the driver could hear better where I wanted to go. Also, Eric had told me that it was safer to sit in the front, not only to monitor what was going on, but also so I could brace myself for the unsuspecting things that happened while driving in Beijing—like sideswiping something, or hitting potholes in the road. Sitting in the front seat supposedly gave the impression that I was scrutinizing how safe the driver was.

Many of the cab drivers I rode with were Beijing family men, usually in their fifties. Born and raised during the Cultural Revolution, they often had Mao Zedong pendants hanging from their rearview mirrors, next to their air fresheners. Their collections of items seemed requisite: glass jars filled with hot water and tea leaves, several newspapers and books, and reading glasses.

These men were proud of their humble and honest vocation. They frowned on the money-hungry ways of Shanghai, the opposing city farther south. Frequenting my favorite street market, I often passed a park near Sanlitun, a popular place for cab drivers to take their breaks. Many read their newspapers and books, discussed politics with the other drivers, and listened to talk radio in their cars.

These fatherly types were the ones who'd always start up a conversation as soon as I got into the cab. The second I opened my mouth to tell them where I was going, their curiosity was piqued by my poorly executed Mandarin.

We frequently got on the topic of my ethnicity. One driver insisted that I was Chinese. "No," I told him, "I'm Japanese American."

"No, you have to be Chinese," he repeated.

After a couple of minutes of arguing back and forth, I caved: "Okay, you're right—I'm Chinese."

"I knew it," he said. He was quiet and satisfied for the rest of the ride.

The drive to school from our new apartment was forty-five minutes when there was no traffic, but it could take up to an hour and a half during rush hour. Those longer journeys gave me plenty of time to cover the basics: where I'd grown up, how old I was, what I was doing in China, that I had a boyfriend but wasn't married, what my dad had done before he retired, where my brothers lived and what they did for a living, and that I had no nieces and one nephew. In return, I would find out where the driver and his wife were from, if his parents lived with them, how old their child was, and where the child worked.

I would never have dreamed of having such personal conversations with cabbies in the States, or have tolerated this line of questioning concerning my personal life, but here I enjoyed refining my language skills and having an opportunity to talk to someone on the long rides. Besides, I knew by then that my Asian features helped them feel comfortable with me—it was one of the few times they came in handy. I didn't mind it, therefore, when the drivers had to work a little bit to understand me. I felt encouraged to try out new words or phrases without being so self-conscious.

I imagined that I reminded these cab drivers of their daughter or a favorite niece. Some of them went out of their way to ensure that I got to my destination safely, especially at night. One evening I shared a long rush-hour commute, followed by a harrowing drive through a pitch-black *hutong,* with a sweet, middle-aged driver with short, bristly hair the color of ash. The location, deserted and dark, just didn't look right to him. He insisted he wouldn't leave until I came back out and told him it was the place I was looking for.

*My relationship and communication* channels with Chu Ping improved steadily, particularly since she'd offered me the lychees. Our months of silence were long gone; now we talked mostly about food, like a neighborhood restaurant I should try.

Our connection grew even stronger when we began cooking together, as we did one midsummer afternoon when Chu Ping taught me how to make braised soy eggplant, a popular dish on most restaurant menus. She took me to the vegetable market, where she showed me how to look for long, smaller Asian eggplant. At home she instructed me on how to cut the vegetable lengthwise, then diagonally.

Over a high flame, I added soy sauce, ginger, salt, and a trickle of water to the wok. As the eggplant simmered, I jotted down the recipe on a piece of paper. The strong smell of the soy sauce awakened my stomach.

"*Ni Zuo fan zuo de hen hao*" ("You cook well"), Chu Ping said, flashing me her pearly whites.

I thanked her and gave her the polite Chinese response: "*Mama huhu*" ("All right").

I pondered the fact that she had never really tasted my cooking before. As if reading my mind, she remarked that she always breathed in the scents of my cooking when I was making dinner.

I wasn't sure if I'd heard her right. Her comment sounded vaguely intimate, as if she were admitting that she had a crush on me, so I simply nodded and smiled, feeling flustered. The light on the rice cooker switched on, indicating that our white rice was finished.

"I cooked for Eric before you came," Chu Ping said, sticking her pinky nail into her mouth to dig for an offending piece of food.

"*Zhende!* Really!" I responded, feigning surprise, as Eric had told me she'd prepared his meals. "I didn't know that."

Chu Ping placed the cooked eggplant on a plate and heated some oil and fresh garlic in the wok. When the garlic became fragrant, she returned the eggplant to the wok and added chili paste and cornstarch.

"The eggplant is ready," she announced, adding the final touch to the dish: a couple of drops of sesame seed oil.

She gave it a gentle stir and, using a wooden paddle, scooped some rice into deep soup bowls and garnished it with chopped green onions. By that point I was so hungry that my stomach felt as if it was about to feed on itself. The steam from the rice filled my nose with a wholesome aroma, like the smell of baking bread.

"Yes," she said. "After you came, he told me to stop cooking, that you would be doing the grocery shopping and cooking."

"That's true," I said, trying not to seem annoyed.

We sat down at the dining room table. A typical Chinese meal would have included several other dishes, but I just wanted to concentrate on learning how to make this one. The eggplant was filling and flavorful with the rice—truly a meal in itself.

"This is delicious," I said in Mandarin. "And so easy."

*I didn't tell Eric what Chu Ping* had said, because my relationship with him was going well. We were settled in our lives in Beijing. And then one day not too long after Chu Ping and I made the eggplant dish, when the summer heat was beginning to give way to the fall chill, Eric arrived home early from work. I thought maybe he was sick, but I saw a sparkle in his eyes and knew he had some kind of news. He told me that some investors from the States were interested in merging with his company. This was the big dream, the big payoff, he had been working toward.

It was all happening very quickly, he told me. "Zhu Yin and I are flying out to California tomorrow to check out their operations."

"Tomorrow?" I asked. A jittery, anxious feeling came over me.

"Don't worry, I'll be back in a week," he said.

That night, we celebrated at a neighborhood Chinese restaurant that Chu Ping had recommended. It was a small mom-and-pop establishment serving typical Chinese fare. Nearly every table was empty. Our waitress swatted flies around us with a bright pink plastic swatter as we talked.

When our food arrived, Eric began talking about our relationship. I knew that the source of my anxiety was the possibility of change. I couldn't define it at that moment, but I would come to realize, over the next few weeks, that our relationship had survived largely because we were living in Beijing.

"Linda, you know I love you," Eric started.

I nodded.

He looked away from me before saying, "I'd like to get married, but I don't think I'm ready to commit to that finality. I feel like I should marry you and you deserve that, but I'm just not ready."

I felt angry that he was bringing this up right now, the night before his trip, putting it on me to absolve his guilt. Also, I was beginning to dislike discussions that ruined my meal.

"Did I say I wanted to marry you now?" I asked, realizing immediately that my words had come out more angry than I meant them to sound.

"No," he said, looking guilty.

"First of all," I said, "after hearing what you just said, I wouldn't want to marry you. It would be for the wrong reason. And if you ask me to marry you within the next year, I'll say no, because I won't have done all the things I'd like to do," I said haughtily.

Eric looked satisfied by this response. I only half believed what I was saying. I knew a part of me was saying it just to appease him, but the part of me that rebelled against this tirade barely raised a hand. My once empowered self was practically gone. How long could I continue waiting for him to want to marry me? And why was I willing to wait as he continued dawdling in a lifelong habit of holding women at arm's length?

Even today, although it's more of a wistful, romantic thought, I realize I'm in love with marriage. Reflecting on my girlhood, I know that I was raised among people who believed that wife and mother was the expected vocation. Women who worked outside the home were viewed as unusual or uppity. Work was a part-time interest that wasn't allowed to get in the way of husband and home. Getting married and having a house were the brass ring of life.

During my freshman year of college, I got engaged to a kind man from my hometown who was seven years my senior. But during a summer internship in Fort Worth, Texas, I got a taste of life outside Indiana and I was gone.

Not until I was in my forties would I envy the strength, empowerment, and self-understanding that embracing feminism engendered. I remember meeting a woman who'd grown up in a conservative part of Cincinnati; she'd been turned on to feminism in her teens, and spoke about how it had impacted her life. As she went on, I could feel myself caving in with embarrassment as I mentally skimmed through the list of men in my life for whom I'd compromised my sense of identity.

My mother always hoped for more for me, but her generation and background had taught her that men and women weren't equal. When I tried explaining to my mother that the burden of trying to make it work with Eric didn't lie solely with me, she commented that I should do whatever I could to make him happy—that the success of my relationship did indeed rest on me.

*By now, Eric and I were* the only people left at the restaurant.

With the sensitivity of a brain surgeon about to wield his scalpel on a patient without anesthesia, he commented, "I have to admit, it worries me how your first marriage ended. I don't understand how you let yourself slide into something you weren't ready for."

I shook my head. It wasn't as if he hadn't brought this up before. How could I explain to someone who had a consistent history of avoiding commitment that taking the leap into marriage doesn't necessarily mean that it's going to work out?

"Why are you dropping all the responsibility of our relationship on me?" I asked. I was digging myself into a hole. Eric was fond of making comments that were best left untouched. More words and explanations only fed his need to justify himself, and for me to see it his way. As our relationship progressed, these types of conversations stressed me out so much that I felt like I was reverting to some infantile space, in which I either couldn't articulate my thoughts or just agreed with him for the sake of avoiding conflict.

With genuine honesty, he continued, "But this whole issue does concern you. You're unsettled and don't know what you want to do." He said it matter-of-factly, not as a question. As usual, he wanted confirmation that I agreed with his views.

"What do you think I've been doing for the past year and a half?" I asked, seething. I was unsettled only because I didn't feel secure in my future with him. I was there for him, and I was making headway in my writing career as best I could. "I've been writing for the city paper, and wrote a restaurant piece for the women's magazine in Hong Kong," I said lamely.

I hated the feeling that I was being put on trial, and that I was starving for his approval. Frustration and quiet anger knotted up in my stomach like tangled metal chains. Our discussion was left unresolved, and Eric left for the States the next morning.

*When a couple of weeks had passed,* it was evident that Eric wouldn't be returning as quickly as he'd thought he would. As autumn gained a foothold, with crisper weather and auburn leaves, my close friend Marybeth arrived in Beijing for a visit. I'd met Marybeth in San Francisco at a writing class, and I'd bonded with her instantly. I loved her wry sense of humor, quirky style, and love of pop culture.

Writing-wise, we'd started off at the same point. While I'd stayed on at my day job at the bank, however, Marybeth had temped and taken on writing assignments, paying her dues by working for publications that eventually folded or couldn't pay her.

During her four-day visit, I gave Marybeth the whirlwind tour of my adopted city, starting with the must-sees: the Forbidden City and the Great Wall. The most fun was taking her to the not-so-known sites, like the peculiar and disturbing natural history museum, my favorite haunt on rainy days. The museum is full of badly taxidermied animals, cross-eyed jaguars, and grinning pandas. The top floor displays a freak show of cadavers without skin or muscles.

We spent one afternoon at the Backingham Palace, a bath and massage emporium and bowling alley. After soaking in deep Japanese-style pools, we retired to the upper-level lounge and restaurant, wearing the establishment's designated terry-cloth baby-doll cover-ups. After we'd finished a bowl of noodles and a beer, a "nurse" escorted us into a dim screening room, where we reclined in Taiwanese massage chairs and received head and foot massages while we watched a Hong Kong action film.

We returned to the apartment relaxed and pampered. One message from Eric was waiting for me on the answering machine. I dialed our service and listened to the message.

"Anything important?" Marybeth asked. Her cheeks were as red as strawberry jam from the hot bath and the late-autumn chill.

"Eric says he's got some important news for me," I said, feeling slightly concerned.

"Well, call him," she said.

"I can't. It's still too early on the West Coast," I explained. "Which means only one thing."

"What?"

"That we have time to run over to the hot pot restaurant," I said, grabbing my jacket.

By the time we got home, I was exhausted. Marybeth wrote some postcards, and I took the opportunity to phone Eric.

I was nervous as the phone connection clicked. I hadn't heard from him in several days. I was occupied with Marybeth's visit and I assumed he'd been busy with work.

"I have some great news," he said. "Something I think you'll be happy to hear." I felt only mildly relieved.

"Tell me. I'm dying to know," I said anxiously.

"The board of the company met, and we're going through with the acquisition here in California. We're going to move back to San Francisco," Eric said.

"You mean now?" I said.

"Yeah." There was a pause while I absorbed the impact of what was being said.

"I thought you'd be happy," Eric said, with a smidgen of annoyance in his voice. "I thought you didn't like it there."

"I didn't at one point, at the beginning," I said, trailing off.

Switching on his business voice, he said, "Well, I don't know what to say, except that I won't be able to come back to Beijing. The project is starting now and I need to be here. You're going to have to organize the move of our stuff back to the States. Will you do that?"

"Of course, Eric," I said, reeling from the onslaught of information. "I just don't understand why you've thought the entire time I've been here that I didn't like it," I continued, clearly choosing to avoid the stress of the bigger picture.

"You just seem unhappy all the time," he answered.

When I got off the phone, I felt a sense of loss, as if I'd just learned that my house had burned down.

"Did you talk to him?" Marybeth asked, emerging from the bedroom in her pajamas.

"I did."

"So what's the news?"

"I'm moving back home," I said flatly.

"You don't seem very thrilled about it," she said in a concerned voice.

"I'm actually not," I said miserably.

For the next hour, over a glass of red wine, I explained to Marybeth how I'd arrived in Beijing wanting very little to do with the culture. I was willing to be here for Eric.

Since Eric had left for California, though, I'd been busy working on my articles and going out almost every night to dine or hang out with friends. Showing Marybeth China's capital city had driven home the fact that I'd created a life for myself here, learning the language and carving out my own niche. I realized that the reason I felt so crushed was that I'd fallen in love with the city.

I looked at Marybeth. "If Eric's leaving, I have to leave, too. My time here is over."

*After Marybeth left for* New York City, I began preparing for the move to California. When I told Chu Ping the news, she appeared emotionless about it. She helped me organize our belongings. We gave her our kitchenware and other items that we didn't care to take back with us. Eric coordinated a job opportunity for her with a nice couple who had recently moved to Beijing from Chicago. Before Chu Ping went home the eve of my last night, we said goodbye to each other as casually as we would have if we'd been planning to see each other the very next day. I couldn't think of any other way to handle it.

On my last night, when I was out with Susan and Gina, memories raced through my mind as we ate our Beijing roast duck. But my recollections came to a grinding halt when I heard a woman sitting near us say in accented English, "Be quiet, I beg you." Susan, Gina, and I stopped and looked at one another. The dining room was small, but it was still difficult to hear people at other tables over the din of conversation. By this time, all the other customers had cleared out and only two tables remained: ours and a table of three Chinese, a woman and two men.

The taller man's eyes were rolled back and the woman was reeling in her chair, swatting her hands broadly as she spoke.

They talked amongst themselves in Mandarin. I could tell by the way Susan was sitting quietly that she was listening to what they were saying.

"Did you hear what that woman just said about us?" Gina asked Susan, turning around to glare at them.

The group was speaking in slang, which I didn't understand at all. I concentrated on rolling up my last pieces of duck in a thin pancake.

Susan and Gina both started laughing.

"What is it?" I asked.

"They're getting really pissed off because you're not reacting to what they're saying. They think you're just being stuck up because you're with foreigners." Gina was amazed. I hadn't told her how often this happened to me, and I didn't want to get into it now, on my last night. "Wow, they're saying some awful things about you, thinking you're Chinese."

"Don't tell me. I don't want to know," I said, chewing my duck and taking a swig of my beer.

"Be quiet," Susan said, waving a hand at Gina. "They're saying we're wearing black, like the Chinese prostitutes, but that we're not worth paying 200 RMB."

Gina and I looked at each other and started laughing. Then Gina said something loudly in Mandarin over her shoulder.

Susan covered her head and told me that Gina had just told them to go suck a dick.

The woman stood up unsteadily and began speaking to us directly. Susan and Gina didn't say a word.

"What's she saying?" I asked Gina.

"That we don't respect their traditions. How dare we intrude in their country? Foreigners make no money here," Gina recited. And then the woman reached for her duck soup and dumped it onto the floor. This display seemed to satisfy her, as she plopped herself down hard on her seat.

"It's so sad, really," Gina analyzed, picking at a piece of cold *heyebing* (thin pancake). "From their office attire, I can guess that they probably work for some foreign country with an office here. Their outrage demonstrates an ugly repressed side. I bet they've never had a chance to express these feelings to foreigners before. It's really quite pathetic."

As Gina continued sussing out the reason for their anger, the two men went out into the courtyard to throw up. The woman stayed at the table, glaring at us.

Susan took the opportunity to whip out her camera and take their picture. In English, the short man said, "No, don't. I'm ugly."

The woman smiled at the camera and said, "Thank you" in that same English accent we'd heard earlier.

As we left the restaurant, the tall man came staggering out behind us to apologize. He said he wanted to rise above his previous conduct and be a good Chinese. Susan told him it was too late, and asked him to please go away.

I decided to take a cab home, so I gave Susan and Gina hugs and said my farewells at the entrance to the *hutong;* the tall man stood in the background, still begging for forgiveness. I hailed a cab and got in the back seat. I turned around to look out the window and saw Gina's and Susan's silhouettes. I wondered if it would be the last time I ever saw them.

*I woke with a start* at four in the morning. An eerie light was coming into the bedroom, and I could have sworn I saw the shadow of someone walking toward my bedroom door. The movers had packed up all the furniture except the guest room bed the day before.

The usual construction noises came from across the way, but over them I was sure I could hear a young Chinese man singing softly. It sounded as if he were walking on the bare, echoing wood floors in my empty living room.

My heart was pounding madly. Had I forgotten to lock the front door? I lay there and decided to jump out of bed and turn on the bedroom light. For a moment, as I looked out into the living room, I swore the front door was open. I almost fell to my knees with relief when I walked across the room and it wasn't.

I couldn't shake off the eerie feeling that morning when I got up. The empty apartment amplified all the noise from the corridor outside. I could hear the crinkling of the stiff plastic bags lining the garbage cans by the elevator, and yet there were no windows for a breeze to make its way through.

I rolled my bags to the elevator and pushed the button. A shiver ran through me when the door opened immediately and the lights blinked on, as if it had been waiting there for me.

The front lobby of the building was deserted. There was no doorman downstairs, as there usually was, but all the Christmas decorations were lit. The window was spray-painted with fake snow that read: MARRY CHRISTMAS. There was even a Christmas tree, complete with lights, wrapped presents, and a tree skirt. The cold stung my cheeks as I walked the distance to the Shangri-La Hotel, where I could get a cab this early in the morning.

Leaving in the pre-dawn hours like this saddened me. I felt as if I were sneaking away from a sleeping lover. I was again reminded of the concubines and their hidden, tortured lives in the Forbidden City.

Just the day before, I'd fielded the movers' questions about a couple of pieces of furniture that I'd purchased. They informed me that because they were antiques, I had to get them fumigated before they were shipped.

I accompanied one of the drivers to the fumigation center. During the drive, I heard a muffled chirp. Then I heard it again and thought maybe it was something related to the truck. I looked sideways at my driver and noticed that he had one hand dug deep in his pocket. The chirping was coming from there.

I looked at him and asked what the noise was. At a red light, he pulled out of his pocket a large cricket, about the size of a Swiss Army knife. Its eyes were as big as beads of osetra caviar.

It was old and strong, he told me. He cradled it in his hand like a delicate Fabergé egg and cooed at it like it was a baby.

I had come to Beijing like the cricket Eric and I had released in the park—with one leg chewed off—but my love and affection for Beijing had turned me into a stronger cricket since then. Several years after I left, I was lucky enough to visit Beijing two more times, but it wasn't the same as living there. To this day, I look back fondly on the time I spent there during the infancy of my relationship with Eric, during that unique period when we felt we had the city to ourselves.

# BRAISED EGGPLANT

*This recipe is great served hot, room temperature,*
*or cold. It's delicious with white rice, but don't hesitate*
*to add it to salad, either.*

INGREDIENTS:

2 tablespoons plus 2 teaspoons vegetable oil

4 Asian eggplants, cut into uniform 1 x 1 1/2-inch pieces

5 tablespoons water

1 tablespoon soy sauce

1/2 teaspoon salt

1 tablespoon fresh ginger, minced

2 garlic cloves, minced

1 teaspoon rice vinegar

1 tablespoon chili paste (optional)

2 tablespoons cornstarch, mixed with 2 tablespoons water

1 teaspoon Asian sesame oil

INSTRUCTIONS:

Heat 2 tablespoons oil in a wok or heavy skillet over medium-low
heat. Add the eggplant, water, soy sauce, salt, and ginger. Cook

for about 10 minutes, stirring gently with a spatula. When the eggplant reaches a soft, loose consistency, remove from heat and set aside.

Add the remaining 2 teaspoons oil to the wok; place over high heat. Add the garlic and stir-fry for a minute or two, until fragrant. (Be careful not to burn it.)

Reduce heat to medium-high. Return the eggplant to the pan, then add the vinegar and optional chili paste; stir well.

Add the cornstarch mixture, reduce heat to medium, and stir until incorporated. Sprinkle with sesame oil and stir gently to blend.

*Serves 4*

*Chapter 8*

# Whore of the
# ORIENT

I REMEMBER MY MOTHER TELLING ME about the nightmares she'd had before she left her life in Tokyo to fulfill an arranged marriage to my father, who was already working in the United States. Their marriage was guided by personal input from family and friends, and the screening process took more than a year before the couple was confirmed as marriage material, but there remained the looming possibility that my mother would be returned to Japan like an incorrect shipment.

Granted, Eric and I weren't total strangers when I went to Beijing to be with him, but similar worries nagged at me. I had traveled great distances, left my job, and subleased my San Francisco apartment. As I prepared for my trip, I anticipated romance and the adventure of living overseas. Combined with the prospects of a bright future, the risk seemed worth it. At night, though, my positive outlook warped like a funhouse mirror. I often woke up gripped with fear. It wasn't the idea of returning to the States without a job or even a place to live that I found most terrifying; it was the explaining I would have to do if the relationship tanked. Normally I don't invest too much in what other people think, but the nights before I left for Beijing, the possibility of returning to the Bay Area and seeing the pity, disappointment, and possible glimmer of glee in another person's eyes about my turn of luck was a sinister consequence that never allowed me to completely relax into my relationship with Eric.

He and I returned to San Francisco in the winter of 1998 with our relationship intact, though, and I felt like a triumphant heroine. It was like a whole new beginning, with another layer added to our expanding history together. Back in the world I was familiar with, I saw how the language and cultural barriers in Beijing had put us in situations new couples hardly ever find themselves in. The scales no longer felt tipped against us; if anything, they were tipped in our favor because we had survived our time together overseas.

We returned to the Bay Area amid the dot-com explosion. It was a celebratory time for start-up companies. Businesses were springing up in every nook and cranny of San Francisco. The air buzzed with energy, prosperity, and a sour whiff of greed. Opportunists were moving in from all over, trying to get a piece of the action. Neighborhoods once thought of as questionable were becoming gentrified as hip new restaurants and trendy boutiques opened seemingly every day. The new Giants' baseball stadium was being constructed, and the Embarcadero was getting a face-lift. All of that, combined with the Bay Area's mild weather, made the city feel invincible.

Garnishing this influx of jobs and opportunities was a housing crunch unlike anything I'd ever witnessed. It wasn't unusual to see renters lined up with applications and financial statements, vying against forty other people for one small apartment.

We stayed with Eric's prep school buddy and his pregnant wife until I could find us an apartment. I was stressed about where we would live, and I devoted all my time to the search. After being back for about two weeks, I saw an ad in the classifieds for a flat in Potrero Hill.

As I climbed the steep hill of Mississippi Street, I tried to control my expectations. The house that matched the ad's address had a spectacular view of the city. My heart pounded from the walk and my growing suspense.

I called Eric from a pay phone as soon as I'd viewed the first-floor apartment. "I found us a great place," I said into the receiver. "We should move on this quickly, before someone else does."

It was an Edwardian-style house with carved built-in shelves and cabinets, a colorful Spanish-tiled fireplace, shiny hardwood floors, and molded high ceilings. What sealed the deal for me, besides the washer and dryer in the garage, were the spacious chef's kitchen with a late-model Viking stove, and an office that extended into the backyard garden. The garden was overgrown, but the scent of the ocean had me visualizing Sunday mornings reading *The New York Times* and sipping coffee. I was drawn to the imperfections, too, such as the musty undertones and the hairline cracks on the walls, because they were signs of the apartment's authentic beauty and charm.

We'd left behind our Corningware dishes and aluminum pots and pans in Beijing, and, like newlyweds, we outfitted our San Francisco kitchen with new flatware, dishes, bowls, and cookware. We replaced our threadbare towels, discolored gray from Beijing tap water, with absorbent new ones.

The first month back home felt like a vacation—a typical day was filled with newfound appreciation and observations of San Francisco, and comparing it with China. Our social calendar filled up with dinners, parties, and outdoor activities with old friends, as well as new friends we'd made in China who'd moved to the Bay Area, lured by the opportunities created by the new economy.

At first, I tried to sustain the momentum of the writing schedule I'd had in Beijing. In China, I'd been busy researching articles for the city paper, crafting pitch letters for future articles, or carrying out freelance assignments. And as a department writer for the English-language city paper, I'd met fairly regularly with Susan and Gina.

I naively thought I could slip back into freelance writing in San Francisco, and that it would be easier for me than it was in China. I was counting on using my United Airlines magazine article as my primary sample, but the piece wasn't scheduled to run for almost a year.

In the late 1990s, China was an obscure place to travel to. More remote areas in China that had been closed off to foreigners were just starting to open airports and encourage tourism. It would be several more years before the country cracked open into the great travel destination it is now. My query letters pitching China travel stories were rejected repeatedly. One travel editor told me that China was a hard sell—no one was going there. I'd experienced this reality firsthand: Planes to China were always half-empty, and I could count on having a whole row to myself. It was frustrating to be met with so little interest, though, having lived there and witnessed the countless gleaming metal cranes across the skyline, and the country's cultural changes and economic emergence.

Mornings were the worst part of my day. After eating breakfast and reading the morning paper with Eric, I'd dress in something besides sweats and a T-shirt to give the impression that I had something meaningful planned for the day.

I'd kiss him goodbye and send him off on his commute to Cupertino, about an hour's drive in morning traffic. Then I'd sit at my desk, looking out onto a clear day, and attempt to craft magazine article ideas. The sunny days depressed me even more; I drafted pitch letter after pitch letter, but I'd ultimately get drowsy from the sheer enormity of my uphill battle, and I'd feel overcome with a sense of hopelessness.

Tiredness followed by sleeping was my way of coping with depression. Sleeping in bed or on the sofa was an indication that I had a problem, so to justify my nap I curled up on a blanket, like a cat, on the floor next to the space heater.

I'd wake up an hour or two later, bleary-eyed and guilt-ridden, feeling like a first-class loser. After lunch, with a renewed sense of motivation, I'd walk or take the bus to run errands.

I'd be home by midafternoon, back at my desk and writing earnestly, with intention and energy, hoping to make up for the time I'd wasted in the morning. Before Eric walked through the door, I ran around frantically, picking up the flat—throwing in a load of laundry, washing the day's dishes, and getting dinner started so it would be ready for him when he arrived.

Over candlelight and chilled California white wine, I'd ask him about his day and tell him about mine. I left out the napping part. It was deceptive, but it was my way of coping.

*Following weeks of rejection letters* and isolation, I knew that I needed to set aside the freelance writing and get a job outside the house, if only for my mental health.

On the bus to the financial district, where the temp agency was, I studied the woman sitting across from me. She had a snazzy haircut and wore a stylish trench coat over a simple sweater and skirt. She had an aura of purpose that I envied. *That used to be me,* I thought.

My first temp job turned into a full-time position as an office manager for a high-yield group within a financial institution. This wasn't what I'd hoped to fall into, but I found the idea of getting up every morning and going somewhere with coworkers appealing, at least for the time being.

As winter turned into spring, my motivation for writing fell away as my workload and stress increased at the office. After a day of meetings, orientation, and administrative work, the last thing I wanted to do was sit in my office at home and pound out a pitch letter. Since I was making my own money, I felt entitled to movies and dinners out with girlfriends and weekends away with Eric. The writing I loved so much nagged me like a festering wound.

Eric and I were at a new level of commitment in our relationship, but the same tremors—my drinking and resentment patterns—resurfaced with alarming frequency. The uncertainty and doubts fueled by my diminished independent self and Eric's controlling behavior that had plagued me in China appeared over and over again across a wide variety of circumstances, as our ongoing problems were never fully resolved.

One early fall evening I shared these concerns with my friend Gill. Eric was working late that night, and Gill and I had a reservation at one of the new eateries on 16th Street in Potrero Hill. We had plenty of time before our reservation, so we decided to enjoy the early-evening light in my garden, snacking on edamame chased with shots of unfiltered Japanese rice wine.

I updated her on almost every aspect of the past two years with Eric. I described the rages I fell into when I drank in Beijing, and my persistent sense of how incompatible we were. I told her how Eric didn't seem to have any faith that we would last, and how I was losing myself in the relationship. "If you question how Eric treats you, why do you stay with him?" she asked.

"Because I love him." I paused, drinking a capful of sake. "He believes I can be a good writer."

Gill raised her arched eyebrows at this, but didn't say anything. She was as loyal as a good friend could be. She had seen me through my divorce and though the rocky year when I'd begun dating Eric.

Gill and I had worked together at the investment bank before I moved to China. She was born and raised in Dublin, Ireland. A petite beauty with long onyx hair, skin as pale as sun-bleached stone, and blue eyes that looked almost gray, she had the face of a wood fairy but the sharp tongue of a picaroon. When one of the many executive types in our old office tried to push his weight around, Gill would look him directly in the eye with a smile and say, in her Irish lilt, something like, "What an arse you are today." The men were almost always flustered and confused, and she'd follow up, eyes fluttering, by saying something to move right past the conflict, like "Yes, the washrooms are over there."

I knew Gill well enough to know what she was thinking: We'd all been there, and love was great and all, but that wasn't good enough when I was always feeling lousy in my relationship.

"I feel like I'm just waiting for Eric to up and leave me," I confessed. "I don't know what it is about him. I would never have put up with this uncertainty and dominance from anyone else, but there's something about him that I just can't let go of. It's like some kind of addiction."

The famous Bay Area winds were picking up as the sun dropped. The air turned blustery and cool. We weren't ready to go into the house just yet, so we wrapped ourselves up in the Mexican blankets I'd brought out earlier. The leaves of the yucca plant whipped in the wind.

Gill looked pensive, but when she didn't open her mouth to say anything, I filled the space with my own musings about why Eric was different. "He's just the first person to believe in me as a writer," I said. "I can't even talk about my writing to my parents. Everyone else is hopeful, but—"

"Linda," Gill interrupted. I realized that she'd gathered her thoughts enough to tell me what was on her mind. "I know you love him, and don't take what I'm about to say the wrong way. But frankly, you've become accustomed to nice things and your life is quite comfortable now." She looked cautious and stopped for a moment, gauging my reaction. "I don't think you believe you can be a writer without his financial and emotional support."

I didn't say anything, wanting to give her some piece of concrete evidence that this statement wasn't true.

"Loyalty is huge, Linda, but I have to ask if it's worth compromising yourself for. Whether we like it or not, in a relationship nothing is ever as equal as we think it is. There seems to be a part of you that doesn't want to go along with the other part of you that's so grateful to him. I just see this split in you, that's all."

I closed my eyes and rested my head against the back of my Adirondack chair. The wind rustled through the rickety trellis, shaking its creaky strips of worn wood. The birds sang an evening farewell, accompanied by chirping crickets.

*Those damn crickets,* I thought. But suddenly, the fact that they kept showing up in my life made sense. I was putting myself, my true self, in a cage—like those crickets that the man on the bicycle was selling in Beijing.

*I can't do this anymore,* I thought. But the idea of leaving Eric made my stomach lurch.

"Are you all right?" Gill said, leaning forward in her chair.

"Yeah, I think it must be the rice wine. I haven't eaten too much today," I lied. "Thanks for opening up to me about what you think. Telling me something like that has to be hard, and I appreciate it."

Gill nodded and smiled solemnly.

"I know what I should do, but for now I'm going to see how things go."

"I know you'll do what you think is right," she said.

She had more faith in me than I did in myself. We sat there, not saying anything, huddling under our blankets and letting the sound of the wind fill our ears and the fresh smell of the ocean seep deep into our lungs. The sound of my landlady, who lived above me, opening a window jarred me back to the present. My loyalty, faith, dependence, and love were wrapped like an impenetrable cocoon around my mind's image of Eric. I locked myself in that golden cage that evening, when I made up my mind to stick with Eric regardless and to do my best to make him happy, despite the toll it might take on me. I didn't fully grasp the level of confinement I'd already accepted for myself.

*The months leading up to* ringing in the new millennium were hectic at my office, as much of my job revolved around finding solutions to the

Y2K bug; it was predicted that computers worldwide would fail on January 1st due to the way they'd been programmed to read dates. Sitting in on boring meetings, I started to miss the simplicity and day-to-day inconveniences of living in Beijing. They now seemed exciting and challenging compared with the life I was living.

I mentioned this to Eric one evening as I sipped my favorite Thai chicken and coconut-milk soup, *tom kha gai*, from Siam's, the financial-district Thai takeout place we frequented. Loading his plate with jasmine rice and red curry, Eric gave me an odd look and said, "I like it here. Remember how hard it was in Beijing? Anyway, all you could ever say was how much you hated it."

I shrugged. "I kinda miss all that now."

As more time passed and the sheen of my office job corroded, the fonder my memories of China became. My disenchantment with work also planted new seeds for my true passions, and, like spring bulbs, my writing ambition began to sprout again.

I began jotting down article ideas in the margins of my Y2K notes during backup-plan meetings. My hunger for writing was as fresh and rousing as it had been when I took my first writing class, at San Diego State University in 1991.

When I discovered my love for writing, I accepted that it would take a lifetime to master. Since that time, to my parents' chagrin, I've considered my day jobs merely work—an emotionless, but necessary, means of bringing in money. Needless to say, this attitude has made countless jobs intolerable. I find peace and commitment only when I turn to the work that I consider my life's passion.

One quiet Friday afternoon during those two excruciating hours before the end of the workday, I was huddled in my cubicle, surfing the Internet, with my ears attentive for my boss's heavy footsteps. I was browsing the newsroom job listings at the *San Francisco Chronicle, San Jose Mercury News,* and *Contra Costa Times.*

A couple of weeks earlier, I'd unexpectedly received an assignment to write a short article about Chinese symbols for United Airlines' in-flight magazine, *Hemispheres.* I'd been turned away or ignored so many times that getting an unsolicited assignment gave me a rocket-powered confidence boost. As with my first article with the magazine, there was a long wait before this one would be published. But this time I didn't mind, because the work renewed my excitement about writing.

A job posting caught my eye: It was for a restaurant reviewer covering the South Peninsula for the *San Francisco Chronicle's* food section. I hesitated for a moment as I weighed my qualifications. I had my restaurant review clips from Beijing and my restaurant round-up for *Hemispheres.* I knew that this position would require me to have stringent criteria for restaurants, and that it would involve an average of three visits to each restaurant in the review queue.

No, I decided, I wasn't qualified for the job. But I applied anyway. I told myself that if I wanted to make it as a freelance writer, I had to start toughening myself up for more rejection.

Almost two weeks to the day after I hand-delivered my resume and clips to the *San Francisco Chronicle* offices, I decided to do something I'd never done before: make a follow-up call.

I peeked over my cubicle wall and spied my boss sitting with his feet up on his desk, yelling into his speakerphone. *Perfect time to make a personal call,* I thought.

After dialing the paper's number half a dozen times before freezing and then hanging up, I thought, *You've got to learn how to do this without taking it personally. Would you rather wait days until you get a letter? No.* I finished dialing and stayed on the line.

"Michael Bauer speaking." The voice on the other end sounded unusually calm. It flustered me, as I had expected to be transferred directly to voicemail.

"Ah . . . " I took a deep breath. "Hi, my name is Linda Furiya. I dropped off my resume a couple of weeks ago for the South Peninsula restaurant reviewer job. I haven't heard anything, so I thought I'd call and see if the position has been filled."

"Tell me your name again?"

"Linda Furiya."

I heard some paper shuffling in the background. "I apologize—I meant to call you earlier," he said. I sat up in my seat. "I set your resume aside."

Was he mistaking me for someone else?

"Hello?" he said. "Are you still there?"

"Yes, I'm still here."

"Yes, well," he continued, "we filled the restaurant reviewer position with a writer who lives down on the Peninsula. But your resume did catch my eye because here we are in a city with one of the largest populations of Asian Americans, and we don't have anyone writing about Chinese or Japanese food."

"Huh." I squeezed my eyes shut, regretting having replied in such an inane way. The editor didn't seem to notice, though, as he went on. "We have an Asian food column called 'East to West.' I think your writing may suit that column. Does this sound like something you'd be interested in doing?" He paused. "Hello?"

Could this be true? I had only called to see if I had gotten the restaurant reviewer job, not a column. Then the wonderful reality started sinking into my brain cells.

"Yes, of course I would!" I exclaimed. The rest of the conversation was a blur. I could hardly contain my happiness when I got off the phone. I looked around to make sure no one could see me hugging myself and tapping my feet rapidly on the floor with glee. I'd known I was a writer at heart before I made the phone call, but now that someone wanted me, I felt like the real deal.

Waves of terror followed my jubilation. This routinely happened when I got an assignment, and the best remedy I'd found was to let the freak-out run its course—and after a couple of hours, like a raging fever, the episodes would subside. Exorcising my demons left me calm and lucid enough to do the work that I felt called to do.

*Eric and I celebrated the arrival* of the year 2000 with his family in Naples, Florida, without falling victim to the feared Y2K bug. We spent the remainder of our winter vacation with friends in Lake Tahoe. The rest of the winter and spring flew past with relative ease and without incident, as if, after the anticipation of impending disaster that was wrapped up with Y2K, the world was able to exhale a collective sigh of relief.

That May, my debut with the *San Francisco Chronicle* began with a feature on *kaiseki* (formal Japanese multicourse meal) cookery. Michael Bauer was patient and guided me closely through this piece. After the article ran, he cut me loose and let me make my own mistakes in order to learn the ropes of newspaper writing.

Turning to the food section that Wednesday morning and seeing my article with color photos was a proud and memorable moment. Eric bought out all the copies of the paper at our neighborhood grocer. Because he had supported me and remained optimistic and encouraging, I felt this achievement was as much for him as it was for me.

As my freelance writing blossomed through these monthly food essays in the *Chronicle* and other work, Eric left his post as chief financial officer soon after his company merged with the California firm. He believed his work was done; following the merger, hardly any remnants of the company he'd started with in China remained.

Eric started going to the gym regularly and enrolled in the professional cooking program at the California Culinary Academy. When he wasn't in cooking school, he drove me to work in the Financial District and picked me up. Now he was the one who had dinner ready for me when I got home. He didn't know what his next step was going to be, and he often seemed at a loss about what to do with himself.

During this time of uncertainty for him, the dot-com bubble burst. As happened with millions of other people, Eric's large stake of stock options, which he'd received during the China venture, became worthless. I made several attempts to talk with him about the stress he might be feeling, but he responded the same way he did with anything that affected him negatively, saying that he was fine and punctuating it with a grin.

That summer, Eric and I decided we were ready to expand our family by adopting two wirehaired dachshunds. We had both grown up with dachshunds, and Eric thought raising two puppies would be a good litmus test for having children. Of course, he disagreed when I suggested that marriage should come first.

The dog breeder we chose was located in the hills near Santa Cruz. When we went down there to pick up our new puppies, we were greeted by a herd of wirehaired dachshund pups, all whimpers and wagging tails. Like two small beacons emerging from the crowd, a silky cream-colored pup aggressively squirmed his way to Eric, and a beagle-looking male pressed his wet nose into my hand.

As it turned out, these pups were the only ones left that hadn't been claimed. It was too early to take them away from their mother, but they'd be ready to leave in early September.

Throughout the summer of 2000, friends of ours—and I myself— wondered what Eric's next endeavor would be. During dinner conversations, he batted away speculation regarding new opportunities with skepticism about the market in the wake of the dot-com crash. He bemoaned the lack of opportunities and shot down lots of suggestions as being not worth his effort.

Despite having been privy to all these conversations, I didn't find out until Eric was getting ready to fly to Shanghai for an interview that he was being courted by a Chinese company that modeled its online auctions after the American company eBay. Ever the consummate pessimist, he said taking the job was a long shot, but still, it disconcerted me to know that he didn't feel like he could weigh the pros and cons with me.

Because Eric was interviewing in Shanghai in September, I ended up driving to Santa Cruz to pick up our new puppies on my own. We'd already named the beagle-looking pup Oscar, and the creamy, soft one Meyer.

I knew nothing about taking care of puppies, but getting up in the middle of the night to let them out, and being attentive to their feeding and bathroom needs, felt enough like caring for a newborn that I resented having to do it on my own.

When Eric came home, I was ready for some relief. I felt like I permanently smelled of dog urine, disinfectant, and newspaper. His first day home, after he got reacquainted with the wiggling pups, we sat on the floor cross-legged and facing each other. He was stroking Meyer, and I was cradling Oscar.

"What do you think about moving back to China?" he asked with a smile. I felt that familiar electrifying sensation of being swept up by wanderlust.

I didn't have to answer. Eric knew I would have gone or stayed anywhere, as long as I was with him, and now with the dogs. When it came to moving and traveling around, Eric and I were incredibly compatible. We shared a desire to pursue whatever challenged us. I didn't feel scared, ambivalent, or insecure about going back to China. I felt instead that I had unfinished writing to do there, and that it would be the perfect opportunity to work on writing a book.

This idea wasn't a new one. Though my clip file was growing, it had become clear to me that as challenging, flexible, and gratifying as freelance writing could be, I was only as good as my last byline. I needed a piece of work that was solid, not fleeting like an article in a magazine or a newspaper. A book would be just that.

My vision of writing a memoir about growing up in Indiana came easily. I had been writing about those experiences in short-essay form for years. And since I'd begun writing for the *Chronicle*, I'd been thinking constantly about article ideas and the recipes that would accompany them. Thus, it wasn't a big leap for me to think about how I might thread the scenes of my life through book chapters complemented by recipes.

Eric's new employers moved quickly to get him started on his new responsibilities. By the end of September, he was working in Shanghai. I stayed behind to organize the overseas move and wrap up any final details. My taking on these tasks had become part of our relationship, but I didn't mind because I was looking forward to living in Shanghai. In early November, the movers came, packed, and took away all our belongings. My last night in San Francisco, I burned a log in the fireplace. I contemplated the past and the future, feeling thankful for all of it. Then I slept on the dining room floor in a sleeping bag with the dogs. The next morning, the dogs and I flew to Naples, Florida, where we'd spend Thanksgiving with Eric and his family. The plan was to fly together to Shanghai from Naples after the holiday weekend.

I spoke to Eric on the phone almost daily during the weeks he was gone, and when I met him at the airport with the pups in tow, there was a renewed vitality to him that was reminiscent of how he'd been when we'd first started dating. Whether it was because we'd been separated for so long, or because we were making a fresh start together in Shanghai, our relationship had somehow been substantiated for Eric while he was away. The day before Thanksgiving, I accepted his marriage proposal.

*My first month in Shanghai,* I disliked the place immensely. Unlike Beijing, with its slower pace, its pride in maintaining artistic and cultural traditions, and its historic highlights, Shanghai seemed too shiny and decadent for my taste.

The city started innocently, as a sleepy fishing village, in the eleventh century. China's defeat in the first Opium Wars brought in the British, French, Americans, and Japanese, who quickly established territories in the city. The Europeans in particular left behind their indelible mark, both architecturally and culturally. Besides becoming the most important port city in Asia, Shanghai was the founding city of the Communist Party of China and, during the 1930s, was notorious as a haven of opium dens, whorehouses, and lawlessness.

Beijing's dust, grit, and unadorned qualities were closer to my heart. The capital city was an understated heirloom, rich with history—she carried herself like an empress. Fun, energetic, and global, Shanghai was the next "it girl," heading into the twenty-first century.

Over time, however, my dislike of the city began to lessen. I found features that appealed to me, such as the French Concession District, where the busy, quaint neighborhoods and charming, tree-lined side streets were flanked by buildings and homes with touches of European detail, such as ornate grillwork on a small balcony, or an art nouveau pattern surrounding a doorway.

Having some knowledge of basic Mandarin was also helpful in my transition. During the two years Eric and I had spent in San Francisco, many of the friends and acquaintances I'd known in Beijing had moved back to the States or moved to Shanghai to take advantage of its burgeoning opportunities.

I was overjoyed to learn that Gina and her husband had relocated to Shanghai. I hadn't seen her in two years, but we picked up where we'd left off. We began meeting once or twice a week at what would soon become our favorite Japanese restaurant, Itoya. There was a large population of Japanese expatriates working in Shanghai, and that made fresh, delicious Japanese food easy to come by.

Not long after I arrived in Shanghai, we met for dinner. As I finished my Japanese steak and started in on my *tekka maki* (tuna roll), I asked, "Have you noticed how now that we've lived in Beijing, life here seems so much easier in comparison?" I slid the small dish of nori- and rice-wrapped raw tuna across the table.

Gina picked up a roll with her chopsticks, dipped it quickly in the wasabi, then dunked it in the soy sauce. She nodded, unable to answer me after popping the whole thing into her mouth. She fanned herself as the wasabi overtook her sinuses.

"What's the difference, do you think?" I asked, sliding her a glass of water.

She took a quick sip. "Money, of course."

"Money?" I hadn't thought of that, honestly, though I had noticed that there were more Western comforts here. "Shanghai feels so much more Westernized than Beijing, which probably explains why I've missed Beijing so much," I said.

Gina dabbed her mouth with a napkin. "I know what you mean, but you'll get over it. I hate to admit it, but since I quit working for Susan's paper, I'm living like a *tai-tai*." (*Tai-tai* is a surname for married women, but it also refers to a well-heeled housewife, or what Americans might call ladies who lunch.)

Even though I was writing, my schedule was flexible and my life wasn't dictated by income anymore. This was a truth I didn't want to accept. I was becoming a *tai-tai*.

"Look at us—we work out in the mornings, and now we're lunching."

"That doesn't mean we're *tai-tais*," I said, a little defensively.

"Okay, what are you doing after this?" Gina asked, her head tilted knowingly.

I didn't answer.

"You're going grocery shopping at the Wellcome Market, right?" she asked, nodding her head. She offered me a cigarette. I took it.

"I was going to pick up a few things and start writing when I got home."

"Listen, don't feel guilty. We deserve this," Gina said.

"You deserve it more than I do," I said. "In Beijing, you worked while your husband studied Chinese. I haven't really done anything."

"What do you call your writing and working in San Fran while Eric went to cooking school? You make his life comfortable. I make my husband's life comfortable. I'm sorry, but that has a price tag." She shrugged. "Hey," she added, a mischievous glint in her eyes, "let's get our nails done."

I gave her a look.

"Just kidding."

I put out my cigarette, hating myself for having had a second one. "Actually, I do have to go to the Wellcome Market. I'm looking for an *ayi*."

The waitress dropped off our check and fresh orange slices stuck with fancy wood toothpicks.

"See, you are a *tai-tai*," Gina teased. "Interviewing housekeepers is the number one *tai-tai* duty."

I walked from the restaurant to the Wellcome Market, which was located at the Portman, an office building development with a T.G.I. Friday's restaurant, a Ritz-Carlton hotel, a Starbucks, and a Western medical clinic.

The Wellcome Market sold most necessities—good breads and pastries; dairy products; meat; and familiar American and European brand-name frozen, canned, and dried products. At the entrance was a large bulletin board with ads for private Mandarin lessons and language exchanges. Urgent pleas to buy or take household goods from families leaving the country appeared alongside employment-wanted ads posted by drivers and Chinese housekeepers.

One such ad, from an English-speaking *ayi*, caught my attention. According to the posting, her name was Emily. I jotted down her number, along with four others that sounded promising.

When I got home, I put the groceries away and immediately went into my office to call Emily.

Emily's voice was soft and slow, like she had just awoken from a nap. I'd later find out that this was just her speaking pattern. Her English was very good, regardless, with none of the choppiness typical of Chinese natives.

"How did you learn to speak English fluently?" I asked her.

"I worked for an American family. The husband and wife had two young children. The wife began teaching me little by little. I learned it quite quickly."

*I'll say*, I thought. I explained what kind of person I was looking for: someone responsible, with initiative, and a quick learner. Emily told me she was working part-time for an American journalist and was looking for extra work to fill in the rest of her week. My voice sounded almost shrill to me toward the end of the call, as a result of my growing enthusiasm for Emily as my future *ayi*. I realized while we were talking that she might be a perfect translator for the China-related articles I'd always wanted to write. I sounded overly eager when I tried to close the conversation by offering to meet her for coffee at Starbucks.

If she'd agree to sign on full-time, rather than part-time, I could make her a good offer: a sizable salary of 1200 RMB, weekends off, and a nine-to-five workweek. But interviewing a housekeeper over a cup of coffee that cost as much as half her daily wages was unheard of. She cordially declined my offer and added that she needed to speak with her current employer before she made any decisions. In my disappointment, I felt like a teenager spurned by a crush. I was surprised by how quickly I'd let myself believe that Emily would be my *ayi*.

Besides searching for a housekeeper, I was trying to get used to my new accommodations. Soon after he'd begun his job, Eric had found a nice, safe apartment for us in downtown Shanghai. It was a twenty-ninth-floor flat in a thirty-six-floor, hotel-managed apartment building. Living in a skyscraper, with a doorman and a concierge in the lobby, was a stark change from being in our garden flat in San Francisco.

Our new home only magnified the challenges of raising two dogs in China. Walking Oscar and Meyer and trying to find a location where they could do their business became a priority for me early on. When the dogs and I had first arrived at our new abode, I'd been relieved to see a grassy lot where I could run the dogs just across the street. Appearances from the twenty-ninth floor can be deceiving, however. When I took them over, the area was littered with garbage, plastic bottles, and broken glass. Although I never saw any canines, there was excrement everywhere. Picking up after dogs, I learned, wasn't a priority in Shanghai.

I began walking Oscar and Meyer along the city blocks in search of a park or a patch of grass. Our situation grew so dire that we took to sneaking into the Xijiao State Guest Hotel, in a 192-acre wooded area with gardens and ponds. Located in Hongqiao, about a twenty-minute car ride away, the hotel grounds were enclosed, with a gatehouse at the entrance. I'd hide the dogs at my feet when the guards at the gatehouse stopped my cab, and I'd tell them I was eating at the restaurant. Then I'd ask the cab to let us out near a quiet wooded area.

The first couple of visits we got away with it, dodging the patrolling guards by ducking into a bamboo grove or heading in the opposite direction. But it was soon all too clear that this wasn't a long-term solution—Oscar and Meyer needed a place where they could roam free, and where we weren't always on the run from security guards.

The average Chinese person wasn't accustomed to having dogs as pets when we lived in Shanghai. It wasn't uncommon to hear stories about someone who'd been bitten by a stray and traumatized by the experience. Almost daily, I witnessed people scrambling out of my way as I approached them with my two small furry friends. And oftentimes people's reaction was even more intense than that, as I'd see them fleeing in the opposite direction or clinging to the edge of the sidewalk, as if my dachshunds were English mastiffs or German shepherds.

For every person who was frightened of the dogs, there were others who'd treat them as if they were strange creatures, never before seen in China. Poor Oscar attracted the brunt of it when people unexpectedly bent down and hit him with their hand, nudged him with their foot, or poked him with an umbrella tip.

This happened when I least expected it. I'd yell at the perpetrators in English, or sometimes shove them away if they seemed particularly aggressive. They'd just look at me like I was the crazy one.

I'm shocked that I didn't get hauled off to jail when I reacted to a police officer who'd nudged Oscar with the tip of his boot. Overcome with anger about one too many hostile attacks on Oscar, I punted the officer back and said in English, "Don't kick my dog!" I instantly regretted it when the crowd waiting to cross the street gasped collectively. Luckily, the policeman just laughed at me.

To this day, even in the States, Oscar barks and growls at Asian men or any man wearing dark pants.

I knew that the *ayi* we hired must be a person who could tolerate dogs, and my hope was that she'd grow to feel the same protectiveness and love toward them as we did. At the very least, I just hoped she felt comfortable around house pets.

The night after I spoke with Emily on the phone, I brought her up during dinner with Eric. I'd made Eric's favorite salmon dish: I marinated the fish in equal parts lime juice, soy sauce, and vegetable sauce, then broiled it, basting it with melted butter, soy sauce, and sesame seed oil.

The salmon fillet turned out perfectly: It had a moist, golden-brown exterior, a slightly moist center, and the finishing touch—a sprinkling of toasted white and black sesame seeds and finely chopped chives. A side of mashed sweet potatoes and sautéed asparagus made it an unforgettable meal.

I waited until Eric was a quarter of the way into the meal and had had a few sips of velvety shiraz before I brought up my desire to hire a new *ayi*.

"She could help around the house, of course, but I could really use someone with English skills to translate when I do interviews and research," I explained. As I described Emily's good English skills and how she would benefit the household, I became even more invested in her.

"Well, can she clean?" Eric asked. "Does she like dogs? It's a great plus that she can speak English, but she's advertising herself as an *ayi*, not a translator."

"Of course she can clean," I said, sounding more exasperated than I actually felt. Since my phone conversation with Emily, I hadn't even imagined her wasting her time cleaning the bathroom or walking the dogs. In my mind, she was going to be my assistant. It was like a dream come true—I could finally revisit the article ideas I had been putting off. I was getting ahead of myself by envisioning taking her with me to Beijing to research stories I hesitated to pursue because of the language barrier.

As Eric cleaned his plate, he said, "Okay, do what you have to, but remember that we need someone to help around the house."

Just to keep my options open, and because I recognized that Emily might not accept the position, I planned interviews with a handful of other candidates. Whether they felt okay with Oscar and Meyer was the make-or-break test, so when the potential candidates came through the door, I was sure to check their initial reaction to the dogs.

The first backup candidate, a young, bookish-looking woman, practically jumped onto the seat of a nearby chair upon seeing them. The second one was a well-maintained middle-aged woman with wavy long hair, carefully applied makeup, and a form-fitting summer dress. As the dogs danced around her feet, wagging their tails and sniffing her shoes, she stood looking down at them with a frozen smile. Amanda, the third candidate, seemed equally uncomfortable, glaring at them as if someone had placed a dirty diaper next to her.

After that, I decided it was time to call Emily again and try to set up a face-to-face meeting to see how she reacted to Oscar and Meyer.

"I spoke to my employer, and she said she would increase my pay to match yours while allowing me to keep part-time hours," Emily said evenly.

I was falling into a familiar trap—pursuing something I couldn't have—and I was breaking every rule about hiring a housekeeper. Heck, I didn't even know what she looked like, but Emily's resisting my efforts to give her a job made me feel like she would slip through my fingers if I didn't act quickly. I felt like I knew enough about her to hire her on the spot, and I wasn't going to be defeated just yet.

I half lied: "I spoke with my fiancé, and we agreed it would be wonderful to have you work for us. I'd like to increase the pay an additional 500 RMB." I didn't have Eric's permission to give her a raise, but I decided that he would be supportive.

I heard Emily gasp softly, followed by a long pause. I felt the triumph of a poker player when she knows she has a good hand.

"Why don't you think about it overnight?" I suggested. We agreed to talk again the following day.

After hanging up, I whacked myself on the head. *I can't believe you're giving her more time,* I scolded myself, but I realized how much I wanted her to work for us, sight unseen.

That evening I took Oscar and Meyer to the corner of Yanan Zhong Road and Maoming Road, just a block from our home. The traffic roared above our heads; the *gaojia* (tall road) was filled with evening commuters.

At that corner I'd found a strip of grass about as long as three pool tables. The blades of grass were flattened, and patches of worn dirt were exposed like painful bruises. There was a *shikumen longtang* there where hundreds of families lived, many of whom had pets. Similar to the *hutongs* of Beijing, the *shikumen longtang* were communities of stone gatehouses, connected by lanes, that were built in the early 1900s and influenced greatly by Western architecture.

"*Ni hao,*" said Mrs. Ting, a middle-aged woman who was accustomed to seeing me there now. She was in her flip-flops and a loose, floral-print housedress, out on her evening walk with her shih tzu named Bang Bang.

Little brown crocheted shoes covered Bang Bang's feet; Mrs. Ting had made them so she wouldn't have to clean his feet every time she brought him home. Bang Bang joined the rest of the dogs milling about.

Mr. Gu soon arrived with his closely shorn Pekingese named Coco, "as in Coco Chanel," he'd once told me. Mr. Gu was also wearing his nightclothes—a crisp, light blue cotton shirt and drawstring pants, with plastic shower shoes. Slipping on PJs and taking an evening stroll was a popular custom in Shanghai. In the summertime, the streets resembled a huge pajama party; I'd even witnessed a few filmy nighties among the parade of airy muumuu-style housedresses and loose cotton shirt-and-pant sets that were favorites among the locals here.

Our mutual dog ownership brought us together, and our conversations centered on our pets. I learned from these neighbors which parks I could sneak into with the dogs, and where I could find salons that catered to them. We commented on the weather, a topic I could handle idly in Mandarin as I watched Mr. Gu's Pekingese mount every dog in the vicinity. Coco, like most Chinese pets, was not fixed. The poor thing was perpetually worked up, his eyes bulging out as he struggled with an erection.

A middle-aged couple strolled by us, giving Oscar and Meyer a double take. The man held up two fingers like he was ordering two ice cream cones. *"Liang-zhi gou ma?"* he asked me. ("Two dogs?")

*"Dui, liang-zhi gou,"* I confirmed, before turning back to my conversation. The couple walked away slowly, looking back at Oscar and Meyer and talking quietly to each other.

I was familiar with this question, since it was so unusual to own two dogs in China. Mr. Gu had explained to me that it was not dissimilar to the one-child policy. Wealthy families will happily pay the penalties for each additional child; just the same, there are those who will pay the fees to own multiple dogs. Pet registration in China is not cheap—we'd paid a hefty annual fee of 2,000 RMB per dog that was almost equivalent to what the average Chinese made in a year. I'd begun to understand, therefore, that having the money for two dog permits was an unmistakable statement of status.

Mrs. Ting asked me how my *ayi* search was going. Before I could answer, a baby-blue taxi drove slowly by. The driver hung out his window and smiled mischievously before beginning to yelp, which caused all the dogs on the grass to look up and start barking back.

Mrs. Ting and I turned and gave the driver our dirtiest looks as we tried to settle our dogs down.

"It's time to go home," Mrs. Ting said, pulling on Bang Bang's leash. "Make sure whoever you hire likes dogs," she yelled as Bang Bang pulled her along. "See you later!"

*I'd already had a bad day* by the time I interviewed Sally, my final backup *ayi* candidate. Amanda had her employer call me to tell me that she had taken a position with someone else. Emily had also called right before lunch. I thought it was a good sign that she was calling, but what she said floored me.

"Miss Linda, I wanted to thank you for your interest in hiring me, but I've decided to keep my present job."

I was disappointed, but also annoyed. I detected a smugness in her careful response: "I spoke to my employer and told her how much you were offering me. She raised my salary also, without adding more hours."

I felt manipulated and frustrated by having lost the bidding war. "Emily, were you really looking for another job when you posted your job-wanted ad?" I said, not even bothering to hide my irritation.

"*Wo bu zhidao ni de yisi.*" ("I don't understand your meaning.") This wasn't the first time I'd noticed the language barrier going up when the mask of niceties was thrown off. This was the first time I had heard her speak Mandarin.

There was a brief silence while I didn't respond, knowing that she knew exactly what my meaning was. Finally, she said in English, "It's fortunate for me that in looking for something better, I actually found it where I started."

"Yes, and unfortunate for me," I replied.

I hung up the phone and went into the kitchen. Deep in thought, I assembled the ingredients for hot and sour soup. Even though it was a warm summer day, hot noodle soup was a year-round favorite of mine. Putting it together was easy—I always had homemade chicken stock in the freezer. After heating the broth, I poured it into a deep porcelain bowl. I added soy sauce, rice vinegar, rice wine, pepper, and chili oil; enoki mushrooms; some cooked vermicelli pasta; bok choy; and leftover meat, carefully mixing everything with a chopstick.

I felt duped, but I couldn't help but give Emily credit: She'd beaten the system by pitting her employer against me and coming out on top.

Standing at the counter, I hungrily sipped the spicy broth and ate the crisp vegetables, noodles, and meat. Hearing the doorbell reminded me that I had an appointment with Sally. By this time, my hopes had been so dashed that my expectations had plummeted dramatically. I was already planning on cutting the interview short.

I opened the front door and found a woman with bright, intelligent eyes standing before me. She had an animated heart-shaped face, and those piercing eyes of hers lit up whenever she smiled. Her Madame Mao hairstyle, slashed blunt across her jawline, looked chic rather than old-fashioned. Dressed in sporty, outdoorsy clothes, she looked like she'd just gotten off work at a Patagonia or North Face store.

She smiled and said, *"Ni hao"* to me, and then her eyes widened and her mouth opened in delight as Oscar and Meyer beelined straight toward her. She plopped right down in the hallway and started stroking and cooing at them. When they licked her face, she laughed uproariously. And I realized that I'd been given a gift at my lowest moment: As it turned out, the perfect *ayi* had saved herself for last.

# SOOTHING
# HOT AND SOUR SOUP

*This is a nourishing and hydrating soup to eat when
you come down with a cold. Marinating the chicken strips
tenderizes and adds flavor to the meat. The vegetables in this
recipe are the ones I like to use. You can substitute any
fresh or frozen vegetables, except for the green onions.*

INGREDIENTS:

CHICKEN MARINADE:

1 tablespoon low-sodium soy sauce

1/8 teaspoon black pepper

1/8 teaspoon garlic powder

1 teaspoon rice wine

1 teaspoon cornstarch

2 boneless, skinless chicken breasts, cut into 1/2-inch-thick slices

SOUP:

4 cups homemade chicken stock or low-sodium chicken broth

Marinated chicken breast slices

3–4 stalks baby bok choy, trimmed and leaves separated

1 5-ounce can sliced water chestnuts

1 5-ounce package enoki mushrooms

2 cloves garlic, minced

1 tablespoon grated ginger

1 tablespoon cornstarch

2 tablespoons rice vinegar

1 teaspoon sesame oil

2 tablespoons low-sodium soy sauce

1 teaspoon white pepper

1 teaspoon chili oil (optional)

1 egg, beaten

1 pack firm tofu, cut into 2-inch cubes

3 cups spinach, washed and stems removed

2 cups warm, cooked vermicelli noodles

3 green onions, chopped

INSTRUCTIONS:

For the marinade: In a bowl, mix soy sauce, black pepper, garlic powder, rice wine, and cornstarch, then combine with chicken and coat thoroughly. Let sit at least 20 minutes.

For the soup: In a large saucepan, bring the chicken stock to a boil, then add the marinated chicken slices. Add the bok choy and water chestnuts; return to a boil. Add the enoki mushrooms, garlic, and ginger. Stir and cook for another 3 minutes.

Stir 1/4 cup of the hot soup with cornstarch, add the mixture to the soup, and stir to incorporate.

In a small bowl, combine the vinegar, sesame oil, soy sauce, white pepper, and chili oil. Pour the mixture into the soup, stir, and cook for another 3 minutes.

Trickle the beaten egg into the soup and stir gently. Add the tofu cubes and spinach and stir gently. Divide the noodles among 4 bowls. Ladle the soup over the noodles. Sprinkle the green onions over the soup and serve immediately.

*Serves 4*

*Chapter 9*

# The
## DAY the
## Sky Fell

ERIC AND I PUT OFF OUR WEDDING for about a year and a half. It was difficult for him to get the time off, and we waffled about whether to have it in Shanghai or in Florida. One thing or another always seemed to come up, pushing the date further and further ahead.

In the early spring, I found us a new place to live. Skyrise apartment living had become a hassle with the dogs. Like any slightly neurotic dog owner, I felt guilty that they weren't able to enjoy fresh grass. During a house tour of Shanghai's old French Concession homes, I made it my mission to find one of these places for us. An American couple we'd met lived in a small renovated house in this neighborhood; its interior, with wood details, high ceilings, and double doors, was like a French cottage's. Eric and I could have one of these charming homes, too, but we had to move fast, as they rented quickly.

One of Eric's American friends who worked in real estate intro-duced me to Kim, a rental agent who specialized in old French Concession homes. Kim was in her early fifties. Her chic, tasteful clothes and fluency in English reflected her mostly Western clientele.

I met her at the café in the hotel next to my apartment. Kim was silent when we first met, peering at me through the amber lenses of her knockoff Chanel sunglasses, which she wore even indoors.

"Maybe impossible to find an apartment with a garden. Just an apartment without garden, I can do, though." She gave the café a once-over as she sipped her cappuccino. "I'll keep you in mind."

I didn't hear from her for weeks, and I didn't know what to do next. But then, a month later, she called and suggested that I meet her immediately to look at an apartment that had come up for rent just that day.

The apartment was in a block-long two-story building located in the Embassy District. I stepped into the pitch-black stairwell and made out the door on the first floor. Kim smiled widely when she opened it.

Directly across from the arched doorway—past a black and white-tiled entryway, French double doors, and a hardwood-floored living room—was a grassy back yard, framed by an expansive picture window. I called Eric and described the place to him. He trusted my sense of taste; he put a security deposit down the next day, and we moved in the next month.

Around the same time, I decided to sign up for a part-time Mandarin class. Why allow my language skills to become rusty when I'd already made so much progress? For a couple of months I took lessons at Jiao Tong University, a school famous for the fact that former president Jiang Zemin was an alumnus. I enjoyed being on campus a couple of times a week; I'd try to get there a little early to watch the students walking to class in groups, carrying backpacks heavy with books, and listening to music through headphones.

The buildings and dormitories and students kicking soccer balls reminded me of universities back home. The only noticeable differences I identified were that a lot of the students carried thermoses filled with hot water for their tea, and that the guards standing along the campus sidewalks barked at the students and teachers to dismount from their bikes and walk them.

My Mandarin class was private, held every Tuesday and Thursday morning for six months in one of the school's sprawling, empty classrooms with chipped paint and old-style tiled floors. The building's spartan, no-nonsense quality reminded me of 1950s elementary schools.

When those initial classes were over, I decided to switch to Fudan University. At Jiao Tong, I was spending too much class time discussing my favorite films and restaurants with my teacher, Huang Laoshi, a stout, middle-aged woman who told me that in her next life she would be a travel journalist. Fudan had an off-campus center for part-time students, and its smaller language program offered group classes, which I'd missed during my private lessons.

The morning of my first class, my cab driver pulled up to the entrance of the building complex that housed the school. I double-checked the address with the driver before I got out. Double-parked along the narrow side street were black town cars with drivers leaning against them, smoking cigarettes. The women who stepped forth from these cars were impeccably dressed, complete with luxurious handbags and dressy shoes. It looked more like a conference of fashion editors than students going to class.

As we all crammed into the best-smelling elevator in China, given the variety of perfumes scenting the air, I half expected these elegant ladies to pour out onto another floor. Instead, we all unloaded together.

The beautifully coifed women should have been the hint I needed that this school wasn't going to be like the grim, utilitarian-style one I'd attended in Beijing or the austere conditions of my Jiao Tong classroom. The cost of the Fudan program was roughly the same price as the Jiao Tong program and certainly didn't reflect the upgrade.

The classroom and student break areas were heated and air-conditioned, and the classrooms had new chalkboards and dry-erase boards, long conference-style tables, and sturdy molded-plastic chairs. The decor, however, was disappointing. I had come to expect no-frills, postcommunist surroundings, not modern comfort and conveniences, when I attended Mandarin school. For me, going to class wasn't just about learning the language; part of the enjoyment stemmed from the idea that I was getting a taste of the local lifestyle. I loved having to wear long underwear because of the lack of heat, or using battered, mismatched chairs and desks. The rustic trappings somehow made my China experience more authentic—because I wasn't brave enough to live like this on a daily basis, like the full-time students did.

The student lounge was furnished with nice sofas and chairs in good condition, and a series of Chinese calligraphy hung on the wall. The coffee room had hot water for tea, as well as a commercial coffeemaker. To add insult to injury, a group of ladies sat in the corner, sipping from Starbucks coffee cups.

Standing with other women in the coffee room, a woman from New Delhi told me that this school attracted women between the ages of twenty-five and fifty. Many were women like her, with husbands who were executives or worked for multinational corporations. The New Delhi woman explained that a live-in *ayi* cared for her two children and freed up her time to study Mandarin, learn Chinese embroidery, and research Chinese green teas.

My classmates were of the same ilk. I had signed up for an advanced class, since I'd studied before in Beijing, and my Mandarin was getting better now that I'd lived in China for a total of four years. My classmates included two women from Finland, a French woman, and a woman from Jordan—all married, with one or two kids. Because the daytime student body was so geographically diverse, we had a chance to sample sweet homemade goodies from all over the world: French madeleines, Japanese sweet bean–filled pastries, Italian biscotti, American chocolate chip cookies, and German fruitcake.

This experience was far different from the one I'd had in Beijing, where every student had seemed interested in a cultural adventure, and where everyone had appeared to be much more hardcore about their mission to learn the language than I was. At Fudan, I overheard tales about the challenges of raising a family in Shanghai, or group discussions at break time about how to find activities to occupy children during the hot summer months. It was an insular world where I almost fit in, but not quite.

I was mistaken as a new teacher several times, and the American English I spoke seemed to confuse all the students, particularly the Japanese nationals and the Europeans. But once word got around that I was Japanese American, not Taiwanese, a group of five Japanese housewives were friendly enough.

One Japanese woman named Yuriko spoke some English, and we bonded once we started discussing Japanese food. In the modest way I've noticed Japanese women do, Yuriko covered her smile with a dainty hand when she laughed. Together we ventured out to several Japanese grocery stores, a hair salon, and a yakitori restaurant.

I learned from Yuriko that the Japanese had more foreign-work-permits than any other demographic in Shanghai, and that Gubei, a sub-urb of Shanghai, was an enclave of shops, restaurants, and other services for the Japanese community.

Yuriko and I kept in touch, but our friendship didn't go much deeper than her showing me around Gubei. Although she was the first Japanese national I befriended and we had a common heritage, we didn't share many interests. She seemed overly reserved and polite, and at times I felt as if my bursts of laughter startled her. I remember feeling frustrated with my mother when she became this way around people outside the family, and wanting her to just shake it off and be herself. Similarly, I kept hoping that at some point Yuriko's true personality would emerge.

Surprisingly, my passing friendship with Yuriko ended up opening my eyes to my own desire to be seen as American. After all those years of wrestling with my identity, especially in China—where I wanted to show and prove to everyone that I was indeed American—I realized that all my efforts centered on fulfilling a sense of belonging.

I grew up alongside the kids I went to school with in Indiana, and yet I felt alienated and detached throughout my childhood and adolescence. As an adult I spent many years vacillating between caring and not caring about how my ethnicity was received, but its importance always remained with me on some level, no matter how much I tried to break free from it.

Briefly befriending Yuriko enabled me to explore whether I could have a natural bond with another Japanese person. When it was clear that we had little in common, except for our race and our enjoyment of

Japanese food, I was disappointed, mostly because it was becoming plain that I'd never find the connection to my Japanese-ness that I'd always sought—an affirmation that would have satisfied a lifetime of struggle and frustration caused by my nationality.

To this day, I still seek this sense of belonging, although my persistent drive to resolve it has become one of those aspects of life that age and experience lessen.

*September 11, 2001,* ended like any other day for Eric and me. I had gone to Mandarin class, come home for lunch, and worked on an article that an international soy sauce company had assigned me.

Tired and hungry, Eric arrived home from work later than usual, when the sky had already darkened to a flint gray. It was still pleasant enough outside to grill the salmon I'd bought for dinner, which we ate with stir-fried garlic shoots and asparagus and noodle gratin. I was cleaning up and getting ready to read in bed when the phone rang. Eric and I looked at each other. Other than Sally, no one ever called us at home. We both used our cell phones instead of the landline.

"Who could that be?" Eric asked.

"It may be Sally's sister. Sometimes she calls thinking Sally's still here working," I yelled from the bathroom, where I was washing my face. I heard the answering machine click on.

From the bathroom, I could hear Eric's brother Steve speaking.

"Eric, this is Steve calling from California." Steve went on for a while, but after a moment I heard Eric get up and race for the phone.

"Steve, it's Eric. Are Mom and Dad all right?" I could hear the alarm in Eric's voice.

Eric yelled at me from the living room to come and turn on the television. I sat down on the sofa, my eyes fixed on the screen as CNN footage showed the two World Trade Center buildings. The south tower had already collapsed. The north tower was burning. At first I thought there had been a bombing, but soon enough, between Steve and the international news, we pieced together that terrorists had hijacked commercial planes.

I don't remember if I said anything, or what Eric said to his brother, or when he got off the phone. Soon he was sitting next to me as the newscaster reported that another airplane had crashed into the Pentagon, and that the White House was being evacuated.

My emotions were running wild. We were halfway across the world. I didn't know what to do—cry, scream, call someone back home? I felt powerless.

We stayed up all night, glued to the television. Both of Eric's parents worked near Wall Street. Eric remained calm, but I knew he was concerned. Steve had said he was working on getting in touch with them, and that we should wait for his next call. We found out late that night that Eric's father was away on a business trip, and his mother was in Connecticut. On TV, I watched the evacuation and people fleeing across the Brooklyn Bridge. I wondered about my cousin Signy and her family, who lived in SoHo, about my aunt Milly in Brooklyn, and about a number of my friends who lived in or near the city. And yet the only thing for me to do, along with millions of other people worldwide, was wait.

We were not getting minute-by-minute coverage in Shanghai; only bits and pieces came through. It was frustrating to have to watch hours of CNN Asia business news in the midst of what was happening back home. I tried to doze on the sofa between the updated U.S. news. Eric switched to CCTV, the Chinese news, every so often to see what was being covered there, but I couldn't understand most of what was being said. All the information I gleaned there was through images of the Twin Towers in smoke, and then collapsing, one after the other. It felt like the wrong time to ask Eric to translate, and he didn't volunteer any information. We were each in our own world, and I noticed that neither one of us went to comfort the other with a hug or with words. We were together, and that should have been enough, but I felt a wall between us that I didn't want to acknowledge.

The beginning of a new day in Shanghai marked the end of that infamous day in the States. I was tired from lack of sleep, and my nerves were unraveled from worrying. I felt like skipping Mandarin class, but I also knew that sticking to my schedule was the best thing to do. I spoke with my parents before I left for school, and I was relieved to hear from Dad that Aunt Milly was all right.

The attacks on the United States were the talk of the school that morning. Everyone grew quiet when I came into class. The French woman was the first to say something, but not by way of asking me what part of the States I was from. Rather, she tsk-tsked terrorism. One of the Finnish ladies was thoughtful enough to ask if my family was fine, and I felt grateful to my classmates for being understanding and compassionate.

When our teacher arrived, I wearily opened my notebook. I didn't want to delve into the lesson, but I was relieved to have something to take my mind off what was going on back home. Sitting behind her desk, Chung Laoshi said in English that she was sorry about the attack on my country. I nodded and gave her a small smile.

She continued, "These kinds of things happen when you are a big, powerful country."

"What sort of things?" I ask.

The smaller of the Finnish women nodded and added, "This is expected if a country thinks it rules the world."

"What?" I wasn't sure if I was hearing them right.

"Yes," continued Chung Laoshi, "I'm surprised this didn't happen sooner."

Hot tears welled up in my eyes. I looked around accusingly at my nodding classmates. "So you're saying that America deserved this?"

The two women looked at me sheepishly, not saying a word. I started shaking my head. The teacher could see that I was getting upset and tried to explain herself further: "No, you're misunderstanding what we're saying." She cleared her throat before beginning, "When you are a great country like America, it is surprising that something catastrophic like this hasn't happened before. That's all we're saying."

Years later, these words actually seem somewhat reasonable to me, but listening to what they were saying the morning after I'd seen my mother country ravaged on television was nearly intolerable. I felt vulnerable in a classroom of strangers who apparently believed they were comforting me. But over the course of the next few weeks, the only comfort I found was from fellow American expatriates, with whom I discovered empathy and a foundation from which to deal with the helplessness of being so far away.

I looked around at the rest of my classmates and felt that we had nothing in common now, other than the fact that we were in China together and studying Mandarin. "I don't know if I can be in a class where people think America deserved this," I pressed, articulating my discomfort.

"No, no, I didn't mean that," Chung Laoshi said, searching out support from the other students but receiving none. "Please calm down and stay," she said to me when I began gathering up my things.

Something told me to stay, that in her own way she was sorry for what had transpired. I sat back down sullenly and continued with the class. But something had shifted in me and seemed unalterably damaged, and I couldn't help it when I found myself glaring at the Finnish woman later in the lesson.

For the rest of the morning, the class was subdued. I left without saying goodbye to the other students. I beat the crowd that usually grew after class to grab taxis.

The cab driver nodded when I told him to take me to the outdoor vegetable market near my home. The usual stream of bicyclists, pushcarts carrying wood beams, cars, construction trucks, and buses competed for road space. I peered out the window, looking but not really seeing all the activity, as I played back what had happened in the classroom.

Had I taken their comments the wrong way? Maybe I was overreacting. Maybe, but I wasn't convinced. I couldn't help but wonder if they would have spoken so candidly if I'd been Caucasian American. I wondered about the ways my Asian face had made Chinese feel safe and comfortable around me—how they'd shared intimacies with me because I didn't seem like a foreigner, at least not completely. When my patriotism for my country reared its head, its depth reminded them that I was American. I hoped it did, at least, and that in the future they would remember that Americans come with all different kinds of faces.

The whole incident left me with a gnawing feeling that increased over the following weeks. I wasn't exposed to the pandemonium of media coverage that barraged American television, Internet, newspapers, magazines, and radio. The news we saw on CNN or the BBC consisted mostly of updates, not the full report. But it wasn't until I moved back to the States that I realized how much information I had missed.

*The noise and colorful produce* displays in the market provided a distraction, cheering me up a bit, but I couldn't shake myself out of my bleak thoughts. My body strolled between the vegetable stands, but my mind was back home. I was overcome with homesickness, the kind you feel when you're a child and you wake up at a sleepover, crying to yourself because you want to be in your own familiar bed. That's how I felt about the United States the day after September 11th.

The issues I dealt with around assimilation and racism in my youth had always left me questioning my mother country. Something shifted for me on 9/11, though, as I'm sure it did for many people. I found that my concern went way beyond my friends and relatives living in New York City; it extended to the state of the entire nation. In this different light, I saw America as an old friend who had many problems and flaws, but toward whom I couldn't help but feel strong loyalty and protectiveness.

*On that day, comfort food was in order.* To me, home was my Midwestern upbringing. Hamburgers and good fried chicken reminded me of America, but now that I was truly deadened by the previous night's events, all I wanted was what reminded me of my mother's home cooking: fresh tofu with grated ginger, chopped green onion, soy sauce, and a squeeze of lemon.

It certainly wasn't typical American fare, like eating a hot dog at the baseball stadium or a hamburger at a drive-through restaurant, but it reminded me of my youth in Indiana, of evening meals with my family after a summer day helping my brothers build forts in the woods and picking lilies of the valley in the cool patch of garden behind our house. At the market, I went straight to the vendor who I knew had the freshest tofu, batches he made at his home every day.

He put the block in a plastic bag; it dangled from my hand, reminding me of a goldfish bought at a pet store. At the nearest vegetable peddler, I selected a bunch of green onions, the bulbs larger than most, with dirt still clinging to the roots, and a piece of ginger root, spread out like coral.

I was relieved when I returned home and discovered that Sally was out walking the dogs. I put my meal together. The firm, dense block of tofu was white as cream and jiggled like Jell-O as I removed it carefully from the bag. I used only half, slicing it lengthwise and submerging the rest in a deep dish filled with water.

Cutting the tofu into bite-size cubes, I grated the ginger, enjoying its fresh, medicinal aroma. The chopped green onions added a clean scent. I sprinkled on a handful of bonito, the color of cedar wood shavings, and added a squeeze of juice from the lemon in the fruit bowl. To me, this was the only way to eat tofu.

I took my dish, a small ceramic dispenser of soy sauce, and a pair of chopsticks into the dining room. Other than the chiming of my chopsticks hitting the side of the dish, the apartment was silent. I piled ginger, green onion, bonito flakes, and a dab of soy sauce on the tofu pedestal, and no one ingredient overrode another as smoothness and crunchiness, spice and zest, danced across my palate. Reminders of home—the smell of soybeans boiling in the kitchen on Sunday mornings and fresh green onions from the garden—cleansed me.

With each bite, from the first to the last, I thought about what a gift it is to be an American.

# SIMPLE JAPANESE-STYLE TOFU

*These ingredients are layered, not mixed together,*
*as indicated in the instructions.*

INGREDIENTS:

4 3-inch cubes of tofu, hot or cold

3 green onions, trimmed and chopped

1 2-inch piece of ginger, finely grated

1/4 cup bonito flakes (optional)

1 lemon, cut into quarters

Soy sauce to taste

INSTRUCTIONS:

Place tofu on individual plates or on a serving dish. Sprinkle green onions on the tofu, followed by ginger and a dusting of bonito flakes.

Set a bottle of soy sauce and lemon wedges at the table so that guests can add it to their liking. Consume immediately.

*Serves 4*

*Chapter 10*

# A
# CLEAVER in
# Every Wok

ERIC AND I WERE MARRIED in February 2002 at his parents' spacious winter home in Naples, Florida. It was the moment I'd been waiting for, and I savored it as I stood there on the landing of the aisle, wearing a simple long ivory dress with no veil or train. On my left was Mom, radiant in a saffron and ivory kimono tied with an aubergine-hued obi. Dad was on my right, looking handsome in a suit and tie.

Ecstatic and buoyant, I felt as if I would float to the ceiling if my parents let go of my arms. As I walked down the aisle, I could feel the soft flower petals under my sandals. With each step I took, I sank deeper into a feeling of completeness. I locked eyes with Eric as he waited and watched from the other end of the room, and I had the sensation of being drawn closer to home. We stayed in Florida for another week, opting to spend time stateside with friends and family members. Rather than moving on to a honeymoon right away, Eric wanted to take it in May, when he would have more vacation time.

*Two weeks later we were back* in our flat in Shanghai. The winter rains were abating, but the masses of commuting cyclists, still in bright red, blue, green, and yellow rain ponchos, that pedaled by were a pleasant sight, like colorful balloons being released into the sky. I opened my eyes one morning and felt a familiar hollow queasiness rocking my stomach. I knew that this particular discomfort could mean only one thing: I was pregnant. Before our wedding, we'd decided that we'd begin trying to have a baby immediately. I'd just never expected it to happen so soon.

Eric had left for work early that morning. He was spending longer days at the office because a possible acquisition was on the horizon. It wasn't fully light quite yet, but the day was awakening, and the sound of pedestrians passing by was extra noticeable against the backdrop of the quiet morning. Sally wasn't due for another hour.

Having our residence on the street level, I had been able to enjoy the sounds of daily life outside my door: the *clang-clang* from the rice ped-dler's bell as he roamed the neighborhood, and the random bellowing of the knife sharpener.

I went to the bathroom and dug out one of the pregnancy tests I'd brought with me from the States. I followed the instructions and held my breath as I watched two lines appear instantly. I hugged myself and squealed in delight, allowing myself to rejoice fully.

That evening, Eric unwound from the day in front of the TV with a highball glass of Jim Beam and soda, and I made his favorite: lamp chops, sautéed spinach, and mashed potatoes mixed with sour cream and chives.

Before sitting down to eat, he uncorked a bottle of red wine.

"Where's your glass?" he asked.

"From now on I'm not drinking or smoking," I said nonchalantly.

He gave me a quizzical look.

"I'm pregnant!" I announced. Eric's eyes flew open and he gave me a big, long hug.

"All right!" he yelled, pumping his fist and raising both arms, the way he did when the New York Giants scored a touchdown.

I sipped a ginger ale with dinner as we discussed where we might have the baby. Having a baby at age thirty-six increased the possibility of complications in every area of my pregnancy, but I was most concerned about the delivery. I felt healthy and strong, and if I was willing, there were birthing centers in Shanghai where I could deliver, but if serious complications did occur, I'd have to be flown to a hospital in Hong Kong.

Delivering the baby in Shanghai would be the most convenient thing to do, but like any overly concerned expectant mother, I didn't want to take any chances. I wanted to approach this physically and emotionally challenging experience with total peace of mind, which for me meant no possible language barriers and the best medical technology available. I was thankful when Eric agreed that, as distressing as it would be to separate the family, I should have the baby in the United States. Our plan was to fly me back to Florida with Oscar and Meyer before it became too dangerous to travel by air. Eric would stay and work in Shanghai and arrive a week before the delivery. I would stay in the States for eight weeks, and then we would all return to Shanghai as a family.

After dinner, sitting back on the sofa, we talked about all that we imagined parenthood to be—the diapers, the feedings, the baby's first steps and first word. When we got into bed, we spooned and continued discussing our future.

"When I make my next fortune," Eric said in my ear, "we can move to France." The stocks from his first China venture were worth nothing, but that didn't stop us from dreaming.

"And while you study French, I'll go to cooking school." I snuggled my back in closer against his chest and imagined what this position would feel like when my belly grew bigger.

"We'll raise our kids there until we run out of money," he whispered, while gently cradling my stomach.

"I'll be writing children's books," I said dreamily. We were allowing ourselves to fantasize, and I felt a security and wholeness I'd never fully experienced with Eric.

"Maybe I could get a job as an accountant for some vineyard," Eric said as he leaned over and turned off the light. I knew we had to go to sleep, but I wanted to keep talking and dreaming.

It was dark and quiet all around us, except for the occasional clicking of the upstairs tenants walking on the hardwood floor or the muffled honking of a car on the main street. I remained quiet and still as Eric's breathing evened out and deepened. I wanted to memorize this moment—the closeness I felt with Eric, the shadows and streetlights casting patterns on walls and moldings, the warmth and weight of Eric's body against my back and legs, his smell of bourbon, cigarettes, soap, and garlic. I wanted to keep all these impressions in my bones so I could share them with our children when they asked about when we'd lived in China before they were born.

Reaching this place of security, love, trust, and devotion felt like it had been a long time coming, but it was starting a family that was the real gift. I believed that the two of us had overcome all of our fears and commitment issues and problems, and that we could strive to create a new life with our children and dogs.

Even years after that magical night in Shanghai as a newlywed and an expectant mother, it was hard not to play out the months leading up to the baby's birth over and over in my head, to scrutinize each frame in an attempt to find what I had missed—a gesture, a word, a facial expression, or a misunderstood mood indicating that Eric was communicating something different from what I'd interpreted. Had I let my guard down too soon in thinking that marriage and a baby meant our relationship was for keeps?

What happened over those next months was like a slow rot, the unrelenting, stealthy kind, and it infested our relationship. It was during my second trimester, during the early summer, that I first detected a whiff of disdain, a clear change in Eric's attitude. Like a shifting glacier, it was subtle and barely detectible to anyone else, but to me it felt like a 7.0 earthquake.

I had a miserable first trimester. Before I was pregnant, I functioned at a high level—writing, walking the dogs, cooking, swimming, practicing martial arts, and grocery shopping. My energy was limitless. Therefore, when I hit a wall during those first three months and felt tired and drained all the time, remembering how energetic I'd been before was difficult. Every morning I'd sit on the edge of the bed, thinking about what I needed to get done, but I couldn't get moving.

My love affair with food and eating took a bad turn, too. The smell and texture of egg, chicken, and beef turned my stomach. I found the idea of eating fish revolting. I craved anything with tomatoes—chopped tomatoes stewed with pieces of white bread, tomato soup, tomato juice, spaghetti with tomato sauce, sliced tomato sprinkled with sugar. I had hankerings for fresh pineapple slices and oranges. Every day I ate toasted cheese sandwiches. I kept a bag of shortbread cookies, a piece of fruit, or rice crackers with me at all times, fearful of the queasiness that would overcome my empty stomach.

I'd always suffered from migraines, and hot, ice pick–like pains in my temples plagued me on a daily basis. I could no longer take my antidote of choice: ibuprofen and nonprescription back-pain medicine chased with a double espresso. The Chinese physicians at the Western-run clinic gave me Tylenol, which was ineffective against the pain.

*Months before our February wedding,* we'd planned to go to Bali in May for our honeymoon. I couldn't wait to swim in the warm ocean water, play two rounds of golf, eat to my heart's content, and bask in the tropical heat. We decided to keep our travel dates even after we found out I was pregnant, because the trip would fall so early in my pregnancy. The villa Eric found for us had a private pool and a beautiful outdoor living area with a daybed and an outdoor shower. Unfortunately, I spent my first morning sprawled in the bathtub with a washcloth on my pounding head. I told Eric to go ahead and play golf without me.

After my bath I tried to fall asleep, hoping the pain would be gone when I awoke. An hour later, blaring leaf blowers reignited my headache.

By the time Eric returned in the late afternoon, I was as exhausted and miserable as I'd been when he'd left that morning. At dinner I picked at the Indonesian meal I'd ordered. The fragrant turmeric, coriander, coconut, tamarind, and lemongrass of the rice dish were making my stomach do cartwheels.

Back in our room after dinner, I attacked the fruit basket on the coffee table. One small fruit's skin—dark purple, as tough as pomegranate—was peeled back to show little pieces that looked like garlic cloves. One bite of that soft interior conjured the flavor of strawberry, pineapple, and citrus all in one. It was nature's version of a sour candy. In one sitting I devoured three of these mangosteens, a banana, a mango, strawberries, and a bowl of lychees. It was the best dinner I ate the entire trip. The only reason I didn't starve was that the hotel staff replenished the basket with more fresh fruit every day.

My lack of energy and disinterest in doing anything started to annoy Eric by the second or third day. During all the trips we had taken in the past, to the Philippines, Thailand, Indonesia, and numerous other destinations, our days had been packed with activities and exploring. This time Eric had to deal with the fact that he was spending a vacation pretty much on his own. Bali's mid-nineties temperatures and humidity exhausted me even further. My body no longer felt like my own.

One cloudy afternoon, as we explored Ubud, the artisans' village on the island, I tried to be lively and energetic. I was relieved when Eric suggested going back to the resort, where he hoped to get in nine holes of golf.

At dinner, couples from all over the world sat at the other tables, looking deeply into each other's eyes. Sitting close to our table were a young couple who were obviously crazy about each other. I watched them out of the corner of my eye as they nuzzled and kissed throughout their meal. I felt a ripple of self-consciousness and sadness pass between Eric and me. I could tell by the way his eyes darted over toward them that he noticed the loving couple as well. The awkwardness between us kept me from making a move to touch his hand or show him affection.

We usually looked forward to eating out during our vacations, being the foodie couple that we were. We pursued local restaurants and preferred to try regional cooking, and we were used to having deep conversations over dinner while savoring every bite and every sip.

But there we were, under a dome of sparkling stars and a clear sky of ink-blue silk, with the warm tropical breeze carrying the scent of exotic flowers, struggling to have a conversation. Eric ordered a freshly caught fish served with stir-fried vegetables, seasoned brown rice, and a glass of pinot blanc. I twirled my fork in my spaghetti plate, which I'd ordered off the kids' menu, and took sips of my ginger ale. That was how we spent the last night of our honeymoon.

On our way home, we had a layover in Hong Kong. We had plenty of time between our flights, so we ducked into a little restaurant and I ordered the blandest thing on the menu, wonton soup. I sipped the clear chicken broth from a plastic Chinese spoon that resembled a rowboat.

Eric was cold and untalkative as I ate. Behind his silence, I sensed pressure to ask him what was wrong. I could tell by the way he moved— a tension that had lately replaced his relaxed movements—that he was holding on to something.

"I don't want to make a big deal out of this," he began. I felt my body tighten up and I braced myself. "But our honeymoon was a disappointment."

"But Eric, you know I don't feel like myself," I retorted. "I'm tired and my stomach hurts all the time. I'm pregnant. Do you think I'm enjoying this?" I knew that the best way to weather a conversation like this was to just keep my mouth shut and let him get it out of his system, but it was too unfair.

"That's the problem. Why can't you be happy about this? All you do is complain about being pregnant and how bad you feel. You're not . . . " he hesitated a moment. "You're not terminally ill."

He leaned forward, and even though he was across the table from me, I shrank back from him. This person wasn't the Eric I knew, and yet it was the only Eric I would come to know as the months went on.

I dropped the spoon I had been holding in midair as Eric continued to spew at me. I got up and left the table. Through tears, I could barely make out the way to the ladies' room. Inside the stall, I hugged my arms to my chest, trying to comfort myself while I cried quietly into my hands.

It was Eric's mother, Dorothy, who'd told me that the duration of a pregnancy is about the only time when a woman can get away with complaining. "We get treated like queens," she'd reassured me. My girlfriends, too, had talked about the way their husbands had been at their beck and call, and I sat in the bathroom and cried over the fact that this wasn't the case with me.

I felt the ominous weight of something unpredictable going on with Eric. My sobs were muffled by the sound of flushing toilets, banging stall doors, water faucets, and paper towel dispensers, and I bit my finger to keep from screaming, "Oh my god—what is happening? What am I going to do?"

I fixed my eyes on the drain in the floor. I just wanted to melt away as I thought about having to go back out there and face Eric. By fleeing to the bathroom, I felt I had rewound our relationship to a place I never wanted to return to. I thought of countless unhappy nights when the only solution to our arguments had been my storming out, feeling unable to cope with the way Eric dealt with things. A desperate fear weighed me down like sandbags.

In the years I had lived with Eric, I had seen him get furious to a point where his eyes darkened with anger and frustration, but behind that I'd always been able to catch a glimmer of love and adoration. That glimmer was the devotion and commitment that anchored us and made us keep trying to make it work. In the restaurant at the Hong Kong airport, though, I didn't see that glimmer. For me, as a recently wed expectant mother, it was the most frightening thing to discover. But at the time, I couldn't and wouldn't allow myself to entertain the thought that he might be falling out of love with me.

*Oh my god, what am I going to do?* Survival mode kicked in. I took a deep breath, rinsed my face with cold water, and took some more deep breaths before leaving the ladies' room.

Eric was looking sheepish, more out of embarrassment about the way I'd taken off, I knew, than out of regret for what had passed between us.

Politely, as if on a first date, he pulled my chair out for me. He asked me if I was okay, but not in a tender, caring way. I felt like a colleague of his who'd abruptly rushed to the bathroom with no explanation.

"Oh, I'm fine," I said, trying to rise out of my numbness and appear normal. "I'm sorry I overreacted to what you said. You're right—I'll try to be better. It's the hormones."

I knew it was what he wanted to hear. I saw relief flood Eric's face and the return of the man I knew. I naively indulged in my long-held belief that nothing had changed: I loved Eric. I was going to have his baby. I wasn't going to lose him.

*After we got home from our honeymoon,* I was able to put the episode at the airport behind me, but there were many more moments of despair when the strain and tension in our relationship expanded like cracks in a wall. I didn't know when it would all come crashing down, but just like I'd done that day in the airport, I rushed to quickly apply plaster, hoping and praying the wall would hold up.

I convinced myself that Eric was pushing himself too hard at work.

He was indeed running himself ragged, burning the candle at both ends. He talked on the phone from eleven at night until three in the morning, and then got up at seven to go to his office for a full day of work.

I tried to make the situation better by letting him come home, have his drink, and watch CNN, and by always having a nice home-cooked meal prepared for him. I reverted to a coping mechanism I was familiar with: communicating with him through food, the way I'd done with my parents when I was growing up. I believed that if I could just show Eric my love, care, and appreciation by making sure the liquor bottles were full and a candlelit dinner with music was ready every night, maybe we could reconnect and make things the way they used to be.

I made the unforgivable mistake of not sitting down with him and making him talk about what he was feeling or going through. Instead, I just prayed that things would turn around by themselves. The one time I meekly tried to communicate with him about what I was feeling, he looked at me with tired eyes and said to be patient, that he was doing all this for us. I knew that he meant making money, so I just nodded. I thought the best way to support him was to leave him alone. And so I allowed myself to believe my fantasy that everything would heal itself once the baby was born. We'd return to Shanghai as a family, and everything would be better.

*A couple of weeks into my second trimester,* my nausea disappeared completely and my body began to radiate warmth and vitality. My eyes were bright as crystals and my cheeks were always flushed, as if they'd just been pinched. I didn't need much sleep anymore, and I started to enjoy the feeling of the baby growing inside me, and the benefits of thicker hair and flawless skin. I could no longer fit into my regular clothes, which had been difficult to give up because the frilly, matronly maternity selection in China was comparable to wearing a bedspread. To help me get by until I flew home, Eric's mother sent me a few items, and I simply bought regular clothes in a much larger size.

No longer did I feel like I was in this by myself. I had a little being inside my body, like a lucky charm. When I sat at my desk to write, I loved feeling the baby's small kicks and stretches; they reminded me to get up and walk the dogs or grab something to eat. A change was happening in me, and it wasn't just about the baby growing inside me.

I knew that once the baby arrived, I wouldn't have time to work on my book, so I established a self-imposed deadline for the manuscript a couple of weeks before the baby's due date. During the summer months, before I left Shanghai for Florida, I worked at my desk every day. Oscar and Meyer were curled up on a Chinese daybed, a piece of furniture I'd had made for the nursery instead of buying a glider chair. The small desk fan stirred the air and brought in earthy smells from the open window that looked out onto the garden. I had never felt so optimistic and happy as I did writing the afternoon away, feeling the weight of life in my belly.

To maintain peace with Eric, I'd ceased talking about the aches and pains of being pregnant many months earlier. Now that I was feeling better, though, I also kept to myself how good I felt. Luckily, Gina had announced that she was pregnant soon after I'd told her I was. Her friendship provided me with the much needed relief of having someone to share the experience with.

When she and I met for lunch at Itoya, smoking cigarettes and feasting on mackerel sashimi were things of the past. During our first lunch out together as expectant mothers, I ordered roasted ginkgo nuts, which Gina said were brain food for the baby, and a sukiyaki beef bowl. Gina suffered from terrible morning sickness and was unable to keep anything down, so she sipped bland fish broth. We fanned away the cigarette smoke wafting from tables of Japanese businessmen nearby.

The waitresses had known us before we were pregnant, but we received more attention now that we were expecting. They showered us with attention every time we came in for lunch.

"How big you are getting," the waitresses told us unabashedly in broken English. "Your legs are heavy and your face is getting fat," Blue, our favorite, said, puffing out her cheeks to make her point.

Our prepregnancy conversations had revolved around our writing progress, story-line development, and endless strategies about how we were going to get published. After she found out she was pregnant, Gina decided to write a romance novel, so now it turned out that we were both working on a book. Our other conversation topic was how Shanghai suddenly seemed dangerously polluted—the streets dirtier, the drivers more reckless, and the parks not child-friendly. As pregnant women, we were starting to see China as an undesirable place to raise a child.

During these discussions, Gina and I fed on each other's fears.

"I had the worst driver on the ride over here this morning. I was yelling at him to slow down, but he wouldn't do it," Gina said during one meal, chewing a mouthful of grilled salmon and rice.

This began a conversation about how climbing into a cab was like playing Russian roulette—you didn't know if you would get a safe driver or a reckless one. But I blanched when Gina insisted that I ask Eric to hire a driver.

"I'll wait until the baby is born," I said. I thought it sounded like a good idea, but I didn't want to put added financial stress on Eric's life at that moment.

To change the subject, I described taking Oscar and Meyer out for their morning walk in the neighborhood that day. I had seen an *ayi* pushing a stroller, then had watched a cab driver cut her off as she was about to push the stroller out into the road.

"This is why Chinese women don't use strollers," Gina said. "They carry their babies everywhere." She motioned for the check.

"You're right," I mused. "I never see Chinese push strollers."

"That's why," Gina concluded, nodding.


*During a dinner party at our house* later that month, I mentioned my change of heart about living in China to Eric. We'd had an agreement that even with children, we would live our life as an adventure. Our children would follow us around as we pursued our dreams.

Day by day, though, as the baby was growing and changing in my body, so were my ideas about child rearing. We had a handful of people over for dinner that night, including Eric's new boss, Bo, and his wife, Jenny, who was hoping to have a child, too. When she asked me if we wanted to raise our children in China or the States, I noticed that I raised my voice so Eric would hear me as he poured snifters of scotch.

"I used to think I wanted my children to be raised internationally, but lately I've become more homesick. It's just a dream, of course, but I would love to just settle in a small town in the States somewhere."

Since I'd left Indiana after graduating from college, I had never looked back. I had always been content and seen myself living in a large city. Now, however, my body and spirit yearned for space all around me, the sweet scent of clean air and soft grass under my feet in the summer, the unique smell of decaying autumn leaves, and the crunch of snow under my boots. I suddenly realized how much I wanted my child to experience what I'd had as a child.

Eric didn't say anything. I didn't mention how much I was starting to miss my parents.

With my delivery date fast approaching, I became more preoccupied with finishing my book. I felt like a robin in springtime: The nursery I'd made in my office was finished, and I put all my time and energy into finishing my manuscript. On weekends I was thankful when Eric went off to play golf and gave me an extra eight hours to write.

By late summer, I was six months pregnant and had a workable draft of my book. In Beijing, Eric had often read over my articles before I turned them in. When I'd started writing my food column for the *San Francisco Chronicle*, he'd reviewed that, too, and made encouraging comments.

On a peaceful Sunday afternoon, after strolling home from brunch with friends, Eric took some photos of me with my protruding belly and the dogs in the back yard. The relaxed pace and ease between us reminded me of old times in Beijing, when the whole day had been open for us to enjoy. It was a typical Shanghai summer day, heavy with humidity that made me think of picnics and barbecuing. Something about the day gave me the confidence to ask Eric to be the first person to read my manuscript.

Showing people my writing has never been easy for me, but I'd relied on Eric's help before, and I respected how well educated and book smart he was. When he'd looked at my writing in the past, I'd always felt that his suggestions helped me make it clearer and better.

I remember reading an article about Stephen King that described how his wife, Tabitha, read one of his manuscripts in a single sitting. His books are long, and I read that article and thought, *That's what a person who loves you does.*

"Of course I want to read it. How exciting," Eric said when I presented him with my manuscript. I felt giddy and vulnerable, and nervous about what he'd think of it. I went to my office and shuffled papers around, thinking about what I would do to keep myself busy and how long it would take for him to finish it. I considered making cookies.

I passed through the living room to go to the kitchen and saw my manuscript lying on the coffee table, open to page five. The television was on. I held my tongue when Eric came back in and started watching the news. *Don't nag him,* I ordered myself.

The next morning, my manuscript still lay open to the same page, untouched. I didn't say anything because I assumed that Eric would take it to work, read some more during his lunch, and continue when he came home.

When it was still sitting there Tuesday morning, I asked him if he was still planning on reading it.

He said yes. To give him an out, I added, "You know, you don't have to if you don't have the time."

He put his hand on my shoulder and said, "I'm dying to read it, okay?"

On Friday, I finally picked up my manuscript off the table. I read up to page five, trying to figure out why he'd stopped there. My head was filled with a numb heaviness. Up to that point, I'd still felt that Eric was one person I could count on to support my writing. I never mentioned the manuscript again. My pride was crushed, and I felt so embarrassed that I hoped he'd just forget about it. I felt that my writing wasn't worth his time.

During the moments when I couldn't ignore the strain in my marriage of less than a year, I reminded myself that we had lived through and shared many experiences before tying the knot. And wasn't the first year reputedly difficult? This was just a bump in the road of married life, a road that we would be traveling many miles on together. But I was finding that as this bump got bigger and longer, my respect for Eric was wearing thin.

*It was Mr. Huang, whom I met* in the first few months after I moved to Shanghai, who gave me the idea to enroll in a Chinese cooking school. I'd thought about it once before, when I'd returned to San Francisco after living in Beijing. I wanted to cook some of my favorite Chinese dishes, and I was craving the challenge of re-creating those meals at home. But getting a new job, coupled with the daily grind of being back in the Bay Area, soon pushed that idea to the back burner.

I met Mr. Huang during a series of cooking classes arranged by the Expatriate Women's Group. It was a six-week class; each class featured a new professional chef from one of the high-end hotel restaurants. Mr. Huang was there to translate the chefs' Mandarin instructions into English, and I liked him from the very first class.

In his day job, Mr. Huang was a professor at the Shanghai Chinese Medicine University. But based on the way he presented information and described Chinese cooking techniques in his work as a translator, his interest in and knowledge of food and cooking were obvious and extensive.

When I got an assignment to write an article for a soy sauce company, profiling a young chef who was responsible for introducing a way of cooking called "new Shanghai cuisine" (basically a fancy name for fusion cooking), I asked Mr. Huang to translate at the interview.

While I waited for the chef to prepare a couple of his signature dishes, I learned more about Mr. Huang. He told me how he'd mastered English to supplement his income. His teaching job at the medical school paid very little, so he'd started doing verbal and written translation work within the expatriate community.

As a food lover, Mr. Huang was a great resource for tracking down obscure Chinese ingredients or finding a specialty market. When I needed help locating a big seafood market I'd heard about, he offered to take me there. As we walked between huge tanks of live seafood, Mr. Huang described to me his experiences attending a Chinese cooking school.

"I wanted to go so much, I took off from teaching," he said, shoving his hands into his Members Only jacket and tucking his black man-purse deeper into the crook of his arm. "I knew losing the income was a sacrifice. But cooking school was something I always dreamed of doing."

He'd attended in the early 1980s, when restaurant cooking required jacks-of-all-trades: Chefs were trained as both butchers and cooks. As we passed a tank of eels, an Asian delicacy, Mr. Huang explained how the students had learned how to catch eels in a tank, as well as how to break the neck of a chicken, then bleed and pluck it.

I was fascinated by his stories, but the idea of learning to make dumplings was what sold me on enrolling. Oh, how I missed the boiled pork dumplings and meat-bread dumplings of Beijing! I was still hoping to leave China soon, and I knew that it was inevitable someday, most likely for Eric to pursue another job opportunity. But having left Beijing in such a rush the last time, I decided that I couldn't leave Shanghai without learning how to make little-dragon dumplings, pan-fried dumplings, and steamed shrimp dumplings. And it wouldn't hurt to learn all the noodle dishes I loved so well, either.

"Would they let a foreigner sign up for the program?" I asked.

Mr. Huang stopped in front of a tank of young eels swarming like seaweed and thought about this for a moment. "I think they would, but you wouldn't receive a certificate."

The school that Mr. Huang had attended was a two-hour drive away, on the outskirts of Shanghai. Its distance seemed prohibitive, given my condition and my distaste for riding in cabs since I'd gotten pregnant. But he also gave me the name of a couple of vocational cooking schools. At home, I had Sally call the Shanghai Meilongzhen Cooking Occupational Training School, which was affiliated with the Melongzhen restaurant, renowned among locals for its authentic Shanghainese cuisine.

When she got off the phone, she said, "Cooking school starts in April!" She was excited for me, since I'd talked about doing the classes for some time now.

"*Haole!*" ("That's great!")

Sally looked at me a little tentatively and said, "But the teacher's Mandarin isn't very good." I wasn't going to let that stop me, and I had an obvious solution: I called up Mr. Huang, who agreed to attend class with me and translate twice a week for the next ten weeks.

*The following month,* the spring sunshine arrived but the temperatures remained the same, and I struggled against the breezy chill as I made my way to the neighborhood where the school was located. Sally had told me that it was behind a restaurant, adjacent to the local middle school and beauty school. She'd wanted to come with me, but I didn't want to show up on my first day of class with an entourage that included both my translator and my housekeeper. Mr. Huang was meeting me there, and as I struggled to find the school, I realized that it might have been better to meet him someplace I was already familiar with.

Soon enough, however, I recognized some of the landmarks Sally had mentioned. Behind a neighborhood restaurant was a large courtyard where some boys wearing the Chinese school uniform, white shirts with red neckties, were playing basketball during recess. Across from the cooking school was the beauty school, indicated by a 1960s-style sign featuring a silhouette of a women's head with a permed coif.

I entered the building next to the beauty school, as Sally had instructed. Walking down a short hallway, I peeked into a theater-style classroom. I knew I was in the right building when I saw fifty desks encircling the demonstration kitchen: A commercial wok stove with a wok resting in a hole over a burner; a chamber ring for the wok to rest on; a faucet for cleaning the wok or adding water; counter space; and mirrors overhead for the students to see what was happening.

White paint peeled off the walls, the floor was dusty and littered, and the windows were filthy and covered with an oily film. Three students were sitting in the classroom: One was asleep, another was playing a game on his cell phone, and the third was a middle-aged woman reading the newspaper. I didn't go inside. I decided to wait for Mr. Huang instead.

A bell rang, and more children poured out of the middle school onto the basketball courts. Talking and yelling echoed through the courtyard. A group of schoolgirls went into Larson's convenient store and emerged eating fish balls on sticks.

As I turned down a walkway separating the beauty school from the cooking academy, a strong smell of garbage hit me. Next to the trash receptacles, which were overflowing with vegetable scraps, was a six-foot wall of used takeout boxes. The stench was overwhelming.

I passed it as quickly as I could, covering my nose. I soon realized that the trash was right next to the windows of the kitchen facility. I held my nose until I got back to the fresh air in the courtyard. My nausea had stopped now that I was in my second trimester, but the smells brought back memories of it. I had smelled plenty of disgusting things in my life, but knowing that I was going to be in close proximity to such a foul stench during the course of my entire cooking-school stay filled me with apprehension. For a moment, I considered that I had made a mistake by enrolling in the cooking school in the first place.

As I contemplated hailing a cab, Mr. Huang walked up, waving and giving me a big smile. I feigned a smile and told myself to buck up and give it a chance before I decided that I couldn't handle it.

All the students had arrived by the time Mr. Huang and I walked in together. We were thirty-five students, not including Mr. Huang, who'd been given permission to sit in as my translator. I noticed immediately that men made up about two-thirds of the class, and that almost all of them chain-smoked. During the entire program, not a day went by when there wasn't a cloud of smoke hovering over our heads. On that first day of class, Mr. Huang asked one of the smokers to open a window. He refused, saying it was too cold and that he didn't want the cold air blowing on him. Mr. Huang and I took seats near the open door.

A chubby man in his early twenties asked me where I was from. When I responded, he nodded and put his headphones back on. He was sitting with a cluster of four high school graduates. One girl of about eighteen was eyeing the three young men, who were knuckle-punching each other. I named them the Three Stooges.

In the back rows were about ten middle-aged people, mostly women, who were chuckling and watching everyone with great interest. Mr. Huang said they were probably looking for an easy part-time job at a neighborhood restaurant or dumpling shop.

Mr. Huang speculated that the majority of the male students between ages twenty and fifty were most likely factory employees who'd lost their jobs, needed to switch careers, or wanted to open their own restaurant. We got a lot of stares from the rest of the class as we conversed in English.

After about five minutes, our instructor, Yao Laoshi, dashed in like a cyclone. In one arm he cradled a baking sheet with a raw chicken on it and his cleaver; on the other he balanced a bowl of vegetables, a red pepper, some bok choy, and a glass jar of tea. He squinted one eye shut, avoiding the smoke from the burning cigarette bobbing up and down in his mouth, as he talked to one of the students in the front row.

Despite Yao Laoshi's high-speed energy, his dark-skinned face was relaxed, friendly, and wonderfully animated. When he laughed, his wide grin and good teeth dominated it. His eyebrows scrunched up when he was thinking. A buzz haircut hid his receding hairline. He had red, hickeylike welts on the back of his neck, apparently from cupping. *"Ni hao, ni hao,"* he said to the class.

He glanced down at my messenger bag, which held my chef jacket, cutting board, cleaver, and ingredients. Holding his cigarette gingerly between his thumb and index finger, he said something very quickly to me in Shanghainese.

"He said you should leave anything valuable at home," Mr. Huang told me. All the items in my bag were things I'd been instructed to bring, so I looked back up at the professor with a confused expression. Then I looked around and saw that almost everyone in the room had carried in their cooking equipment in plastic grocery bags. I realized it was the messenger bag he'd interpreted as valuable, and from then on, it stayed at home.

Yao Laoshi began speaking in Shanghainese. Mr. Huang leaned over, his breath smelling garlicky, and whispered, "The rules of my class are these: In my class you can sit anywhere you want—just in the same seat, and you must always use the same counter space in the kitchen. I will call out your number at roll call. At the end of every class, I will assign someone to sweep out the lecture room. Sharpen knives before and after use and keep them away from water. Wipe water off as soon as possible with a towel."

He picked up his cleaver. "Today we're going to sharpen our blades."

Yao Laoshi dropped his burning cigarette on the floor and rubbed it out with the sole of his shoe. Three of the men sitting closest to him jumped out of their seats to offer a fresh cigarette to the teacher.

"Are they trying to get brownie points or kill him?" I whispered to Mr. Huang, hoping he'd know I was trying to be funny.

Mr. Huang smiled. "It's *guanxi*, or having connections. They're showing a sign of respect to the teacher by giving him this luxury. He has to take it or it's a rejection."

Without skipping a word, Yao Laoshi took the cigarette closest to him. Within seconds, the same three men pulled out their lighters and held them out in front of his face. Over the course of my ten weeks in cooking school, Yao Laoshi never went without a cigarette in class—the students wouldn't let him. Whether his hands were occupied or dirty, a student was always there to gently place a new cigarette in his mouth, and the same or another person would follow up and light it.

In many ways, the cooking academy felt like what I imagined a disorderly inner-city public school to be like. I seemed to be the only person who noticed the talking during class. The Three Stooges bantered loudly. The young woman took incoming phone calls. No one turned off their cell phone during lecture. Two of the older women sitting beside each other in the back row opened lunches they'd brought, taking their food out noisily from plastic bags. Yao Laoshi talked over them all, stopping from time to time to take a deep, thoughtful pull from his cigarette.

*After Yao Laoshi showed us* the basics of knife sharpening, it was the students' turn to put his words to use as we moved to the prep and kitchen area. The kitchen comprised two sparse, tile-floored rooms. The first room, where we would do our prep, resembled a school chemistry lab, which it probably had been or still was for the middle school across the courtyard. Along a wall of shelves on one side of the room were stacks of woks, dishes, bowls, and plastic tubs of cooking utensils. The next room had three commercial wok stoves where we would cook. Faucets built into the walls allowed the woks to be cleaned with fresh water.

Yao Laoshi walked slowly among the islands that served as our individual stations, running his thumb lightly against the blade of his knife as he spoke. "A sharp blade comes with time and continuous sharpening," Mr. Huang repeated for me in a low voice.

As Yao Laoshi held up his cleaver by its sturdy wood handle, we were all in awe of the handsome rectangle of steel brawn. The blade was polished smooth, and its razor-sharp edge was as shiny as a silver dollar.

Yao Laoshi continued strolling the floor. "This instrument is all you need for Chinese cooking. You don't need spoons, or even chopsticks. This cleaver works as a hammer, a spatula, a knife, or a spoon. It's an all-in-one tool."

During one lecture, our instructor compared Chinese and Western cooking: "When you learn Western cooking, you have several sizes of knives, different spoons, and cups to stir and measure. In Chinese cooking all you need is a cutting board, a cleaver, a teaspoon, wok, and a spatula. In fact, you don't even need a spatula.

"The cleaver is heavy and strong enough to crack through bone, yet delicate enough to split hairs. You can use it to stir a soup and scoop. Using it in different ways makes you one with it, so it becomes an extension of your own hands."

Before the first day of school, I'd gone to the kitchen equipment store to purchase a chef's jacket and cleaver. The store was a state-run operation, a dark room with a couple of dangling exposed lightbulbs. I told the saleswoman, who was munching an apple, that the cooking school had sent me. I handed her a list of items written in Mandarin. She sucked on her tooth and pointed to a cardboard box in a dusty corner. The first cleaver I picked up was completely orange with rust. It took us a while to find one that was in decent condition.

*Yao Laoshi sprinkled some water* on the whetstone, held in place on a wet towel, and demonstrated how to sharpen our knives. "Push away from you at a slight angle," he said, yelling over the Three Stooges, who were horsing around in the back of the room.

Using whetstones provided by the school, everyone fell into their own rhythm of sharpening, pushing the metal back and forth along the slick, silty surface. I examined the edge of my blade and gingerly pushed a finger against it to test it.

I worked on my blade for fifteen minutes before taking it to Yao Laoshi for examination. He took one look at it and said, "Try to cut this with it." He handed me an eggplant. I pressed the shiny knife edge into the dark purple vegetable. It wouldn't budge past the skin; it left only a dent.

I spent the next hour and a half sharpening my cleaver and learning the feel of my blade, as well as the appropriate amount of pressure to apply while I sharpened. My arms felt heavy and my lower back ached. My hands and forearms ached, too. I was actually sweating from the vigorous but controlled act of pushing the blade, but I was determined to get my knife to sink into the eggplant.

Mr. Huang was talking to some of the other students and dodging the Three Stooges, who were testing the sharpness of their blades by trying to cut locks of hair from one another's heads.

I felt extremely satisfied when I put the eggplant back on the cutting board and witnessed my blade slip easily into its flesh, without any force on my part except for the weight of the knife.

Once the cleavers were sharpened, transporting them to and from class posed a challenge. Each student devised their own version of a blade cover. I made a sheath for mine out of an old Nike shoebox and duct tape. One ingenious student tucked the sharp edge of the blade into the spine of a paperback book and held it in place with a rubber band.

For the rest of the first class, we practiced slicing the vegetables we'd been instructed to bring. The school wouldn't supply the raw materials we needed to make each dish; we were all responsible for bringing the main ingredients to each class. At the end of class, I asked Yao Laoshi to write out the grocery list, which included five items: ginger root, one *jin* of lean pork, two pieces of dried tofu, a cucumber, and a couple of potatoes.

In Chinese cooking, cutting the ingredients to perfect uniformity is essential for even cooking. And the only way to master knifing skills is to practice. Our classroom reverberated with different chopping rhythms: machine gun *rat-a-tat-tats*, horseshoelike clomping, and hammering like nails into a wall. We learned several cutting, slicing, chopping, and julienning styles. We learned how to score and slice patterns on seafood and dried tofu so they shrank and curled inside out when boiled or cooked, which gave them their finished flower shapes and curlicues.

As the weeks passed, the class separated into cliques. The men and women in their fifties sat opposite me, while the men in their late twenties and thirties sat near the windows. Then there were the Three Stooges, who made up a little group along with a couple of other high school graduates, and me, pretty much on my own.

Several weeks in, the classroom atmosphere during instructor demonstrations took on a picniclike quality. We learned how to make local Chinese dishes, such as braised fish belly and pork threads and mushrooms, as well as dishes like *gong bao ji ding* (kung pao chicken) and braised eggplant, which are familiar to the Western palate. The class was always eager when it came time to smell and taste the four or five dishes that Yao Laoshi prepared. The older group started bringing in their own bowls, dishes, chopsticks, and sometimes cooked rice. One of the men even brought beer. The aromas were heavenly and my mouth watered, tempting me to take a taste. But the first time I reached in to try something with my chopstick, Mr. Huang stopped me.

"What are you doing?" I asked. "I've eaten street food the entire time I've lived in China."

"That was before you were pregnant," Mr. Huang insisted. "Look at that wok. I don't think it has ever been properly cleaned. The cutting board is wood and only gets washed with plain water. Do you see how when he adds water to food, he uses tap, not bottled?"

"Good point," I said, resigned to the idea that all I'd be savoring were the smells. Mr. Huang never hesitated to give me medical advice. One afternoon before class, he peered at me closely and described my skin as "sad looking."

I touched my face. I thought my skin looked radiant.

"Steamed fish. Yes, that's what you need. Freshwater fish, to be safe. It's cool." Since I'd gotten pregnant, he'd started asking me about my intake of cool and warm foods. He explained how in Eastern medicine, expectant mothers are yang (warm) and therefore need to be balanced with yin (cool) foods.

Like learning the masculine and feminine designations of objects in European languages, understanding how foods are considered yin and yang felt just as hazy to me. Once during class, I pulled a banana from my plastic shopping bag and Mr. Huang gave the cool fruit an approving nod. I hadn't realized before then that bananas were yin.

I don't know if the steamed fish cured me of my lackluster complexion, but the moist, flaky fish infused with fragrant Chinese rice wine and ginger was bland enough for my unpredictable digestive system, yet just flavorful enough to satisfy my deprived palate.

Of course, the students started to insist that I take some once they saw that I wasn't eating Yao Laoshi's food. Mr. Huang told me they thought only an idiot or a stuck-up foreigner would pass up free food, but, he asked, hadn't I noticed that the teacher never tasted his own dishes?

I had been in China long enough to know that a dirty wok just wasn't a good enough reason to not eat—not in this country, where people greeted each other with the question *"Ni chi fan le ma?"* ("Have you eaten yet?") My excuse of having already eaten before coming to class was met with shrugs. Little did my fellow students know that after class, I'd race home to re-create the dishes we'd learned, in an attempt to sate the hunger that all those delicious aromas had stirred up.

After all the students had filled up on the demonstration dishes and relaxed from the beers, we'd enter the kitchen to make the food ourselves, using the ingredients we'd been instructed to bring from home and one of the kitchen's woks. The wok is iconic in Chinese cooking—a single vessel used for stir-frying, braising, and steaming. Caring for a wok is like caring for a violin: With time and attention, the carbon-steel or cast-iron veneer transforms into a lustrous nonstick surface and seals out rust. This patina, the soul of the wok, produces that sublime flavor unique to Chinese fare, the way a musical instrument can produce breathtaking sounds.

The school's kitchen contained the same commercial-size equipment we would use if we worked in a restaurant. The woks were three times as big as the one I used at home. In class, we'd nestle the woks deeply into the stove's heat source, a flaming hole that made me think of childhood stories of fire-breathing dragons.

All the students tried their best to re-create what Yao Laoshi had demonstrated. Before we went home, we were to show our prepared dishes to Yao Laoshi; he would check them for presentation, color, and aroma. If he was unsatisfied with the result, the student had to remake the dish in the next class.

The last week of class ended with a bang when two of the Three Stooges broke out into a full-on fistfight. One minute, they were playing an innocent knuckle-punching game to see who could hit the hardest. The next minute, they knocked each other over onto the chairs and into the older students' part of the room. One of the guys had to be held down by three students while the teacher and another student dragged the other guy out of the classroom. After the class settled back down and the boys made up, Yao Laoshi looked at them and said, "Next time, use your knives and get it over with faster."

Class ended early for me because I wasn't going for the certificate. The rest of the students had to pass a series of written and cooking tests in order to work in restaurants or start their own business.

I don't think Yao Laoshi expected me to say goodbye to him on my last day of class. Mr. Huang translated my farewell. I thanked him for allowing me to be in his class, and for accommodating my poor language skills. He nodded sheepishly. I could tell by the way he looked down and rubbed his head that he felt embarrassed. He told me it was nice having me in class.

As I turned to leave, I said, "*Xiexie ni. Zajian.*" ("Thank you. Bye.")

He replied by saying goodbye in heavily accented English. One of the Three Stooges standing near him snickered, and Yao Laoshi turned to swat him on the head with a dishtowel.

# STEAMED WHOLE FISH

*Healthy and great tasting, this is one of my favorite dishes*
*I learned in cooking school. If you don't like the look of a*
*whole fish, you can cut off the head and tail, but keep the skin on.*

INGREDIENTS:

1 1/2 pounds whole fish (I use perch, but you can use any firm-fleshed freshwater fish), rinsed and patted dry

Sake or Chinese yellow wine *(huangjiu)*

Salt and pepper to taste

1/2-inch piece fresh ginger, peeled and finely julienned

1 green onion, trimmed, cut into 2- to 3-inch lengths, then slivered lengthwise

3 teaspoons soy sauce

1/2 teaspoon Asian sesame oil

INSTRUCTIONS:

Set your steamer, with lid in place, atop a wok or skillet half filled with water. Place over high heat.

Cut two or three slashes on each side of the fish, then rub the skin with sake and season with salt and pepper. Place the fish in a glass pie plate or other heatproof dish.

Mix together the ginger, green onion, soy sauce, and sesame oil. Pour over the fish, piling the ginger and green onion slivers evenly atop the fish.

When the water in the wok comes to a boil, lift the lid carefully. Let the hot steam settle for a few seconds before placing the plate in the steamer. Cover and steam for about 15 minutes per pound. Test doneness by sticking a chopstick into the thickest part of the fish. The flesh should appear white, moist, and flaky.

Serve portions of fish with some of the broth that collects in the pie plate.

*Serves 4 as part of a multicourse Chinese meal*

Chapter 11

# PRELUDE
## to Winter

TAILS WAGGING AND NOSES SNIFFING, Oscar and Meyer trot-
ted along the wide, tree-lined sidewalk outside our two-story apartment
building, on our usual morning route through our neighborhood of em-
bassies and antique shops.

Snowfall was a rare sight in the port city of Shanghai, but that early
October morning, tiny snowflakes, stirred by cabs, cars, and bicycles,
were suspended in midair like children's soap bubbles.

The sky, cast with a pewter tint, reminded me of the winter sky
in Beijing. Lately, as the day when I would leave Shanghai for Florida
approached, Beijing had been occupying my mind the way home did.
Though it hadn't seemed like it when we were there, something about the
isolation and simplicity of that time had made it the happiest era in my
relationship with Eric.

As the arrival of my child drew closer, my change of heart about staying in China became even more pronounced. Shanghai possessed all the conveniences I could ask for, but I felt far removed from my friends in the States who were also married and having children. If we remained in Asia, I wondered how often my parents would see their grandchild—once a year at the most?

As I walked the dogs, the sweet, velvety aromas of yeast and steam rising from meat buns mingled with the smell of gas fumes and blacktop. I held tight to the dogs' leashes as we passed the snack stand where I used to buy my favorite breakfast: crispy fried dough, tart pickled cabbage, and brown sugar stuffed in the middle of a bun-shaped roll of sticky rice. Before I was pregnant, I would wash down this treat with a couple of little glass jars of homemade yogurt, but now I didn't eat street food or yogurt, for fear that I'd catch some nasty bacteria or parasite that would wreak havoc on my system.

Despite my growing ambivalence about China living, we would be departing for the United States that morning, and I was feeling particularly sentimental about what I was leaving behind. I wouldn't be coming back until the following February, when the baby was strong and healthy enough for the long overseas flight. I remembered how when I'd first come to China, the country had felt like a stranger I didn't care to get to know. But so much had changed, and over the years I'd experienced my own memories and adventures free of Eric. The feelings of attachment I'd developed made leaving feel as if I were saying goodbye to a best friend whom I had grown apart from.

I was due in December, which made October my last window of opportunity to leave China before the risk of flying pregnant became too great. I noticed how winded I got while walking the dogs, even at a slow pace. The baby had noticeably less room to move around in, and my body jolted sideways whenever he changed positions. When he stretched or kicked, I winced as if someone were poking my internal organs. Other times I was mesmerized by the imprint of a little body part pressing against the wall of my belly.

I'd learned I was carrying a boy from the amniocentesis I had received in Hong Kong. Because of my age, the possibility of birth defects was greater, so we'd opted to travel to Hong Kong for this procedure. Chinese hospitals were banned from performing amniocenteses because of the risk that parents might abort if they knew in advance that they were having a girl.

Now the time had finally come to move forward with our initial plan. Eric and I were going to travel together to Florida over China's National Day, and then he would fly back to Shanghai on his own and stay there through Thanksgiving, until the first week of December. His employer would allow him to spend one month in Florida after the baby was born.

The previous spring, when we'd concocted the plan, it had seemed great, but I was leery of my two-month separation from Eric. In the darkest part of my heart, I was genuinely worried about what this time apart would do to us. My developing maternal instinct wouldn't allow me to dwell on such poisonous thoughts, but it was there, like a spider weaving its web.

That summer, we'd played the role of happy expectant parents in front of our friends, but behind closed doors the distance between us was growing as wide and deep as a sinkhole. Our intimacy was practically nonexistent, and my discontent about living in Shanghai was increasing by the day. When I look back on the concentrated time surrounding our marriage, immediate pregnancy, and an anticipated windfall of money,

I believe these circumstances may have caused Eric to doubt the person he had chosen to share them with. I'll never know for sure, but what I do know for certain is that something was terribly wrong when, as newlyweds, we acted like a miserable couple who'd been married far too long.

*Passing under an awning* of changing leaves, I slowed my pace. The dogs took advantage of the situation and lunged for some chicken bones left by construction workers who'd just been lunching along the curb.

Regardless of my situation with Eric, I was ready for the baby's arrival, and all my affairs were in order. The long hours I had put into writing the book over the last year had paid off. The manuscript was finished. It just needed editing and a book proposal to accompany it, which was what I was planning to keep myself busy doing while I was in Florida without Eric.

The baby's nursery, which occupied half of my office, was furnished with a crib and a changing table that my friend Michele and her husband, Mike, who were moving to Seattle and unloading lots of baby stuff, had passed down to us.

The day they came over to drop off the table, Michele was carrying her six-month-old son on her hip. Glancing at my midsection, she said, "I won't be surprised if you end up back in the States."

"No, we're staying here. This is where Eric works," I answered, a little too automatically.

"If you say so." She paused. "I hate to say it, but once you have a kid, things feel totally different."

I didn't admit it to Michele, but things were already starting to feel totally different. I was missing my parents and my friends, and I'd started to feel paranoid about how unsafe the city was. But my growing desire to move back home only brought on arguments with Eric, so I kept it to myself.

In the beginning of our courtship, I'd felt that our life overseas had a romantic, sugary-sweet, us-against-the-world quality. I didn't dare say it out loud. I didn't tell even my closest friends, because it seemed so cheesy and impossible to explain. And I'd always thought I would want to raise my child internationally, with all the exposure and culture that brings, so I couldn't have imagined how dramatic my almost 180-degree shift would be.

The topic kept coming up, of course, because even though I knew it bothered Eric and was conscious of trying to squelch it, part of me—the last trace of the defiant me—wanted to scream at the top of my lungs and have Eric recognize that my needs and desires had changed. Lately it was becoming even more of a sore spot because I couldn't take my mind off something Eric had told me about when we were first dating—that he and his best friend from high school had built a house in rural northern Vermont.

"I want to create it for my future wife," he'd told me on one of our earliest dates, while we sipped martinis in an upscale restaurant in San Francisco's Mission district. He told me about the 175-acre parcel of rolling hills, wild fields, and untouched nature. I remember melting at this and thinking how lucky his future wife was going to feel. While we were dating, Eric took me to the property four times. I loved the area, with its expansive views of Jay Peak, trees, pastureland, and grassy knolls. Its isolated, small-town Americana feel reminded me of my own rural upbringing. Now that I was his wife, I couldn't shake the idea that we should live there—that *I* should live there.

I began bringing it up from time to time, talking about how nice it would be to take the baby there in the summers, and how great it would be for him to experience the place on a yearly basis. I thought Eric's ties to what he proudly referred to as The Property, and my fondness for the area, would make it a place where we could mend the fissure between us. I fantasized about the way Eric used to be, when he was delighted by me, rather than easily angered. But when I brought up the idea that perhaps the baby and I could go to Vermont for the whole summer, leaving a little early to have more time in the States, he accused me of planning a trip without him. I had wrongly assumed that we'd be among the expatriate families we knew who got up and left hot, muggy Shanghai during August. Some expats even managed to cut deals with their companies that allowed them to work away from China during the summer. But Eric's reaction was such that I added The Property to my ever-growing list of things to never mention to him.

*Luckily, in Sally I found someone* with whom to share some of the trivial but meaningful joys of future motherhood. In September, the month before I left, she and I began discussing what duties she'd need to be responsible for during the months when I was away.

We initiated this conversation over my favorite lunch of hot, spicy beef noodles. Although I was still craving pineapple and foods with a tangy tomato base, my body was starting to want spicy flavors, too, although this sometimes meant I had to deal with unpleasant results. My favorite hardcore Sichuan dishes, such as *shuizhuniurou* (cooked pork slices and cabbage in a chili-infused broth) and *liang ban huang gua* (spicy cucumber and garlic) upset the baby and kept me awake all night with his kicking, but when Sally came home with takeout from my favorite neighborhood restaurant, I couldn't resist.

Sally and I ate at the dining room table overlooking the yard, where the dogs enjoyed the sun as they sprawled out on the patch of lawn next to a small rock garden. I savored the soup's homemade noodles, green leafy vegetables, and slices of tenderized beef. It had the texture of tofu, and I stirred in red pools of chili oil and specks of chili peppers before digging in. I informed Sally in part English, part Mandarin, about the duties she needed to accomplish while we were away and when Eric came back, but also, and more important, the things I anticipated when I returned with the baby.

These kinds of conversations between us took forever, and I was never quite sure if she actually understood all the things we discussed. But Sally was happy as a spring chicken to be doing anything regarding the baby, it seemed. She'd been unwavering in her support since the day she'd found out I was pregnant. She'd told me that caring for a newborn would be like caring for her own child, and I trusted her implicitly, the way I would a close relative.

We paused and picked up our long Chinese chopsticks to eat the noodles. I hunkered over my bowl. It looked sloppy, but we weren't going to win any awards for good manners, and this was undoubtedly the most efficient position for eating noodles.

As I leaned over and stirred the abundance of noodles, fresh cilantro and chili scents rose up in a puff of steam and tickled my nose. The first bite was always the best. The savory, rich beef broth and zesty spices and onions were like a melody that played on my tongue, but it was the fresh homemade noodles, cooked to a perfect softness, that made the dish. I'd learned to order the noodles from the restaurant early, so I wouldn't be crushed if they ran out. I scooped up some of the broth with my porcelain spoon. It was so delicious, I couldn't imagine trying to reproduce it when I was back in the States.

Sally and I sat there like two teenage boys in an unspoken contest to see who could slurp the loudest. Sally was the reigning queen, of course. I was amazed at how she could blow quickly a couple of times on the steaming noodles dangling from the tips of her chopsticks, then vacuum a bite with her mouth without burning her tongue or cutting the noodles with her teeth.

If my mound of noodles wasn't cooled just right, I scalded my mouth and dropped the noodles back into my soup. Whenever this happened, Sally just smiled politely at my neophyte noodle eating and set her elbows on the table to show me how it was really done. As I lost the contest yet again, I wiped my mouth and dabbed at the chili oil that had splashed on my shirt.

Sally's portable English phrase book, which had a photo of a young Paulina Porizkova on its cover, sat on the table nearby. She had told me some time ago that she would enroll in an English language class, but I realized in that moment that she hadn't said anything about it for a while. We both knew she was doing this for my benefit. But she had seemed interested, so I'd offered to pay for the class, give her time to study, and help her learn.

I chewed on a tender morsel of meat when Sally told me that she couldn't find a class. That didn't make any sense; I knew there must be a wide variety of English language classes, especially in Shanghai, since it was such a big city. I told her I'd help her find one.

With her eyes downcast, Sally admitted that she'd gone to one class, but she'd realized it wasn't for her.

"Everyone was from university," she said in English. "I'm not smart."

"Yes you are!" I exclaimed, setting down my chopsticks. She shook her head like a little girl. I knew there was nothing I could say to change her mind. She carried the burden of satisfying what society expected of her as an *ayi*.

My wushu instructor, Zhang Yi, told me a similar story about something that had happened to him. When he was eight, the government had selected him for admission to a martial arts academy. He was chosen because of his weight, height, and other physical specifications. After he graduated and began teaching wushu, he decided to enroll in a management class to help him learn how to run his business. He had a change of heart, though, after he ran into an acquaintance who told him he was an athlete, not a student, and that he should stick to what he knew or be disappointed when he flunked the class.

We sat in silence for a few moments. "I will learn English with baby," Sally said with a grin. She leaned over to pet Meyer's soft underside. She had so much love to give.

"You're excited about the baby coming?" I asked in Mandarin. I knew I hadn't constructed the sentence accurately, but the best part of our relationship was that we each got the gist of what the other was trying to say.

I already knew the answer to my question based on the way she eyed the baby clothes, nursery bedding, and plush toys my friends and relatives had mailed to me. From my writing desk, I'd watched Sally carefully tying on the crib bumper, putting on and smoothing the bedding, and arranging the stuffed animals, looking at each one before placing it carefully in the crib. She'd hand-washed all the new clothing and ironed each piece, and she'd worn a smile as she carefully folded and put away each garment. I knew that setting up the nursery is considered a mother's sacred privilege, but allowing her to help me made me feel like we were in this together. At the start of such an uncertain period in my life, Sally was like a friend and confidante to me.

"You know one-baby policy?" she asked. I nodded.

"I have no more," she said in English with a sad smile. When I'd hired her I'd seen her resident papers, which had stated her age: thirty-six. Same as me. She'd told me that she was twenty-one when she'd married and had her daughter, Xiao Zhu.

"Were your husband and daughter with you in Beijing when you worked for the other family?" I asked as well as I could in Mandarin.

She answered with the nonchalance of someone who's had much time to accept her situation: "I was by myself," she said simply. I'd seen Xiao Zhu occasionally, when she stopped by to visit Oscar and Meyer; she had her mother's quick smile and sloped eyes. She was tall, with a strong, compact physique, and was very poised and mature, until she let out her soft girlish laugh. Like two best friends, she and Sally would take Oscar and Meyer on their late-afternoon walks, talking and laughing the entire way.

I thought about how to ask Sally what I wanted to ask her as I did the math in my head. I proceeded gently: "When I hired you, you said you worked for the Beijing family for nine years."

Sally laughed uncomfortably. "Yes," she said, with a finality that was an obvious cue that she wanted to end the conversation. She'd told me once that she and her husband had met with some financial difficulties during the first year of their marriage and after their daughter was born.

I'd never made the connection that this was why she'd taken the job as an *ayi*. I now realized how silly it was that I hadn't put two and two together. Of course she'd had to make whatever sacrifices had to be made, even if that included being separated from her family.

So for nine years, Sally had worked in Beijing, raising a little boy named William as if he were her own.

"When did you see your daughter?" I had to ask.

"Once or twice a year, on national holidays." To reassure me, she added slowly in Mandarin, "Xiao Zhu was with my parents, and on the weekends with my husband. I quit my job when she turned thirteen. I told my employers I couldn't be separated from my daughter any longer."

I dropped the subject and gave Sally a warm, understanding smile.

At the time, I never could have imagined that I would someday feel the empty, bone-splitting sorrow that comes from being separated from one's child.

After we were finished with the noodle soup, Sally collected the bowls and chopsticks, packing them up so that she could take them back down to the restaurant. She turned toward me abruptly as I stood to return to my office and continue writing, as if she realized that the moment to say what she wanted to say would pass. Hesitatingly, she explained that she had posted her job-wanted ad on a supermarket bulletin board when she learned her daughter had been hand-picked to join the national sailing academy.

It was like the government's version of sending your child to boarding school. Chinese parents rarely refuse the government's invitation to place their children in these programs, because all of their needs—food, shelter, clothing, and education—are taken care of. The education guarantees the student mastery of a skill, and employment after graduation.

Over time, Xiao Zhu's training would evolve from classroom studies to ocean sailing. Sally sought work to occupy her time while her daughter was away at sea. My heart sank when Sally said, in a voice that reflected her sadness and resignation, that rather than seeing her daughter every day, as she had before the academy, she anticipated seeing her only during brief shore leaves. As someone who was about to have a baby, I couldn't imagine the pain of that kind of separation.

*I steered the dogs back down* to Fuxing Road as we finished our circuit. I knew I shouldn't be loitering and daydreaming when there was still much to do before I left for the airport, but the nearer I got to the house, the less possible it became to shake off my overwhelmingly foreboding feeling.

I stopped the dogs at a street corner several yards from the entrance to the apartment. The men sitting outside the nearby antiques store were looking at me. I nodded at them; they nodded back. No matter what the weather, these five middle-aged men sat outside on whatever chairs or stools they were selling, playing cards and spitting sunflower seed husks. They were better than any security guard. When I'd return home from grocery shopping, they'd often ask questions about a certain foreigner who'd come by that day, or they'd let me know that Sally had run to the market to buy tofu. Or that my dogs were suffering from the heat and needed a haircut.

I stood completely still while a vortex of scattered dead leaves spun around my feet and flapped the dogs' ears. It was plain and simple: I didn't want to go back to the States. All of a sudden, I wished I were having the baby in Shanghai, rather than leaving Eric for several months. I had the sense that if I left, everything I had would be taken away from me.

I passed by the men sipping their tea from tall glass jars and slipped into our building. *Everything will work out,* I told myself. I tried to convince myself that my feelings were just preflight jitters.

The snowflakes were still dancing around like dandelion seeds as Eric and the cab driver loaded the baggage and dogs.

"Okay, bye, Sally," Eric said in English. He'd be back in a few weeks and wasn't much for farewells anyway.

I turned to give her a hug and saw that she was crying.

"Don't cry, Sally," Eric said in Mandarin. "She'll be coming back with a baby."

Sally seemed to sense that I didn't want to leave, so we stood on the sidewalk as pedestrians walked around us, clinging to each other for our own reasons. Finally, I knew I had to get in the car.

As the cab pulled away from the house, I stared out the window and saw Sally smiling, waving, and wiping away tears with a tissue.

*"Welcome home!"*

As we pulled into the driveway, Eric's mother, Dorothy, lean and spry and two years retired from her job as director of a charitable foundation, came bounding outside.

"Oh my, Linda, you look terrific! Look at your beautiful stomach." Although she'd lived in New York City most of her life, Dorothy had held on to her charming Southern accent.

Dorothy was tall, like Eric, and when she leaned into me I smelled the hairspray in her short, wavy do, and her favorite moisturizer, cocoa butter. Both aromas had become synonymous with Florida for me in the years I'd known her.

"C'mon in. I want to hear about your trip," she said, picking up one of the lighter bags. As Eric rolled the two larger suitcases through the French double doors, she remarked, "But first, Eric, I must tell you about my golf game, or lack of one." In their retirement, my in-laws had taken up the sport.

"I'll be in in a sec," I yelled. "I want to take the dogs around the block. They need the exercise after the trip."

The flight from Shanghai was thirteen hours to San Francisco, with a five-hour layover there. Then we'd had another five-hour flight to Miami, followed by a three-hour drive across Alligator Alley to Naples. I felt a new level of exhaustion. As the sun was on the verge of setting in Shanghai, it was just morning here, and I felt in dire need of a second wind.

I was using the excuse that the dogs needed a walk to help me transition into my new surroundings. I walked among swaying palm trees, elegant calla lilies, groomed streets with majestic landscaping, and the shiny, well-maintained cars of the gated community where Eric's parents spent their winters.

The lush tropical greenery, the white clouds floating against the blue sky, and the golden cast of waning sunlight, so vivid and colorful, felt dreamlike compared with the gigantic neon signs and monochrome of Shanghai's urban sprawl. The heady scent of gardenia and the soft aroma of freshly mowed grass teased my nostrils, which were used to the smell of gasoline exhaust, burning coal bricks, rotting trash, and fried cooking.

Back in the house, Dorothy heated up some food she had picked up from her favorite caterer. As we ate the salmon loaf, potatoes, and vegetables on the enclosed lanai, Dorothy went over the details of what I needed to know during my stay alone in the house: How to set the house alarm, what day to take the trash out, the schedule of repairs and water delivery, and emergency numbers. I was disappointed to hear that she was leaving the next morning to go back to New York City, where her husband, Frank, was still working.

"Dear, will you be all right by yourself?" she asked, holding her fork in midair, picking up on my reaction. "I would usually be here, but I've got two annual meetings to make."

"Don't worry," I said, regaining my composure. "Finishing up my book will keep me busy. You'll be back for Thanksgiving; then it'll be time for me to have the baby. The days will fly by. Please don't worry about me." I was reassuring myself at the same time. I took a big drink of water and helped myself to another piece of fish.

The first time I'd met Dorothy was at her Connecticut home. Eric and I had begun our long-distance relationship and were on our way to The Property in Vermont to meet his best friend, who wanted to build on a deck. For some reason, Eric had led me to believe that his mother was a stay-at-home mom like mine. I was intimidated when I learned that she was actually a fund manager for a nonprofit foundation.

The first time I met her, she was standing at her kitchen table, opening boxes of new shoes; she had three of the same style in various colors. Before we had even been introduced, she caught me staring at the footwear with a look of wonderment. She looked at the boxes and then at me, and said matter-of-factly, "If a style works for you, I say buy it in every color."

Putting aside the fact that she was Eric's mother, I was drawn to Dorothy, and she to me. I learned about who she was as a careerwoman, wife, and mother. I came to think of her not as Eric's mother, but as a go-getter, a strong, determined woman to admire and emulate.

Over the years, I pieced together her inspiring story. One evening in

Florida during the Thanksgiving holiday when Eric proposed, when just the two of us were cleaning up after dinner, she told me how she was the only child of teachers who lived in rural Tennessee. After she'd graduated from Vanderbilt University, she and a girlfriend had set their sights on New York City.

Dorothy's stories of life in the Big Apple during the 1950s and '60s were accentuated with details of the clothes she wore and the colorful settings she found herself in. As she told me her life story, I pictured it in my mind as if I were watching *Breakfast at Tiffany's* with a wardrobe designed by Edith Head. Dorothy described wearing a sweeping, pale caftan and wide-brimmed hat to protect her fair skin during one beach vacation in the Hamptons, the trip when she'd met her future husband. Her strategy for talking to him was to out-sit all the other women, until she and he were the only ones left at the beach as the sun set.

She'd worked on Wall Street until she started having children, and she was one of the few women included in the analyst training program at the large investment bank where she worked. Her tactic for being taken seriously as a woman banker, she told me with a spark in her eye, was to serve coffee and tea as sloppily as possible, and to never learn how to type.

What impressed me most about Eric's mother were the openness and vulnerability behind her honesty. As we food shopped one day at a gourmet store in Florida, she told me that after she had her three boys, she'd go to a cocktail party, mingle, and feel like a complete nobody.

"I couldn't wait to go back to work. As much as I loved my sons, I needed a place to go and a place to feel important. Some mothers get their validation from staying at home with their kids—more power to them. As for me, I wasn't getting it being a housewife," she said, gently putting a ripe cantaloupe into the cart.

"Unfortunately, it's the same with cooking. I'd rather be cooked for than cook," she confessed. "I love nice restaurants and the work the chefs put into it, but I have no desire to re-create it myself." The way she said things like this always made me laugh.

For someone who wasn't interested in cooking, Dorothy still understood and appreciated what went into preparing a meal. During our visits in Florida, she bought all the ingredients and equipment Eric and I could ever want or need. If we mentioned a particular type of pan we liked, we'd find it in the kitchen the next day. One morning, the week after our wedding, I was flirting with the idea of making a berry tart, but we didn't have the tart pan or a rolling pin. That afternoon, I found a bag from Williams-Sonoma with the items I needed inside.

*Before Dorothy left the next morning* for New York, she took me aside in the lofty foyer of the house, where I'd stood on my wedding day, just ten months earlier, before proceeding down the aisle.

As considerate and thoughtful as Dorothy was, she wasn't the gentle-earth-mother type. She could be tough and rough around the edges. But that evening she sat me down in one of the comfortable, elegant love seats in the living room.

"Now, I want you to really take this time to enjoy yourself, go to the spa, eat out, sleep. Life's going to change once the little one comes." She looked me directly in the eye, and I felt the relief of being taken care of.

"I'll be back in a month, and all of the aunts, uncles, and cousins will be here for Thanksgiving. The week after, Eric will return and he can take over before the baby arrives." She patted my hand.

"Yes, I know." I stopped breathing for a moment as I contemplated telling her that it wasn't being alone that I was concerned about—it was my marriage. I knew she and I were friends. The way she had accepted me into the family long before Eric and I married made her like a second mother to me. Along with the New York Giants' football game videotapes she sent to Eric in Shanghai, she included articles she had clipped from the *Wall Street Journal* and *New York Times* food sections, thinking I might find them interesting. It was one aspect of a mother-daughter relationship that I had always wanted, but never had, with my own mother.

Ultimately, though, Dorothy was Eric's mother, and as much as I needed someone to talk me through what was going on, she wasn't the appropriate person to have that conversation with.

"Have a great trip. And thanks a lot for everything." I gave Dorothy a big hug before climbing the staircase to my bedroom.

*Eric took golf lessons* and practiced every day for the rest of his stay. I was too far along in my pregnancy to play, but I tried anyway, getting tired and cranky after nine holes in the blistering sun.

Since we'd arrived in Florida, we were getting along much better. Eric was more relaxed away from work, and I was thankful to be back in the States, despite my misgivings during the week before we'd left Shanghai.

Looking back on this time when we were alone—truly alone—together for a whole week, it seems natural that we would have discussed what was happening to us. But we chose not to, each for our own reasons, I'm sure. My denial ran so deep that I thought it was all behind us, and that bringing it up would only make matters worse.

Eric's departure date came quickly. His ride to the airport pulled into the driveway at that time of the morning when the sky is just awakening, with soft, puffy pink and orange streaks along the horizon. It's always been the time of day when I feel most vulnerable. I sat on the edge of the bed, watching helplessly, as he dressed. Eric was awake and chipper as he gathered magazines and paperwork in his bag.

Sitting down next to me, he put his arms around me and I sank into his chest, the way I had when we lived in Beijing.

"It's time for me to go," he said. He drew back slowly and stood up. I held on to his shirt, my two hands clenched together as if I were gripping jail bars, as if he were leaving me behind and I wasn't allowed beyond the confines of the space I was destined to stay in. I started to cry.

He chuckled and stroked my hair. "Oh, sweetie, don't cry. It's going to be okay."

"I don't want you to leave," I sobbed into his shirt.

"You know I don't want to leave, but I have to finish the acquisition. It's for our future."

I nodded and slowly released his shirt, smoothing out the wrinkles I'd made. The sense of impending finality I'd felt the morning we left Shanghai was back upon me like a tidal wave. I remembered how Dorothy had reassured me that everything was going to be all right, but everything felt far from it.

Now that Eric was inches from walking out the door, I found myself at a loss for all the words I should have said over the past week; the months' worth of feelings, impressions, and misunderstandings didn't want to come out of me. I had a strong desire to push an imaginary button that would stop time momentarily and give me the chance I needed to express everything I hadn't said. If I'd had such a device, I would have pushed that button countless times during that summer.

Once the baby was growing inside my body, all the rules of my relationship with Eric seemed to change. The baby, all by itself, was suddenly reason enough to believe in Eric and me, despite all the indications to the contrary.

*Outside, the driver honked.*

"I'm going now. You'll be fine," Eric repeated, giving me a peck on the mouth. "Take care of Oscar and Meyer."

The sky had turned gold and azure as the town car drove away on the cobblestone street, where gardeners were arriving to begin work on the neighborhood lawns. Oscar and Meyer looked up at me with their soft caramel eyes and perked-up ears resembling apostrophes. "C'mon, let's go for a walk," I consented.

*"What? You haven't packed* your hospital bag yet?!" Mom screeched over the phone.

"Mom, remember, I told you when you came down to visit that I've been trying to finish my book before the baby comes," I answered sheepishly, knowing that it was a lame excuse for not being prepared for one of the most physically taxing events in a woman's life.

I saw Dorothy pass by my bedroom. She was back in Florida for the rest of the winter, and she and I were rattling around in the big house alone until Frank arrived later that weekend. Sitting in a deep leather wingback chair, I turned back to the phone.

"There are still some items I need to buy—like slippers. I don't have slippers to wear at the hospital."

"Buy slippers, then," Mom scolded me.

"I still have plenty of time," I insisted. "The book, believe it or not, is finished. Three days ahead of schedule," I said, even though I knew she still thought my writing was a hobby.

"Forget book, think about the baby!" Even though I was a grown woman, I couldn't help but roll my eyes like a defiant teenager. I knew she meant well, and that this was just her brassy way of communicating, but it still drove me crazy. Since I had returned to the States, I had tried to talk to Mom and Dad regularly, mostly in an attempt to relieve my guilt about missing Thanksgiving with them and not choosing Indiana as my son's birthplace. I'd decided that my parents' house was much too small, and the winter weather too unpredictable, considering that they didn't live near a hospital.

"Mom, don't worry, my doctor thinks the baby will be late, so I'm scheduled to be induced in a week. Eric is flying out of Shanghai today. He'll be in Florida the day after tomorrow." Eric had decided to stay in San Francisco for one night to attend a business meeting.

"Are you excited?" Mom asked.

"Yes," I said, trying to hide the ambivalence in my voice. Phone communication with Eric over the last month and a half had been perfunctory. I'd excused it, as I always did, by telling myself that he was busy with work—and I was feeling guilty myself, since I'd used my monthlong solace before Thanksgiving to concentrate fully on finishing my proposal and manuscript. Every kick and movement was a reminder that I'd better hurry. Once everything was completed, I told myself, I would be free to forget about the book and enjoy motherhood and the baby.

By that point, I found no comfort in lying down, sitting, standing, or walking. My sleep was erratic; I woke up every couple of hours to go to the bathroom. I'd read it was nature's way of preparing the mother for night-time feedings. Unfortunately for me, though, I'd often forget that I had an extra thirty pounds on me when I awoke. I'd roll myself out of bed and feel those first initial steps weighing me down like a sopping-wet parka. My only relief from the weight was floating in the ocean like a piece of drift-wood, which gave me the sensation that I wasn't carrying a baby at all.

In my weeks alone after Eric left and before Dorothy returned, I enjoyed reacquainting myself with southwest Floridian food. I filled up on my favorite coconut shrimp, shrimp cocktail, batter-fried fish, fried-oyster sandwiches smothered with tartar sauce, and baskets of hush puppies. By the time my parents flew down for a visit, I had worked out all my crav-ings and was eating healthier. Their trip was brief, but comforting and much needed. Dad walked Oscar and Meyer for me and went for a swim in the ocean every afternoon. Mom brought Japanese ingredients, even rice, in her suitcase so that she could cook my favorite meals. I took them to a shrimp shack–style restaurant reminiscent of the ones we'd eaten at during our Florida road trips. Of course, when they left, my mother stashed a pound of fresh scallops in her handbag.

*Mom sighed on the phone.* "I have to go now. Your dad is coming back from swimming and will be hungry. I'll call in a couple of days."

When I hung up, I looked over at the red duffel bag on the armchair. I had laid out a gown, a bathrobe, and a pair of socks for myself, and a baby gown and baby socks. I still needed to pack my toiletry case and daytime clothes.

My finished manuscript was on the desk in a nice neat pile. I felt light and free—finishing my book had been like a birth in itself. Then

Dorothy and Frank had arrived, several days before the Thanksgiving celebration with Eric's huge family began. Eric had remained in Shanghai to work through the holiday, since he would be away from work for the month after the baby's due date, but a round of festive family-hosted pool parties, cocktail parties, lunches, and dinners at the beach club had kept my mind off my approaching delivery.

Now that the holidays were behind me, everything was happening as planned: Eric was finally arriving in a couple of days, and all I had left to do was pack my hospital bag. I had been dragging my feet for weeks. I had heard from other mothers that they'd had their bags ready two months ahead of time.

Somewhere in the back of my mind, I thought that putting off packing my hospital bag would somehow push back my delivery. A packed bag symbolized that I was ready to go—and I wasn't. Eric wasn't there yet.

At my final examination before my delivery, my doctor told me I wasn't dilating, yet my cervix felt like only a thin layer of membrane was holding the baby inside me. I imagined that the only thing containing him was something that looked like the skin that forms on the surface of hot milk. With every step I took, I felt like it was on the verge of tearing, and even though I wasn't dilating, I felt like gravity was speeding up the process.

Eric had invited his best friend for a visit to play golf the week before we were scheduled to induce. I'd thought about how poor his timing was, how maybe he should spend time with me before the baby was born, but at that moment all I cared about was that he be there for me. I had one week left. I finally felt ready to finish packing. I decided to drag Dorothy to the mall with me the next morning, to buy those slippers and a few things for the baby.

*I found a pair of fuzzy blue slippers* at the mall. I was surprised when Dorothy sat down on a bench after stopping at a couple of stores.

"You go on ahead. I'm just going to rest for a bit," she said, waving me on. I was surprised that she was tired so soon; she was in her early seventies but had the energy of someone thirty years younger.

"Okay, I'll be just a minute."

"Take your time," she answered cheerfully as I waddled off to a nearby kids' clothing store.

A minute turned into two hours as I scrambled from store to store, looking at baby clothes and taking advantage of sale bargains. Instead of feeling tired, which was the usual result when I exerted myself, I was exhilarated and charged with energy. I felt as if I could go all day.

That evening, I still didn't feel any of the fatigue that had come to seem almost normal over the past couple of months, so I offered to make Dorothy dinner—my lion's cub head meatballs with sautéed Swiss chard and a pasta "mane." Classic Chinese lion's head meatballs are the size of tennis balls, but I made bite-size meatballs instead, and jazzed up the "mane" with angel hair pasta, instead of the traditional cabbage. It was a recipe I was working on for a *Chronicle* food column installment. Dorothy devoured it.

*I looked at the clock as I slid into bed.* It was past eleven. I had planned on getting to bed earlier after my day of shopping, but after dinner I'd decided to wash and dry all of the baby's new clothes. I'd folded the clean, tiny shirts, pants, bibs, and socks and put them away. I still wasn't fully packed, but I had the slippers I wanted. The thought of having the entire next week to myself felt wildly decadent. For once, I felt like I could look forward to relaxing, easing into motherhood, and catching up on my sleep before the baby arrived.

With Oscar and Meyer curled up under the sheets, I turned off the bedside lamp and pulled the sheets up around me. Just as my head settled into the downy pillow, I felt a sudden surge of wetness between my legs. At first, I thought the baby had pressed on my bladder; I'd heard that expectant mothers could wet themselves uncontrollably.

And then, suddenly, I had another thought: *Oh no, not now—my water couldn't have broken. It's too early. Eric isn't here yet.* For about five minutes, I held on to denial. I even lay back down in the bed.

But after another minute, I decided to call the maternity ward. "Hello, my name is Linda Furiya, and I'm registered to deliver my baby there in a couple of weeks. I was climbing into bed and felt some wetness all of a sudden. I'm not sure if the baby pushed on my bladder. I don't think my water broke. Should I come to the hospital or wait a few hours?"

"Linda, you need to come on in," the nurse said. "We'll be waiting for you." This was not what I wanted to hear. It was the middle of the night, for Pete's sake.

I suddenly felt panicked at the thought that I hadn't gotten any sleep. My mind was racing. *Eric isn't with me. This is not the way I planned it to happen.*

I gave myself an additional five minutes of luxurious denial. *This isn't happening, this isn't happening.* I lowered my face into my hands. "Okay, don't panic," I whispered to myself. "The doctor may just send you home." *Yes,* I reassured myself, *this could be a false alarm.* I had heard stories of expectant mothers' being sent home to wait for their contractions to begin. *Maybe when I get to the hospital, they'll just tell me to turn around and go home. Okay, that sounds good.*

By this time, it was near midnight. Calm came over me as I finished getting everything I needed for my hospital bag. Noticing that I was up, Oscar and Meyer stuck their heads out from under the covers. I scratched under their chins and gave them a kiss before changing from my pajamas into my sweat suit.

Before I went downstairs to wake up Dorothy, I took one last moment to compose myself for what was about to happen. I sat down on the edge of the bed. The crickets outside soothed me with their songs, reminding me of nighttime's peace. I held on to the moment, the stillness, before my life would change.

I knocked on Dorothy's bedroom door and pushed the door open a crack. "Yes," she answered in her soft Southern accent. I could tell she had been in a deep slumber.

"Dorothy, my water broke. I have to go to the hospital." There was no easy way to put it. I cringed when I heard the bed covers fly off. She reached for the light switch.

"What time is it?" she asked.

"Around midnight. I'm packed and ready to go."

She nodded, alert now, gathering her things as quickly as she could.

We didn't say much on the drive to the hospital. Dorothy and I had never discussed what we would do if the baby came early—because of my older age, it was certain to be late. I realized in the car that night that we'd never talked about it because we both had an underlying fear that it might actually happen.

Dorothy was not going to be a hands-on grandmother. She interviewed and hired baby nurses and childcare providers, but she refused to change a diaper or soothe a screaming baby. We both knew that she didn't want to be present during the delivery, but I also knew that she would do the best she could to step up and provide whatever support I needed.

The nurse took my blood pressure and a blood sample and examined me. She said I hadn't dilated at all, but when I remarked that I hoped that meant I would be going home, she informed me that my obstetrician had instructed that I be induced right away. "But my husband isn't here!" I wailed. Then I was informed that my obstetrician wasn't on duty that night, so her partner, whom I had met only once, would be delivering my baby.

My heart sank. I still couldn't grasp that this was happening the way it was. I needed Eric to be there, to share in this experience we'd created together. *He's supposed to hold my hand through the pain. We're supposed to cry together when the baby emerges. I'm not supposed to do this with my mother-in-law!*

I was wheeled into a private room, where I changed into a hospital gown. I set out the slippers I had bought that morning. A nurse came in and performed the procedure to induce labor. Dorothy winced when she saw the needle plunging into my arm.

Dorothy had left messages with Eric about my water breaking. Eric's friend was arriving that morning; Dorothy tried desperately to call him and tell him not to get on his flight.

All I could do now was try to sleep and wait. I knew Dorothy was as scared as I was, so I felt required to put up a brave front, but all I wanted to do was crumble.

I was thankful when, at two in the morning, Dorothy offered to run home to let Oscar and Meyer out, and to pick up some personal effects she needed.

The nurse turned down the lights while we waited for the induction to work. After she left, I was finally alone to have a good cry. Sobbing quietly, I cursed the timing, and my being deprived of a delivery with my husband present. I wouldn't be telling birth stories of how he'd encouraged me through the whole ordeal and handled all the important decisions that came along. But most important, I knew, was that I wanted the magic of this event to bring us back together.

My crying ceased as the magnitude and clarity of the monumental task at hand took over. I had to pull myself together, to access a strength deep down inside me, in order to endure the birth of my child alone. I wiped away my tears and took a deep breath, understanding that I needed to conserve my mental strength and accept the way things were turning out.

I slept fitfully over the next several hours as the morning light leaked through the blinds. A woman came into my still-dark room with Dorothy. It was Sandy, a former maternity nurse whom Dorothy had hired to help me with my newborn. Apparently, Dorothy had phoned her and told her about our situation. Sandy advocated for me during the delivery and was like an angel sent during my darkest hour of despair.

Before I was given an epidural, I went through a couple of hours of agonizing contractions. Once the anesthesia took hold, the crashing tides of pain gave way, wave by wave, to a blissful stillness. I felt such physical relief that, like a rag doll, I fell into an exhausted, sweaty half-slumber. As I slept for forty-five minutes, my body relaxed until I became fully dilated.

When the obstetrician arrived, I knew it was time for the most difficult part—the pushing. I'd heard of women pushing for hours and knew that I couldn't last that long. I had to make each one count.

After forty-five minutes, Manfred emerged. Bluish-red and slick with mucus, my tiny, writhing, screaming baby was placed on my stomach. I examined his egg-shaped head and counted his fingers and toes. Sandy was beaming and Dorothy was snapping pictures from every angle. When the nurse took Manfred away to clean him up, the doctor approached me with such a big needle, with a piece of string so long, that it looked as if she were going to do some darning.

After I was sewn up, Manfred was returned to me. His head was covered with a crocheted hat, his feet with booties. Sandy showed me how to swaddle him in the softest of baby blankets.

This was my first chance to get a good look at him, and his first chance to experience being out of my body after his shocking entrance into the world. His alert eyes moved around, seeing but not seeing. He made an O with his mouth, as if he'd just discovered his lips. All warm, content, and swaddled, he dozed in my arms.

*Around me, nurses and attendants* were wheeling away equipment, drawing curtains, and cleaning up after the delivery. Dorothy was taking photos of the staff and making calls on her cell phone. Sandy was talking to the nurse. I was in the hospital room, holding a sleeping Manfred, my mind in another country, another world.

*Sing in the summer and autumn, die in the winter.* Where had I heard that before? It wasn't the words to a song. A vision of the old man with the splintered teeth and watery eyes who'd sold us the crickets my first week in Beijing came to mind, and with it a vivid memory of the intoxication of being loved and in love, my unforgiving uncertainty about why I was in Beijing in the first place, and the headiness of feeling alive.

The old man, Eric had told me, wanted to make sure I understood the crickets' short life span. I remember thinking how odd it was that he assumed we didn't understand that the crickets wouldn't live long. Had he actually been talking about the short span of relationships—of *my* relationship?

Eric's plane was scheduled to land in a couple of hours, when our future together would begin unfurling. I felt myself turn cold, as if I'd been hit by a blast of frigid air. The old man was right: My summer and autumn had indeed ended, and ahead of me was a long winter of uncertainty and depression.

I felt my life reshaping itself already. Rather than shrinking away from the thought, though, something inside me—the self-sufficient, forward-thinking part of me I'd lost somewhere along the way—was roused from a long dormancy. Being mostly on my own these last two months hadn't felt all that bad, and I wondered what that meant for Eric and me. I didn't know what the future held, but I was a mother now, and that was what mattered. I could only hope for the best, but I knew, with more conviction than I had ever felt in my life, that my son's priorities came first. Call it maternal instinct kicking in, but this knowledge didn't make me feel trapped—I felt full of power and purpose. I was welcoming back a vital part of myself. This consciousness would surge and withdraw like rapids at different times over the years following, but it would never leave me.

A lot of the details of that afternoon have faded over time. Although I'm not positive, I think I spoke with Eric on the phone. But my memory focuses only on the image of cradling my precious baby boy. It was just he and I—my future was right there. As I moved forward into uncertainty, I learned my first and hardest lesson: I had to know and give myself what I needed emotionally. And so my next journey began with my comforting both of us and repeating, "We're going to be just fine on our own."

# LION CUB'S HEAD MEATBALLS
# WITH VEGETABLES AND PASTA "MANE"

*I've added more vegetables to this classic Chinese dish.*
*The meatballs can be formed into any size, but I find the*
*gumball size daintier and more child-friendly.*

INGREDIENTS:

MEATBALLS:

1/2 pound ground pork

1/2 pound ground turkey

1 cup fresh crabmeat

1/4 cup plain breadcrumbs

1/2 teaspoon salt

2 teaspoons sesame oil

1 tablespoon rice wine

6-ounce can sliced water chestnuts, drained and minced

3 green onions, chopped

1 teaspoon grated fresh ginger

2 tablespoons cornstarch

2 1/2 tablespoons soy sauce

1 tablespoon water

## PASTA AND VEGETABLES:

1 head napa cabbage

5 tablespoons vegetable oil

Rice wine, as needed

Salt, to taste

3 carrots, peeled and julienned

1 small daikon, peeled and julienned

5 Swiss chard leaves, sliced into 1/4-inch-wide strips

1 cup chicken stock

4 cups hot cooked angel hair pasta

1 tablespoon finely grated lemon zest

## INSTRUCTIONS:

### FOR THE MEATBALLS:

Preheat oven to 350°. In a medium-size mixing bowl, combine pork, turkey, crabmeat, breadcrumbs, salt, sesame oil, rice wine, water chestnuts, green onions, ginger, 1 tablespoon of the cornstarch, and 1 tablespoon of the soy sauce. Mix well, making sure ingredients are evenly distributed. Form into 16 meatballs, each about 2 inches in diameter. Place on a cookie sheet or baking pan.

In a shallow bowl, combine remaining tablespoon of cornstarch, remaining 1 1/2 tablespoons soy sauce, and water to make a meatball–coating liquid. Set aside.

### FOR THE CABBAGE AND VEGETABLES:

Remove 2 whole leaves from the cabbage and set aside. Cut remaining head in half lengthwise, then julienne leaves to the point where the tough white core begins.

In a deep sauté pan or wok, heat 1 tablespoon vegetable oil over high heat. When oil is hot, add julienned cabbage, a dash of salt, and a splash of rice wine. Stir until cabbage becomes slightly limp. Transfer to a 3-quart Dutch oven or casserole dish with a cover. Repeat the procedure individually with the carrots, daikon, and Swiss chard, adding more oil and rice wine as needed. Add stir-fried carrots and daikon to casserole dish. Place Swiss chard in a separate bowl and keep warm.

Using the same pan, heat remaining 2 tablespoons vegetable oil over medium-high heat. When oil is hot, whisk cornstarch mixture, then dip meatballs into it and add them to the pan. Fry until brown on all sides, about 10 minutes.

Transfer meatballs to casserole dish and pour chicken stock over them. Drape reserved cabbage leaves over meatballs. Cover and bake for 30 minutes.

While meatballs are cooking, reheat pan containing the meat drippings over medium-high heat and pour in remaining meatball-coating liquid. Add pasta, tossing to coat thoroughly. Add lemon zest and toss well.

Divide pasta among serving bowls. Discard cabbage leaves, then top each serving with meatballs, Swiss chard, and other vegetables.

*Serves 4–6*

# EPILOGUE

THE YEAR AFTER MANFRED WAS BORN, I had a recurring dream. I'm sitting at the tail of a sailboat. The vessel moves quickly and smoothly, cutting through the waves as if chasing the buttery yellow sun on a late afternoon.

Eric is seated just ahead of me. He looks handsome with his hair all tousled and a relaxed grin on his face. One arm is hooked securely on the polished wood railing and the other is around Manfred, who is squirming and gurgling on his lap. Watching them, I'm bursting with tremendous joy, well being, and belonging.

Over the roar of the snapping sails and the battering wind I hear a flat tone, like static, playing like background music. It's not annoying, as it would be if I were awake; instead, as it strengthens, like the cricket's song, it somehow intensifies my extreme happiness.

At the point when I realize it's all a dream, the tone becomes louder still and my elation is suddenly replaced with raw fear. I wake up the instant my mind identifies the static noise as a flatline.

Those first couple of seconds immediately upon waking are the worst. Before I move a muscle, my mind thinks I'm lying in our bed in our Shanghai apartment, Eric by my side, Oscar and Meyer curled up under the blankets, and Manfred asleep in his nursery. My impulse is to tell Eric about my dream, and then I roll over and the remembrance of the past year comes crashing down on me like a mudslide.

*We returned to Shanghai* a couple of months after Manfred's birth. Any hope that Eric and I might be able to rebuild our relationship was crushed. Eric wanted a divorce.

That late spring, the outbreak of SARS (Severe Acute Respiratory Syndrome), and worry over Manfred's susceptibility, led the baby and I back to the States—without Eric. I spent the summer at my parents' home in Indiana. I tried to maintain a steady grip on my frayed nerves by focusing on taking care of Manfred during the day and working on my book at night.

I didn't return to Shanghai once the SARS outbreak was contained. My parents suspected something else was amiss, but they didn't press me for information. Instead, they showed their support by feeding me all my favorite Japanese dishes from the bounty of fresh vegetables from my father's garden. When I eventually broke the news to them, their faces mirrored all the fear and uncertainty I'd been holding back for months.

I did return to Shanghai in the fall, and arranged to have my belongings and some furniture sent back to the States. The world as I knew it was coming apart. I felt completely numb. Eric and I were estranged, and I didn't recognize Shanghai as the city I knew before. My life there was finished.

Manfred's first birthday came that December. Eric and I slept in separate rooms at Eric's parents' Florida home, the same house where I'd spent many holidays, had my wedding, and awaited Manfred's birth.

Though my decision to leave Shanghai felt abrupt, I couldn't go without visiting my favorite restaurants one last time. I lingered over each meal, savoring them like a farewell kiss. Most of those dishes I could never re-create, nor would I even want to attempt making. I was confident that I would return someday, but I knew it wouldn't be soon.

*Every so often, I think about China.* In the beginning, I wallowed in the nostalgia of being romanced in Beijing, distorting those memories to mythic proportions. But as more time passed, and as the pain of the failed relationship faded, the subtle details of that life began to stand out in a different way, like the lines of an ancient fresco: Chu Ping singing the Cultural Revolution songs as she cleaned; Susan and Gina being tailed by the drunken restaurant patron in the *hutong;* bespectacled Ding Laoshi telling a goofy joke in class; and Sally slurping her lunchtime noodle soup.

These treasured memories of my time in China are my mementos, which will remain with me forever. As frightening as starting all over seemed at the time, I heeded the words of the cricket seller and moved forward with the knowledge that there would be another spring and summer, when I would sing to my heart's content.

# About the
# AUTHOR

LINDA FURIYA is the author of *Bento Box in the Heartland: My Japanese Girlhood in Whitebread America*. She writes a food column for the *San Francisco Chronicle* and teaches Asian cooking and tofu-making in Shelburne, Vermont, where she lives with her son and three wired-hair dachshunds.

318

# Acknowledgments

To my editor, Brooke Warner, much gratitude for your professionalism, direction, and objectivity.

To my agent, Carole Bidnick, many thanks for your expertise and practical advice.

Sharon Harkness, Trina Webster, Laura Gigliotti, Terri Petrie, Anne Stevenson-Yang, and Anita Ritchie, thank you for your encouraging words and immeasurable support, both in the present and throughout the years.

Thank you, Miriam Morgan, Martin Yan, and Tara Lee.

Lastly, I'd like to extend my thanks to my friends in the People's Republic of China, for making my experience living abroad an unforgettable one.

# SELECTED TITLES FROM SEAL PRESS

For more than thirty years, Seal Press has published groundbreaking books. By women. For women. Visit our website at www.sealpress.com. Check out the Seal Press blog at www.sealpress.com/blog.

*Bento Box In the Heartland: My Japanese Girlhood in Whitebread America*, by Linda Furiya. $15.95, 1-58005-191-X. A uniquely American story about girlhood, identity, assimilation—and the love of homemade food.

*Tango: An Argentine Love Story*, by Camille Cusumano. $15.95, 1-58005-250-9. The spicy travel memoir of a woman who left behind a failed fifteen-year relationship and fell in love with Argentina through the dance that embodies intensity, freedom, and passion.

*Mexico, A Love Story: Women Write about the Mexican Experience*, edited by Camille Cusumano. $15.95, 1-58005-156-1. In this thrilling and layered collection, two-dozen women describe the country they love and why they have fallen under its spell. Also available, *Italy, A Love Story: Women Write about the Italian Experience*. $15.95, 1-58005-143-X and *France, A Love Story: Women Write about the French Experience*. $15.95, 1-58005-115-4.

*Tales from the Expat Harem: Foreign Women in Modern Turkey*, edited by Anastasia M. Ashman and Jennifer Eaton Gökmen. $15.95. 1-58005-155-3. Female expats from different countries describe how the Turkish landscape, psyche, people, and customs transformed their lives.

*Waking Up American: Coming of Age Biculturally*, edited by Angela Jane Fountas. $15.95, 1-58005-136-7. Twenty-two original essays by first-generation women caught between two worlds. Countries of origin include the Philippines, Germany, India, Mexico, China, Iran, Nicaragua, Japan, Russia, and Panama.

*Homelands: Women's Journeys Across Race, Place, and Time*, edited by Patricia Justine Tumang and Jenesha de Rivera. $16.95, 1-58005-188-X. An insightful and thoughtful collection of essays on what "homeland" means for women in search of a deeper connection to their cultural pasts.